MAYBE YOU KNOW
MY TEEN

Also by Mary Fowler

MAYBE YOU KNOW MY KID

A Parent's Guide to Helping Your Child with
Attention Deficit Hyperactivity Disorder

MAYBE YOU KNOW MY TEEN

A Parent's Guide to
Helping Your Adolescent with
Attention Deficit Hyperactivity Disorder

MARY FOWLER

BROADWAY BOOKS
New York

Broadway Books titles may be purchased for business or
promotional use or for special sales. For information, please write to:
Special Markets Department, Random House, Inc.,
1540 Broadway, New York, NY 10036.

Visit our Web site at www.broadwaybooks.com

Library of Congress Cataloging-in-Publication Data

Fowler, Mary.
Maybe you know my teen : a parent's guide to helping your adolescent
with attention deficit hyperactivity disorder / Mary Fowler—1st ed.
p. cm.
ISBN 0-7679-0514-8 (trade pbk.)
1. Attention-deficit disorder in adolescence—Patients—Care. 2. Attention-deficit
hyperactivity disorder—Patients—Care. 3. Parenting. I. Title.

RJ506.H9 F683 2001
616.85'89'00835—dc21
2001025466

FIRST EDITION

Designed by Erin L. Matherne and Tina Thompson

10 9 8 7 6 5 4 3 2 1

With love and gratitude to
my sons David and Jonathan,
my sister Margaret, my brother Joseph

•

For my nephew
Mitchel John Fowler
June 3, 1994–March 28, 1995
Your light still shines.

Contents

Foreword

Several years ago, I was addressing a group of parents at an elementary school cafetorium. We were discussing the unique pressures and challenges of raising children who have Attention Deficits.

During the question-and-answer session, a young mom raised her hand and, hopefully, asked the "will he grow out of it?" question: "Mr. Lavoie," she said hesitantly, "isn't it true that ADHD adolescents are just like *all* adolescents?"

I gave her a direct answer, one that I have given to countless struggling parents since: "Yes! ADHD adolescents are like all adolescents . . . only more so!"

Adolescence is a period of turmoil, confusion, and angst in the human life span. Your teenager with ADHD will navigate the craggy shoals of social rejection, peer pressure, academic challenge, homefront conflict, increased independence, and burgeoning sexuality. And all of these challenges will be exacerbated and further complicated by ADHD. "Just like all adolescents . . . only more so."

Interestingly, the field of ADHD is now entering its *own* adolescence! This area of exceptionality is currently the darling of the lay press, scholarly journals, and medical research labs. But fifteen short years ago, ADHD was virtually unknown. The field's "adolescent period" is filled with conflict, confusion, identity crises, and rejection of old ideas . . . similar to the adolescent period of the human being. Parents need a wise and compassionate guide in order to navigate the labyrinth of differing opinions, strategies, and approaches. Mary Fowler offers that guidance in her remarkable book *Maybe You Know My Teen.*

Mary's earlier book, *Maybe You Know My Kid,* sits on my desk along with a handful of other classic works in the field, dog-eared from constant use. This book provides information and inspiration to parents who struggle daily with the unique needs and behaviors of school-age kids with ADHD. Her new book offers similar blazing insights into the world of teenagers whose attentional problems cause them to view and understand their environs in a unique way.

Adolescents are "managed by the moment." They perceive no past and no future. Whatever event is occurring in their lives at that moment in time is viewed as the single most important event in the history of humankind. I conduct a workshop for parents of adolescents entitled "Never Say 'It's Only a Dance.'" The title comes from an anecdote that I include in the seminar:

Fifteen-year-old Sally stands in front of her mirror on Friday evening, admiring her outfit (the fifth one that she has tried on in a half hour!), her hairstyle, and her makeup. She is preparing to go to the Thanksgiving Dance at her high school. Every moment of her waking time for the past two weeks has been occupied by dreams, thoughts, and peer conversations related to *the* dance. Plans are made . . . modified . . . altered . . . finalized . . . and adjusted yet again. Who will I dance with? When will I arrive? Important—no, *crucial*—issues for Sally.

As she completes her final primping, Dad passes her room and notices the activity:

"Why are you so dressed up, honey? You look terrific!"

"Tonight's the dance, Dad. The Thanksgiving Dance. Jeannie and Sasha are picking me up in ten minutes!"

"Oh, no! Sally, I know you mentioned something about a dance this weekend. But I thought that it was *tomorrow* night."

"No, Dad! The high school dances are always on Friday."

"Well, Sally, we have a problem. I invited Grandma and Grandpa to come to dinner tonight. They leave for their trip to Europe on Sunday and I want all of you kids to be here. Mom made a special meal . . ."

"But, Dad . . . *the dance* . . ."

"C'mon, honey . . . it's only a dance . . . there will be others . . . you can go *next* Friday. . . ."

CRISIS! DISASTER! CONFRONTATION!

Dad failed to understand or appreciate Sally's perception of the dance. To her, that singular event is more important than air pollution, the Renaissance, or nuclear fusion. The Middle Ages and the invention of the internal combustion engine pale in comparison to the significance of that evening's dance in the gym. (By the way, she will doubtless have a terrible time at the dance, describe it as "boring," and pledge to "never go to a high school dance again!" upon her return home!)

The world of the adolescent is a mysterious one. I have shepherded three of our own kids through adolescence and have worked professionally with countless more. But—despite (or perhaps *because* of) this experience—I find that I still have more questions than I have answers. Mary's book provides wise responses to many of those questions.

I have long felt that adolescence is the most difficult and challenging period in the life span of a person with a learning or attentional problem. I cite two reasons for this:

a) ADOLESCENCE IS THE ONLY PERIOD IN THE LIFE SPAN WHEREIN YOU ARE EXPECTED TO DO ALL THINGS WELL!

The American public high school celebrates the generalist. The valedictorian is the student who has extraordinary skills in the sciences, language, mathematics, and history. The "well-rounded" student receives the awards and the plaudits.

Kids with learning and attentional problems are generally not generalists. They are specialists. They often possess extraordinary skills in specific, well-defined areas. As a result, their high school years are often characterized by failure and frustration. He is not allowed to take advanced art courses (where he excels) because he must take remedial math sessions in order to pass Algebra II. In fact, his successes in art are often used as evidence that he "simply doesn't try hard enough" in math.

The ADHD adolescent faces the daily frustration and anxiety of—quite literally—being a square peg attempting to enter a round hole. A *specialist* in a world that honors the *generalist*.

b) ADOLESCENCE IS THE ONLY PART OF THE HUMAN LIFE SPAN WHEREIN "DIFFERENT" IS AUTOMATICALLY REJECTED, ISOLATED, AND MISTRUSTED.

Consider. Younger kids love anything that is different. The six-year-old is instantly attracted to the clown in the mall food court. Adults also celebrate differences. Note the crowd that invariably envelopes an exotically dressed stranger at a cocktail party.

But adolescents insist that their peers adhere closely to the culture and mores that have been established. Deviation from group norms are branded "uncool" and are rejected. The ADHD adolescent is often isolated by peers because of the atypical behavior that he manifests. This inability to "connect" with his peers often leaves him lacking the acceptance, support, or camaraderie that is crucial during this developmental period. At a time when he feels alienated from his parents, he is also unable to establish relationships with his classmates. I once asked an adolescent with a learning disability to describe himself in a single word. "Lonely" was his instantaneous response.

High school students with ADHD often find themselves on a collision course with the curriculum. The course of study places focused emphasis on memory, organization, time management, concentration, independence, long-term assignments, and integration skills. *All* of these skills are long-recognized areas of weakness for students with ADHD. Ironically, as the curriculum demands increase . . . the availability of remedial service generally decrease—a school version of Catch 22.

Most impressive among this book's structure is Mary's use of a "medical model" in examining ADHD. This approach is far different from the traditional educational method of examining a syndrome. I have three degrees in Special Education. When I review my transcript, I realize that 90 percent of my course work was an exploration of exceptionality, deviation, and disability. I was required to take but a few courses in normal, typical development. The "medical model" approach is quite different. A medical student, for example, will spend several years studying normal, healthy human anatomy. Only then will he undertake the study of disease and illness. The bias of this model is: "ONE CANNOT TRULY UNDERSTAND THAT WHICH IS ABNORMAL UNLESS HE FULLY UNDERSTANDS THAT WHICH IS NORMAL."

Mary wisely utilizes this approach by providing the reader with an insightful and invaluable exploration of normal adolescent development. She then contrasts this with the development of the teenager whose growth is complicated because of attentional problems. This reasoned and readable approach makes this book an invaluable addition to the literature and a must for every parent's bookshelf.

Mary brings clarity and genuine wisdom to challenging issues including driving, curfews, delinquency, drug abuse, anxiety, home/school communication, sibling relationships, and accessibility of resources. *Webster's* defines "wisdom" as "having good judgment based on knowledge and experience." The reader will gain much from Mary's knowledge and experience. She possesses both in full measure.

As a parent, it is your right and responsibility—your duty and your privilege—to shepherd your child through this puzzling and challenging period. You must be his or her advocate, while simultaneously teaching your child to self-advocate. In order to be an effective and responsive guide, you must read and learn about the dragon that your child fights daily. But, if your relationship is going to be a successful one, I advise you to remain mindful of six things:

1. Any adolescent would prefer to look like a *bad* kid than a *dumb* kid.
2. The pain that a troubled child causes is never greater than the pain that he feels.
3. Negative feedback only *stops* behavior. . . . Positive feedback is an agent of *change* in behavior.
4. Listen.
5. Listen.
6. Listen some more.

With every good wish,
Richard D. Lavoie
President
Riverview School
East Sandwich, Massachusetts

Acknowledgments

I am deeply appreciative to the many people who contributed to this book. Foremost, I thank the teens and parents who took me into their lives, tape recorder and all, so that I might capture their stories. They spoke openly, honestly, and with great courage. I would like to recognize each of these contributors personally, but we agreed that pseudonyms would be used in the book. Although I can't name each of you, please know that your contributions have been a great help to me and to those readers struggling for hope and answers.

I am also very grateful to researchers and professionals who generously shared their expertise and gave their time to me. Their commitment to their work greatly improves the lives of those with ADHD, their caregivers, and their loved ones.

My sincere thanks to:

Russell Barkley, Ph.D., director of psychology and professor of psychiatry and neurology at the University of Massachusetts Medical Center, director of the Center for Attention Deficit Disorder.

Thomas Brown, Ph.D., associate director, Yale Clinic for Attention and Related Disorders, Yale University.

John Curry, Ph.D., associate professor and director of clinical training, department of psychology and social health sciences, Duke University Medical Center.

Margaret Feerick, Ph.D., Child Development and Behavior Branch, National Institute of Child Health and Human Development, National Institutes of Health.

Lisa Freund, Ph.D., program director, developmental psychobiology and neuroscience, Child Development and Behavior Branch, National Institute of Child Health and Human Development, National Institutes of Health.

Lili Frank Garfinkel, associate director, EDJJ: The National Center on Education, Disability, and Juvenile Justice.

Marsha Glines, Ph.D., dean of the College of Education and executive director of TAP, Lynn University.

Stephen Hinshaw, Ph.D., director of clinical training program, University of California, Berkeley.

Richard L. Horne, Ed.D., senior policy adviser, Presidential Task Force on Employment of Adults with Disabilities.

Peter Jensen, M.D., Ruane Professor for implementation of science and director of the Center for Advancement of Children's Mental Health, Columbia University. Former associate director for child and adolescent research, National Institute of Mental Health.

David Keith, M.D., director of family therapy, interim director of child and adolescent psychiatry, SUNY Upstate, Syracuse University.

G. Reid Lyon, Ph.D., chief, Child Development and Behavior Branch, National Institute of Child Health and Human Development, National Institutes of Health.

Bruce McEwen, Ph.D., professor and head of the Harold and Margaret Milliken Hatch Laboratory of Neuroendocrinology, Rockefeller University.

Sheri M. Meisel, Ph.D., associate director, EDJJ: The National Center on Education, Disability, and Juvenile Justice.

Sallie Montgomery, Psy.D., senior clinician, Hazelden Center for Youth and Families.

The Honorable Gerald Rouse, immediate past president, National Council of Family and Juvenile Court Judges.

W. Michael Nelson III, Ph.D., chair, professor of psychology, Xavier University.

Arthur Robin, professor of psychiatry and behavioral neurosciences and pediatrics, Wayne State University School of Medicine, chief of psychology at Children's Hospital of Michigan.

Joseph Sergeant, Ph.D., president of Eunythydis, the European Network for Hyperkinetic Disorder, professor, Klinische Neuropsychologie, Vrije University, Amsterdam.

Robert Silverstein, J.D., director, Center for the Study and Advancement of Disability Policy, and former staff director and chief counsel for the subcommittee on disability policy of the U.S. Senate Committee on Labor and Human Relations.

I also thank the excellent clinicians who added a "chairside perspective": clinical psychologists William Bumberry, Ph.D., St. John's Mercy Medical Center, St. Louis, MO, Drew Yellen, Ph.D., Richard Zakreski, Ph.D, and Patricia Quinn, M.D., author and co-editor, *ADDvance* magazine.

My appreciation to Ross Greene, Ph.D., Katherine Kennedy, Ph.D., Barbara Posner, Helene Reynolds, Marsha Bartolf, and Eileen Vogel; Lt. Kristie Etue from the Michigan State Police Prevention Services Section and the staff of Sorenson's Residential Treatment Center.

Many thanks to James Swanson, Ph.D., director of the Child Development Center, professor of pediatrics at University of California, Irvine; Thomas Spencer, M.D., Timothy Wilens, M.D., and Eric Mick, Sc.D., of Harvard University and Massachusetts General Hospital; Ann Masten, Ph.D., director of the Institute of Child Development, University of Minnesota; and William Pelham, Ph.D., SUNY Buffalo, for providing me with stacks of articles that provided much background and foreground for this book.

I am also grateful to the following publishers and organizations for graciously supplying me with books and access to information: The Resolving Conflict Creatively Program, the National Center for Children and Youth with Disabilities, Guilford Publications, Brooks Cole Publishers, O'Reilly Press, and PIRI (Public Information Resources, Inc., www.edupro.com), sponsors of the nationally recognized annual Learning and the Brain Conference.

Special thanks to Richard Zakreski, Ph.D., for reviewing the text; Robert Silverstein, J.D., for his assistance with the special education law chapter; and attorneys Michaelene Laughlin and Pete Wright for fact checking the special education chapter; Heather Ringeisen, Ph.D., at NIMH; and William Cope Moyers, who graciously helped me with interview sources.

For the wonderful support, I thank my former students, and the staff, administration, and school board of the Oceanport School District.

Much appreciation goes to my family, especially my mother, and to David and Mollie; to my friends, especially Sandy Thomas for her bottomless supply of moral support, care, and concern; and to Joyce Block, Cat Doty, Stevi Lischin, Helen Pike, and Bobbie Van Anda.

I also wish to thank all those involved in the publication of this book, including Hillel Black for encouraging me to write it, my agent Wendy Lipkind for her patience and wisdom, Tracy Behar for her initial interest in this work, editorial assistant James Benson for his considerable effort, my editor Tricia Medved for her commitment, care, and help in bringing this manuscript to form, and Rick Lavoie for writing the foreword.

Introduction

I wish I had this book when my children were teens. Alas, as the old proverb goes, we grow too soon old and too late wise. My parenting, from the very first day, seems to have been the type of challenge that one has to live through before answers come. Perhaps you can relate to this experience. Though I knew a lot about attention deficit hyperactivity disorder (ADHD) by the time I became the parent of adolescents, our family faced extraordinary challenges that went beyond ADHD and that complicated the disorder. Knowledge plus experience has definitely made me older. The writing of this book has made me wiser. May it ease your journey.

Unlike my first book, *Maybe You Know My Kid,* which is full of personal revelation, I deliberately chose not to write about my family's experience with ADHD in this book for two reasons. First, most adolescents don't like to be "discussed" or "exposed." Issues of privacy are important and to be honored. Second, no single account can tell the story of ADHD during these highly complicated years. If I had told my story, you might not find the personal relevance you need. Still, you will find that I write from the vantage point of one who's been there.

My children's adolescence has taught me that these years can be quite complex. I know what it's like to be in over my head. In this book, I wanted to be sure that any parents who turned to these pages for answers would find their problem and the appropriate recommendations. As a result, this book grew into a big book. *Maybe You Know My Teen* is not a simple treatment of ADHD. It is, however, written in easy-to-understand language. Nonetheless, there's a lot of information to digest. So I divided the book into three parts. The first part is basically an overview of ADHD in adolescence, along with information about related disorders. It tells you where to go, what to do, and why. The second part covers the disorder as it relates to matters in the family and between parent and teen. The third part addresses ADHD in school and work. Read the book once from cover to cover. Then I suggest you use it as a reference. When different problems arise, you can look to the index or the introductory comments in each chapter to locate the particular subject area that may be causing you concern.

Throughout the text, you will also find "Information Links." These links are meant to help you find other reliable resources and information about specific topics. I could not possibly include all the available sources to go to for your needs. There are many good publications, materials, organizations, and Web sites that I may not have mentioned, but that you may find helpful. Like the Web, the links I've supplied will no doubt take you other places as well.

You can read this book with confidence that the information provided comes from widely respected sources. I interviewed the leading researchers here and abroad to be sure that you received the most accurate, up-to-date information available on ADHD. However, guidance, information, or suggestions in this book should not replace medical counsel. If you have a question or concern, consult a licensed treatment professional. I also spoke with many teens with the disorder and their parents. They graciously opened their lives to me and answered extremely personal questions with no restraint because they wanted you to have the benefit of whatever experience and wisdom they had gained. I have given them pseudonyms, but their experiences couldn't be more real.

In closing, I share part of a poem I wrote for my sons. Its sentiment represents the spirit of this book. Though it's about mothers, it's for fathers, too.

If I could write you a fairy tale,
your mother would not be locked in the castle.
She would be a searchlight
who travels the night sky
looking for nothing in particular
just you for whatever reason.
You would look for her steady arc
across your night sky.
And she would give you your bearings
until your morning came.

PART ONE

Adolescence and the Nuts and Bolts of ADHD and Related Disorders

CHAPTER ONE

Normal Adolescent Development—Whatever That Is

Parenting is a story of change, and adolescence is a dynamic developmental stage. When the teen years arrive, many parents are not so sure they recognize their kids anymore. This chapter charts the course of typical adolescence. It provides an overview of the physical, social, emotional, and cognitive changes all teens undergo, along with the shift all parents and teens experience in their relationship. This chapter is meant to give you a sense of "normal" adolescence so you understand the nature of the changes you and your teen are navigating, ADHD aside.

On the day that I plan to write the first chapter of this book, a phone call interrupts me. My neighbor is in labor. Both she and I are about to begin an intense journey. While I drive to the hospital, my neighbor rubs her belly. She imagines a son at Stanford University on a full golf scholarship. I'm struck by the irony of the day. My job is to write about adolescents—and not just typical teens. I am writing about teens with ADHD and related disorders. I have personal experience with this disorder. Both my son and I know that ADHD can bring a sizeable helping of struggle to life.

The task of this book is to talk about some pretty difficult issues in depth, exposing all. Escorting an expectant mother to labor and delivery means talking about healthy babies, good futures, and great expectations. When we become parents, we sign up for a minimum twenty-year commitment to assist in the development of a life. In between the dreams for our children and the reality of their plans for themselves lies a wonderful opportunity. Whether a child has special needs or not, parenting offers a great chance to learn and to grow in love and through struggle. We find hope to help us meet each challenge. Dreams do come true. And some expectations become reality.

Adolescence is usually seen as a stage that kids go through on their way to adulthood. I believe parents and teens pass through this stage together. As our teens grow into their lives, we parents grow out of our expectations. We put aside some of the dreams that never belonged to our sons and daughters. As our teens struggle to cut the cord and achieve their identities and independence, we parents tug at the other end of that rope. When do we let go? When do we pull harder? Ultimately, we have to move to the sidelines of our sons' and daughters' lives. There we sit, watch, and advise when appropriate.

Raising our children seems to have as much to do with our own childhood, adolescence, biology, and outcome as it does with the experiences our kids have and their biology. My neighbor with her visions of her son sailing off to university on scholarship money makes me smile. I had similar ideas for both my sons.

Then came the grocery store days. Life turned into a Cracker Jack box with a surprise that my children fought for on every grocery store line. I can still hear the warnings of the mothers ahead of me at the checkout: "Enjoy them now. Wait until they are teens." I'd smile with gritted teeth, not quite sure what to make of such comments. They seemed so jaded.

When my children got older, the problems *did* become more serious and the answers less clear. I learned that the warnings given me by the women in the grocery store had a basis in truth. This stage of life can be absolutely hellacious. But a grain of truth is not the whole story. Yes, there are struggles. Especially when ADHD is present. It can cause more twists and turmoil. Teenagers with ADHD may be harder to manage. They may get in trouble, be their own worst enemies, be grossly misunderstood, or be mishandled. Family peace may be hard to come by. Still, imagine the message we send to teens with or without ADHD when we view this very important stage of life as one of major trouble and upheaval. Parents of teens need a positive attitude and to keep things in perspective.

This notion of the teen years as terrible times has deep roots. An early-twentieth-century psychologist tagged the period as one of "storm and stress," characterized by emotionality. That was during the Victorian era, when emotion and improper behavior were perhaps synonymous and propriety meant a lot.

Since conflict makes for a good story, I think it has been easy to continue to fuel the myth that adolescence is a thoroughly tumultuous period where all parents can expect the worst. As 16-year-old Eric Stoner observes, "I honestly think that adults don't give teenagers enough credit for being good people. My parents have a lot of respect for what I do, but a lot of my friends' parents expect their kids to freeze them out, to go get drunk, get laid, you know, to be the cliché teen."

Some teens are the cliché teen. They and their parents experience these years as tougher years than others. Some of this book is about the cliché teen. Most of it has to do with raising teenagers who have problems that begin in childhood as attention deficit hyperactivity disorder. It's about what we parents can do when faced with minor skirmishes and major life-threatening issues. It's also about attitude, acceptance, love, and how to navigate through the wide variety of challenges ADHD brings to a family.

For this book, I spoke with a range of parents and teenagers, some with mild problems to troubles so severe that these teens would be considered juvenile delinquents. The kids on the severe side of the spectrum get off track for many reasons, some of which will become clear as you read. In addition to offering specific guidelines for what to do under the toughest of circumstances, this book also provides ideas and tips for all situations in between the extremes. Before diving in, it's important to have some knowledge about this phase called adolescence, which derives its name from the Latin *adolescere,* "to grow up."

At the Crossroads

In between writing *Maybe You Know My Kid* and writing this book, I raised two teenage sons and added another six years of teaching experience to my life. I taught middle school. The developmental issues of early adolescents both challenged and stimulated me. They continue to be a source of inspiration as well. Actually, these 11-, 12-, and 13-year-olds taught me that before I could help them deal with the challenges brought by this life stage, I needed to know what's normal for the stage and what's not. I realized (and it's almost with great embarrassment that I admit this fact to you) I had entered my own parenting with a particularly bad assumption: that because I had been a teenager once, I knew what was going on.

It takes only a month or two with seventh graders to understand why they scoff and roll their eyes when they hear those famous words, "When I was your age." Teens seem to know something adults forget: The early and middle parts of the teen years are like a game of toss.

During these years of great change, their fates seem very much up in the air. They are not sure what ball they are trying to catch. They only know they have to reach. They are pretty sure that I don't get "it," whatever "it" is, because they are teens and self-absorbed and certain that no one quite understands what they are going through. And I think I do get "it" because I have gone through this passage. But I forget that a key element of adolescence is that it is a period of time when each of us lives straddled between a clearly definable world and another world full of uncertainty.

As a middle school teacher, I have observed that many teens shake with nervous anticipation at the thought of becoming teenagers. With good cause, I might add. These years bring a rush of changes in the way teens look, act, think, and feel. These changes in turn create differences in the ways they see themselves. Their relationships with family, friends, teachers, the outside world, and even *themselves* transform. With so many changes, figuring out what's normal or not can be tricky for a parent.

The remaining pages of this chapter provide a brief overview of what normal adolescence appears to be. That way when something happens and you're not quite sure if it is normal or not, you can look to this chapter as a baseline. That's important because a lot of adolescent ADHD issues are normal—only multiplied perhaps even ten times or more. I suggest you read some books totally devoted to general adolescent development, especially since what we hear about teens today tends to focus on extremes. Demystification will help you not take personally some of the teen's angst, which frequently gets directed at the parent, often the mother. Knowledge may also reduce your fear and worry. Nonetheless, if you have questions or if you or your teen is having trouble, seek outside counsel. Don't second-guess.

The Newness of It All

In the *Handbook of Child Psychology,* author Harold Grotevant notes that the primary changes during these years fall into three categories:

1. Physical development and sexual maturation
2. Change of social status from child to adult
3. Potential development of more sophisticated reasoning abilities

Physical development and sexual maturation happen automatically, but not necessarily on a given time schedule. I used to laugh privately when my seventh graders walked into class each new school year. It is not unusual to have girls tower over boys. Some boys have face fuzz, while others still sport baby fat. Many wear braces. One memorable student coordinated her metal mouth with a nose ring. A girl wearing a T-shirt in the fall might find the same garment exposing her navel months later.

Then there's the teenage nightmare. I still vividly recall one sophisti-cated-looking young lady who seemed more like 17 than 12. She bounded up to my desk and in a loud voice asked, "Is this a zit?" Mirrors and combs come out without thought about the appropriate time and place. Muscle flexing is a favorite activity. In addition to rapid growth in both height and weight, early adolescents contend with body parts that don't all grow at the same rate. Thus, a teen who may have been athletically capable in fifth grade might find him- or herself uncoordinated just a few years later.

In a curious twist of nature, with so much changing and "Am I nor-mal?" a major preoccupation, early teens have a "pack" mentality. They want to fit in and be the same as everyone else. As 17-year-old Emily Rus-sell recalls, "When I was in grammar school I didn't get my period until late. I can remember being sooooo embarrassed." Puberty—marked by nipple swelling, the onset of menses, and the development of pubic and underarm hair in females—begins earlier for girls (usually between the ages of 10 and 13), as does the growth spurt. Generally boys add hair and inches and muscle tone beginning a year or so later than the girls. Females, who also add inches to their hips, thighs, and buttocks, finish growing before males. Boys, whose voices deepen, may experience the cracking voice as both a welcome sound and a source of embarrassment. I've had more than one young man turn beet red when in the middle of answering a question his voice rose from a low drone to a squeak. It occurs to me that the reason so many boys seem to mumble in seventh grade might actually have to do with fear of voice failure.

By the middle to late adolescence, teens have more control over their physical bodies. They grow into them, so to speak. Physical changes continue to occur, but they don't seem as dramatic until you look at old home videos or photo albums. Child-development researchers have found that an easier adjustment in puberty occurs when girls develop on schedule and boys begin early. Similarily, when girls develop early and boys late, they seem to have more trouble adjusting.

Hopelessly Hormonal

A subterranean sea of hormones, among other biological processes, triggers physical and sexual maturation. When puberty begins, different chemical systems impact on behavior and thinking. Teens may appear to get a bit squirrely. In light of the massive physical, social, emotional, and cognitive changes of adolescence, we can understand why the early teen years have much conflict and reservation. Like summer storms, chemical imbalances occur temporarily and destabilize the adolescent. What's the result? Well, you see emotionality and mood swings, teary faces and downright hysterics. Girls might be "bitchy," and if you have sons, you might see anger flashes or need to replace doorknobs and hinges that loosen or fall off from being yanked open by young men who don't know their own strength.

Sleep

According to adolescent sleep researchers, the average teen requires nine hours of sleep a day. Most get two hours less. Lack of sleep isn't their only problem. During the teen years, biological clocks change. Teens not only need more sleep; their circadian rhythms tell their bodies that they need to go to sleep later and get up later. Of course, most high schools require them to get up earlier than ever before.

Consider a day in the life of Emily Russell. "I'm exhausted," she says. "I wake up at 6:15, go to school from 7:30 to 2:30. I have sports after school until 5:30 or 6:00. Then I normally come home. I used to shower and stuff, but now I just forget it. I eat dinner and try to do my homework, which is tough to focus on when you're so tired. I try to get to bed like 10 but usually it's 11. This week I have a research paper due, so I'll be up to the wee hours tomorrow night." Emily's average sleep time is seven hours. And she's doing a lot better than most of her friends, some of whom have jobs, too. "A lot of kids don't get to bed until 12:30 and they are up at 6:30 the next morning," she reports.

Adolescent sleep researchers find that lack of sleep affects the adolescent's ability to concentrate, think clearly, and control emotions. It also makes them more vulnerable to accidents and depression. The National Highway Traffic Safety Administration estimates that almost half of the 100,000 car crashes a year linked to sleepy drivers involves late adolescent and young adult drivers. Given the potentially devastating effects of lack of sleep, the obvious solution seems to be that teens should go to bed earlier. But, as explained before, that's not what their biological rhythms require.

What do many adolescents do? They try to make up for lost sleep on weekends. However, irregular sleep patterns actually may make matters worse. Sleep researchers Amy Wolfson and Mary Carskadon note that teens with irregular bedtimes report academic difficulties, daytime sleepiness, down feelings, and sleep/wake problems. Girls also seem to miss school more due to sickness. Boys have a greater number of injuries requiring treatment.

A *USA Today* article offers this advice from Dr. Carskadon:

- Have a sleep plan that allows at least eight and a quarter hours per night.
- Limit extra sleep on weekends to one or two hours.
- Don't perk yourself up just before bedtime.
- Limit light exposure in the late evening and increase it in the morning.

Getting to Me

Another primary change involves the changing social status of the adolescent. One main job of the adolescent is to move from dependence to independence. Transitions like this one come with upheaval, power plays, and negotiation.

Achieving independence is a long process of trial and error. It begins with the discovery that parents are people, and thus imperfect beings. I would have loved it if my teenage sons had come to me and said, "Mom, I'm a teenager now. I need to get on my own path. As wonderful as you are, I now see that you sometimes make mistakes. I'm also not so sure I agree with your beliefs or the way you vote in elections. I honor your opinions on abortion and gun control, but lately—and darn, I just can't seem to help myself—I've been having a few opinions of my own, which don't entirely match yours. I hope you don't mind. And while I respect your rules, based on the extensive reading I've done in growth and development, I really need to test them a bit. Please don't be upset. I'm sure we will be able to negotiate and work out a compromise that we both can live with." Ah.

But early adolescents themselves don't know what's going on. Many fall into a period of confrontation, which may include angry exchanges, arguing, hiding their lives, giving parents the silent treatment, or flashing a look that says, "You are dorkier than the dorkiest dork." Most of this behavior is normal, unless it's to a significant degree or rebellious beyond most if not all rules. And this initial behavior does tend to diminish around ages 14 or 15, when the teen is better able to use newly developed thinking abilities. (More about that later in this chapter.)

Peace in the family in part requires that parents understand what's going on in their teen's developmental world. In the book *You and Your Adolescent*, Laurence Steinberg and Ann Levin advise parents to expect teens to do the following:

- Reject your efforts to help, reassure, or give affection
- Be hypercritical of your personal weaknesses
- Choose friends before family

- Turn everyday decisions into tests of your trust and their competence
- Appear "parentless" in order to look older and more independent

Enter the Peer Group

Meanwhile, as our sons and daughters busily reject us, they also live in identity nowhere land. So they become tribal and put on the identity of the clique they hang with. Young teens especially gravitate to groups. They tend to think of every member as an intimate friend.

For younger teens, life can pretty much be an in-or-out experience. Usually, they don't choose to be on the outs with their group. In fact, the very idea of social rejection creates incredible fear and anxiety. It is one reason why teens may cave in to pressure to do things they really don't want to do.

I've watched these group dynamics up close in the classroom. Many a 12-year-old girl has come to me in tears because her "best" friend has a new best friend, which threatens the girl's group status. Instead of tears, boys tend to get into angry interchanges when one group member threatens another's social standing. With both genders, potential and actual fights erupt, especially when the "he said/she said" rumor mill begins to spin. Social rejection devastates young teens, and they do lose control. The trick is to intervene early on.

Older teens also group together, but by the mid-teens, their clusters become smaller, as does the circle of friends. Tenth grader Eric Stoner loves the social part of school, but he also notes that for some people, school is a fearful place. "Judgment is horrible. You are sorted into cliques depending on how you look, or dress, or if you play sports." Eric doesn't really want to be part of the "popular" crowd. "I don't think I could trust them because they are so obsessed with physical things," he explains.

Here we can see where cognitive changes enter into the picture and help the teen make judgments that are more appropriate. Peer pressure doesn't really bug Eric too much. At 16, he has more self-confidence. Also, he may be helped by the differences between the way males and females experience socialization. Females are encouraged to be a part of a group. Males are pushed toward independence.

For instance, Eric views peer pressure as "the pressure you perceive and put on yourself—like I'm not going to be accepted unless I drink." He explains, "I've been to parties where people are kicking down shots. They look at you and offer a shot. You say, 'Nah.' They're cool with that. It's really not like, 'Oh, then go leave the party.'"

Senior Emily Russell finds her friends are growing apart. She believes that's partly due to the natural transition high school graduation brings. But perhaps a more immediate reason for separation is the change in her group's behavior. "A lot of my friends are into new types of things," she explains. "I think almost everybody likes to drink and drug once in a while. But now it's not just smoking pot. It's taking it to the next level—doing Ecstasy."

She's also disillusioned with the sexual behavior. "Sex isn't an issue until you hit a certain point. Then, even people you didn't expect are doing it because like 'Oh, you are 17, 18. You should be at the next step.'" Of course, sex and drugs may be issues even for middle schoolers, but Emily's point is well taken. Her way of dealing with this pressure is to separate from the pack. Middle schoolers may not have the confidence to go it alone.

The term "peer pressure" is mainly associated with negative behavior, but peers can be positive influences on your son's or daughter's behavior. They also serve an important role in developing intimacy and friendship skills. For instance, when Emily has a problem, "I go to my mom with certain things, or I'll talk to my friends about it and give my mom the restricted version." Emily leaves out just enough stuff so that she can still get the point across. But for problem solving, she finds that "somebody your own age is really important because they understand more." We adults might have a knee-jerk disagreement with Emily's perception and think that we should be the main confidants for our sons and daughters. Perhaps we need to remember that growing up does require us to practice problem solving and to learn from mistakes.

In addition to peer pressure, teens also face parental pressure. Some parents expect their teens to be older and wiser than their years. They may also look for excellence in academics or extracurricular activities. Thus, some teens perceive their parents to be demanding.

What Are They Thinking?!!

Each fall on back-to-school night, I'd stand in front of a sea of parents. They all paid more than perfect attention to what I had to say. While interested in the curriculum, grading policies, and homework policies, most of these parents of seventh graders had one overriding concern: "How will my child do?" So after a couple of back-to-school nights and a few barrages of frenzied phone calls following first-marking-period progress reports, I began to talk to parents about an observation I had made after some years of experience with kids. In many cases, marks go down in seventh grade, or the student finds he or she needs to spend a lot more effort to make the grade. I would tell the parents before the first progress report, "Don't be surprised if you see a decline, and don't be too hard on your child, especially if he or she is trying."

I also told my students not to be surprised if they found the academic world tougher in seventh grade. School and curriculum demands require a lot more sophistication in thinking, planning, organizing, and following through. Middle school happens to be the gateway to demands for very complex thinking and processing abilities. As happened in their child-hood days when they learned to read, most early adolescents are bound to wobble until they fall into sync. Just as all teens don't physically mature at the same time, changes in their cognitive abilities occur at different rates as well. That's a point often overlooked.

At home, we parents often observe a certain "spaciness" in our early adolescents. They seem to be able to keep track of the most insignificant minutiae about what someone wore, or who spoke to whom in the hall, or what band had what hit single on the top-500 countdown. Doing chores, remembering what to get when sent on an errand, and putting the bike where it belongs rather than on the ground in the driveway behind the car just seem to flow right past them. Fortunately, these thinking patterns are neither terminal nor unusual.

Different areas of our brains develop at various periods in life. Neuroscientists recently discovered that the rapid brain development once thought to be characteristic only of a child's earliest years continues into the teen years. Neurons, or brain cells, are the brain's basic building blocks. Our brains always look to make patterns and sense out of information. To do so, networks of neurons form. In early childhood, our brains take in a lot of information, but the neural networks are fairly simple, like the single stalks of new raspberry bushes. During late childhood, these networks experience rapid growth and become dense, like raspberry bushes left unattended for a few years. A lot of these neurons will have no purpose, and so gradually these dense networks go through a self-pruning. By mid-adolescence, the neural networks are less dense but far more intricate and capable of quite sophisticated "thinking and doing" operations.

What adults observe in the preteen and early adolescent years is the characteristic change in thinking capability. Children's basic intellectual ability doesn't change. Rather, it's the way they think and do that changes. Margaret Feerick, Ph.D, an adolescent specialist with the National Institute of Child Health and Development, explains: "Teens are able to muse about and think through all the possibilities of a problem. They can reason about abstract things. This ability affects their moral development. When approached with a moral problem, they have the ability to think about more possibilities, more solutions, and more abstract resolutions."

This enhanced ability to reason doesn't necessarily mean, however, that teens act accordingly. Think about your own son or daughter for a minute. Can you remember a time when he or she ardently condemned someone's "amoral" behavior, perhaps even yours, and then went ahead and did something similar?

During these years, teens also develop an increased memory capacity, better problem-solving strategies, and improved verbal ability. Overall learning improves. The down side of this change in logic and reasoning ability, especially in the early teen years, is that many parents find little they say accepted at face value. A simple no may no longer exist. As they begin to flex their brains, these teens can be quite argumentative and get stuck in a position, especially when their newly found idealism kicks in.

Conflict can frequently erupt, but disagreement and argument should not be confused with defiance, which is quite another problem and not typical teen behavior. (More about defiance in Chapters 8 and 9.)

We parents can be fooled into thinking that better reasoning means better judgment. These are not the same. Consider a recent adolescent/adult study conducted by Harvard researcher Deborah Yurgelun-Todd. She used imaging technologies to see what areas of the brain are activated when a person is shown a series of pictures of faces with various expressions. Overall, adolescents had exaggerated responses, poor ability to accurately identify the feeling expressed in the picture face, and poor insight and judgment. When shown a face with a fearful expression, the adolescent brains reacted from a brain area associated with emotion, while adults relied on judgment and reasoning areas in their identification process. Clearly, reasoning and judgment are under construction in teens.

"Failure to understand changes in the way young adolescents think is a leading cause of conflict between parents and teenagers," write Steinberg and Levin in *You and Your Adolescent*. Adolescent specialists generally offer the following advice:

- Don't confuse debate with argument.
- Don't take it personally.
- Find issues on which you can safely defer to adolescent judgment.
- Encourage curiosity, inquiry, and independence.
- Expect mistakes.

One of the scariest aspects of parenting any adolescent is the "it won't happen to me" mentality of teens. They know enough to be dangerous to themselves. It's the gap between what they have done and what they think they can do that makes for dangerous decisions and parental shortness of breath.

What are they thinking? Well, they're thinking great thoughts; that they know it all; that you are not all-powerful, all-knowing, all-anything; that if given a chance they could make the world a better place; that if they are seen in public with you, someone may find out that they have parents; that if you only understood them . . .

When they approach early adulthood, they are thinking maybe you're not quite as out of it as they once thought; that you might be more than a meal ticket; that family matters as much as friends. Occasionally they drop their egocentricity and consider your needs, too. Having said this, I have to make a qualification. Writing about humans means using generalizations. What I've just described may not be entirely accurate in your experience. In some parent–young adult situations, it may not even be partially the case. A lot of factors enter into the primary changes associated with adolescent development.

The Parent-Teen Relationship Shift

Adolescents tend to see themselves as existing in present time only. Still, much of what they do and how they do it has many influences. The parent/child relationship is among the most powerful influences. It also undergoes significant changes as adolescents work on their major developmental tasks of autonomy and "de-cloning," or what is typically called identity achievement. Suffice it to say, families undergo significant changes in the ways they interact. Still, as Dr. Feerick points out, "People tend to think of these years as this period where kids are rejecting their parents. Typically, it's really not that extreme."

The relationship between parents and teens undergoes a bit of a cycle that may repeat many times throughout these years. When new issues over autonomy and identity arise, whether large or small, there's a point of disagreement that creates tension. This misalignment may continue until all parties work it out, make adjustments, and fall back into sync.

In addition to the changes in the parent-child relationship, around the time our sons and daughters become teenagers many of us are busy reexamining our lives. Mothers may be beginning or actually going through menopause. Careers may change, as may marital status. Illnesses, some of them grave, become more common in midlife. Many of us are sandwiched between taking care of our children and taking care of our aging parents. Not only does the teen's developmental process affect home life, but home life will impact on the teen, and it may be particularly hard during these very vulnerable years.

The Good Parent

When I asked 16-year-old Eric Stoner to tell me what makes a good parent, the wisdom of his answer surprised me. "You set a guideline. That is what you should do, because if you make set-in-stone rules, these will be broken. But if the set-in-stone rules aren't there to begin with, then that doesn't lead to rebellious behavior."

With his voice growing higher and his speech pattern becoming more rapid-fire, Eric finishes his description. "Parents have to listen. They have to respect what we do, and that we are emotional people. We are not going to do whatever you say. We're not robots. But we are not going to ignore everything you say, either. There's that boundary, and you just have to find that and respect it. It's that simple." If only . . .

If you read between the lines, what Eric describes is a parenting style that most psychologists agree is well suited to the development of well-adjusted young adults. For most types of teens, this style works really well. Below are descriptions of common parenting styles. See if you can pick out which one Eric advocates.

Permissive: These parents are nice, but they don't set limits, make rules, or give consequences. They think teens will learn through trial and error. They don't have much regard for the concept of authority.

Authoritative: These parents are loving. They make rules but also offer explanations and encourage their teen's involvement in the decision-making process. They can be flexible, but they make non-negotiable rules for issues of safety. They foster independence but still provide guidance. They impose consequences when necessary.

Authoritarian: These parents are in total charge and intend to raise perfect and obedient teens. They expect the teen to do as they say. All hell breaks loose when that doesn't happen.

Disengaged: These parents may be bodily present, but they are not there for their kids. They may be extremely emotionally needy or self-focused to the extent that their needs come before those of their children. Some may even be negligent.

Authoritative is the style Eric advocates. He is not asking to live in a rule-free environment. He's really suggesting that rules be considered guides to behavior, and that teens be involved with the creation of those guidelines. Eric doesn't want to be rebellious, but he's also aware that at times teens will do things that go against their parents' wishes. When that happens, he realizes that there will be consequences. Some of those are natural, like getting ill from getting drunk, and some of those are logical, like being grounded for crossing the line. Obviously, no parent is 100 percent in any category. It is the good and good-enough parents whose teens tend to have better outcomes.

Also, the degree to which parents are more authoritative and less authoritarian regarding limits and consequences has to do with the age and maturity of their kids. Early adolescents need (and seem to want) clear limits. In fact, these can actually be a comfort, as it allows them to get off the hook of negative peer pressure. I've overheard lots of seventh graders say something like, "I can't do that. I'll get so busted if they catch me."

Older teens want to have more of a voice. Having a say and being listened to are really important to them. Adolescents involved in the negotiation of rules and limits tend to honor them more. When they do choose to break a rule, they often seem to accept the responsibility for their actions. In fact, when asked by an adult to come up with a consequence for misbehavior, many teens actually give tougher penalties than those in authority would ever think to give.

I Gotta Be Me

Teens become increasingly more concerned with who they are separate and apart from a peer group and parents during middle adolescence. By late adolescence and early adulthood, our sons and daughters are supposed to be leaving home, either for education or for work. They should be assuming responsibility for their lives, entering the career loop, and maybe even meeting a future partner. In short, they develop an identity.

According to author Harold Grotevant, "Development of identity is an on-going process with antecedents in childhood, dramatic changes in adolescence, and the potential for on-going change and adaptation through adulthood." The challenge is to blend social, emotional, cognitive, and intellectual aspects into a unique and distinct self. As explained by Dr. Feerick, adolescents go through various stages in search of an identity, beginning with being clueless about who they are. Then they move to an experimental stage where they try on different identities until they fashion one that is a unique and customized fit.

Not all adolescents, or adults for that matter, achieve an identity separate from the world around them. Researcher Erik Erikson called that an "identity crisis." Some teens and adults never quite figure out who they are. Others don't fully explore their identity. Rather, they sort of adopt identities—often, but not always, based on what their parents expect, which is known as identity foreclosure. Such individuals become who they are expected to be rather than who they are meant to be.

An identity crisis can also be temporary, as in the case of people who delay finding their identity. Late bloomers may fall into this group. These people don't adopt someone else's plan for them. Instead, they coast until they figure out who they are. "Identity achievement for men is a predictor of long-term stability, good emotional outcomes, and good psychological outcome," Dr. Feerick explains. With women, for whom there is more emphasis on adopting roles, she notes that both foreclosure and identity achievement predict positive outcomes.

Harold Grotevant reports that certain family characteristics are associated with adolescents who achieve identity—meaning they become responsible, independent, productive members of society. These families encourage and provide opportunities for self-expression. They support individuality rather than seeing autonomy as a form of separation. They hang in, even during the most difficult of circumstances, and tolerate unwanted and unexpected emotions. They can also handle novelty, ambiguity, and uncertainty.

Carl Dodson, a college sophomore with whom I spoke on his twentieth birthday, is well on his way to identity achievement. He's found the greatest challenge of college to be "more of a rite of passage than of academic achievement." At the end of his freshman year, he realized the school he thought would be a perfect fit barely fit at all. So he packed up and moved to a new school. He's learning what really interests him. And he says, "I try not to freak out about making decisions that might not be popular."

A Disability Consideration

Now that we have an idea of what's normal for these dynamic years, we move to how ADHD adds challenge. So many parents struggle with the question of what's normal and what's ADHD. I'm not so sure we need to focus our attention on this query. Really, the issue has more to do with changing our expectations of our adolescents and understanding their struggles. We don't want to limit our kids or make excuses for what they do or do not do. If you find yourself wondering if a behavior is normal, ask yourself, "Does it matter?" Then quickly ask a second question: "What can be done to help my son or daughter?" We want to maximize their potential, not make them "disability excused."

I came to think this way because of a teaching experience I had at the high school level in a building that had many classrooms without four walls and a door. I couldn't help but notice an eleventh grade student with bright red hair who always seemed to walk around and disrupt his class and others. No one ever said a word to him. One day I happened to be covering for his teacher. He came late to class, so I told him to get a pass. He was outraged at what he perceived to be my unreasonable request. He really thought I had some nerve to hold him to the same standard as everyone else. A colleague came up to me afterward and reminded me that this young man had "learning problems" and was in the school's disability program, commonly known as special ed. "Oh," I said, and asked benignly, "Does that mean he's not capable of getting to class on time?" Well, I'm sure you know the answer.

Having a disability does not entitle the person to a different set of rules when he or she is quite capable of following the rules in place and meeting appropriate expectations. To allow otherwise is to do a great disservice. I stuck my neck out with the administration to advocate for this boy. I reminded my colleagues that he would be held accountable in the outside world. Certainly he deserved whatever we could do to help him become a productive member of society and to feel good about himself. After I made my case, the administration tried a slightly different approach. Lo and behold, he stopped being late to his classes because we held him to a standard he could reach. It is important to emphasize "a standard he could reach." I do believe he actually felt better being treated like everyone else.

As parents, we have to know our teens' limitations. We have to understand that ADHD is a neurological disorder. Thus, we have to expect the types of problems described in the remaining pages of this book. We want to help our teens normalize to the best of their abilities. In so doing, we take the *dis-* out of *disable* and create *able*. Within the pages that follow, I hope you find the help you need, but not just practical "where to go and what to do when" help. May you find comfort and support.

 INFORMATION LINK

For a wonderful report on the teen years and parenting principles (free of charge and easy to read): A. Rae Simpson, Ph.D., *Raising Teens: A Synthesis of Research and a Foundation for Action,* Project on the Parenting of Adolescents, Center for Health Communications, Harvard School of Public Health, www.hsph.harvard.edu/chc/parenting.

CHAPTER TWO

ADHD—The Potentially Powerful Problem

ADHD has the potential to create serious lifelong problems, especially when it goes undetected and untreated. Consider this chapter a basic guide to the diagnosis of ADHD. It describes what ADHD looks like, what it consists of, and the recommended methods professionals should use as part of a good diagnostic practice. The chapter also contains an explanation of the current thinking about the nature of the neurological processes affected by the disorder.

"She ran away three times, and I wish I didn't have to wake up until she was 25," says Sylvie Lovitch earnestly. Until her teen years, Sylvie's daughter Lucy had been fairly easy to raise, especially when compared to her hyperactive younger brother, who had been diagnosed with ADHD at age 6. She did great in elementary school and had been in the gifted and talented program. Then came the middle school years. Problems surfaced. Life for this family became conflict laden.

Despite knowing a lot about the disorder, her parents were thrown a curve by Lucy's behavior. Her once excellent grades began to slide and eventually tanked. Lucy changed friends. She refused to bring any of them home to meet the family. There was the hostility at home, especially toward her mother. "She was so nasty and called me the most godawful names," Sylvie vividly recalls.

Based on their daughter's horrendous behavior and what they had heard about her newfound friends, the Lovitchs figured Lucy must be into drugs and alcohol. In fact, they were so certain about this idea that they began to attend Parents Anonymous meetings.

Lucy has a different take about this period. She felt unsupported and judged by her parents. She shut them out because, she explains, "All I would hear is how I'm not doing what I'm supposed to be doing, that my friends are crazy, and what's wrong with me." Lucy knew her parents thought she was on drugs. She was not.

Lucy's defiance successfully masked her core problem. Undetected attention deficit hyperactivity disorder (which led to poor school performance) plus well-meaning but ineffective parenting practices had set the stage for the years of uproar. By the time of her diagnosis at age 22, Lucy felt depressed, anxious, and defeated.

"It's surprising that it took so long to find out I had ADHD," says Lucy, who guesses about the reason why it wasn't picked up sooner: "I didn't have the hyperactivity, and I didn't have the acting out in classes." Instead, Lucy says she daydreamed. "I would be taking notes and then just zone out. I had number one and number ten, and I'd be like, 'What happened to two through nine?' I either got A's in my classes or just barely made it. It's not like I had a problem learning in high school," she observes. "It's just that something went wrong and I couldn't figure it out."

Lucy went to an open-enrollment community college after graduation. Too much pressure and too much partying led to trouble there. It took this very bright student with an IQ over 140 twice as long as it should have to make it through. "They'd hand out the syllabus and I could feel the anxiety build inside me," Lucy remembers. The work piled up beyond her ability to stay on top of the situation. In a sad tone she says, "I would just get sucked into this hole. I felt like I was never going to get out. Over time I stopped going to classes—even math, which I was doing well in." Logically, you would expect her to salvage what she could, but at this point Lucy felt her chances for success were almost zero.

"Eventually I started wondering if I had ADHD because I had a problem paying attention and organizing for classes. When I got bored, I left because I couldn't concentrate." She sighs. Lucy sought help from the college's counseling center. She recalls that they always gave the same advice: "You need to do better." As she looks back, this nonresponse makes her angry. She feels someone at the college should have recognized her problem and said, "Well, it seems to me there's a pattern in the classes you passed and the classes you failed. There must be a reason for this." Lucy stumbled along and got more depressed. She decided to go for counseling. That's when an evaluation led to her diagnosis.

Lucy's life has made a turn. She is just about to get her associate's degree. She's also coming to terms with the aftermath of poor judgment and trouble resisting temptation. These impulsive behaviors led Lucy to run up a $2,500 credit card debt and to buy a car without a title. It can't be registered, so it sits rusting in her parents' driveway. In between classes, Lucy works two jobs to pay her bills.

I can't help but wonder what Lucy's life might have been like had someone only recognized her ADHD earlier. Fortunately, her life is improving. Remarkably, this family has recovered from the battle they once knew. They laugh now. They freely talk about their most intimate ghosts without bitterness or shame. Their story reveals a family that has struggled and come to terms with its problems, many of which stemmed from ADHD but became more complicated due to adolescence.

The Legacy of Myth and Misconception

Attention deficit hyperactivity disorder. Often when I hear these words, especially from people who haven't lived with it in one way or another, I hear the haunting sounds of a Greek chorus. "Yes, but . . ." "Is it real?" "Okay, so she has ADHD. But she should still pay attention like everyone else." "What's wrong with those parents?" "I mean, why give this kid just another excuse?" "They should discipline him more!" "I know someone who has this and he doesn't act that way!" "ADHD, no big deal!" "Well, lots of people have this problem and they do just fine." And when I hear "If that was my kid . . ." I say to myself, "If only it was."

Some people call ADHD a fad, the diagnosis du jour, a big excuse. I disagree. Still, I have seen kids labeled without the benefit of a thorough diagnostic procedure. I have heard adults call themselves ADHD because they have been a little scattered from time to time, or because they prefer interesting things to monotonous activities. No wonder skepticism surfaces.

Sadly, the term *ADHD* (or *ADD*, as it was known before 1994) has been bandied about with little regard to the knowledge and understanding gained from rigorous scientific scrutiny of this disorder. Scientists don't yet know all there is to know about this neurobiological condition, as well as many others. Critics argue ADHD's validity. The effects of this ADHD-bashing can be devastating. As one father remarked, "I find it very hard to tell people that my son has ADHD because I think there is a stigma." This dad believes people think that ADHD is the excuse for an ill-behaved teenager and bad parenting.

ADHD has even been called a cultural phenomenon. Of course it is not. ADHD exists worldwide. A panel of international experts notes that the differences in prevalence rates between countries are quite small. The United States estimates that between 3 and 5 percent of the population has the disorder.

Another source of controversy about this disorder stems from the use of medication as a treatment. Mention Ritalin, a medication widely and effectively used in the management of ADHD, and opinions fly. Those critical of medication therapy often do so with the belief that drugs are being given to youth whose behavior falls within the spectrum of "normal." They are not. The medication topic is discussed extensively in Chapter 4.

Maybe I'm preaching to the choir here in discussing the myths and misconceptions about ADHD. But even I sometimes get lured by the "ADHD is overdiagnosed" headlines. It is not. An April 1998 Special Council Report of the *Journal of the American Medical Association* (JAMA) looked into these claims of overdiagnosis and overprescription. The Council concluded:

> *Although some children are being diagnosed as having ADHD with insufficient evaluation and in some cases stimulant medication is prescribed when treatment alternatives exist, there is little evidence of widespread over-diagnosis or misdiagnosis of ADHD or of widespread over-prescription of methylphenidate (Ritalin) by physicians.*

What do adolescents make of ADHD? Well, it varies. Hallie Banks, 15, tells me, "It's actually my fault. If I tried to pay attention, I probably could." She doesn't truly believe these words. Rather, Hallie uses them as a defense. She finds calling herself lazy and such actually lessens the likeli-hood that others will criticize her. She beats them to the punch.

Other teens echo the sentiments of 12-year-old Marty Prior, who finds that ADHD "is just another way to say that people are bad." In fact, he thinks the letters *ADD* stand for "adult deficit disorder." I chuckled when he said so, and almost thought he might be playing with me. He wasn't. In fact, Marty voiced another myth that skeptics and critics use as a way to make their points: that the kids are fine and that ADHD is noth-ing more than a child's failure to meet adult expectations.

At times I can fall into the illusion that ADHD is no big deal. Some-times I even forget what I am dealing with. Maybe that's because we par-ents of teenagers are more removed from our kids than when they were little. They are developing identities separate and apart from our visions of who they are or should be. We don't intervene in their every waking action. We have less control. Our adolescents *do* have more say and more independence. It can become easier to see them as masters of their uni-verse, creators of their own hard times. If you are struggling with a tough teen or a teen with difficulties, you might easily lose sight of the current moving underneath the troubled waters. You might find yourself think-ing, "I know my teen has ADHD, but he or she should _____."

Separating normal adolescent behavior from ADHD behavior is not easy. Frankly, I'm not sure it's even advisable. We have to deal with whole people regardless of what causes the issues and problems. Whether symp-tomatic of ADHD or simply adolescent shenanigans, problem behavior must be dealt with.

Signs and Symptoms

When it comes to making sense of human behavior, the signs we see—what somebody does or does not do—are not so easy to figure out, espe-cially as children age. For instance, not turning in an assignment can be seen as a sign that the teen chooses not to do the work. Or interrupting another person can be seen as rudeness. As interpreters, we have to ask why before we can make a good determination of what we think we see. We color our answers with our own prior knowledge or lack of it, and with our experience. We make educated guesses, like Lucy's parents. Based on the behavior their daughter showed, they guessed drugs to be the culprit. A good guess, but incorrect. A well-trained diagnostician was able to look at the whole range of Lucy's behaviors and determine that she had undiagnosed and untreated ADHD. Her picture became further complicated due to family problems, poor communication, Lucy's own anxiety stemming from her difficulties, and the onset of adolescence. All in all, hers was not necessarily an easy puzzle to solve.

How Can We Tell If Somebody Has ADHD?

When clinicians diagnose any mental health disorder, they follow the guidelines suggested in the *Diagnostic and Statistical Manual of Mental Disorders, Fourth Edition (DSM-IV-TR)*. Clinicians understand that the behaviors associated with ADHD are often associated with other problems. In ADHD, these symptoms cluster into two main domains:

Inattention

often failing to pay careful or close attention to details
often making careless errors
often having problems paying attention for sustained periods
often appearing not to listen
often failing to finish tasks or follow directions
often losing needed things
often distracted easily
often forgetful

Hyperactivity-Impulsivity

often fidgety or squirmy
often out of seat when sitting is expected
often restless, running excessively, climbing
often noisy
often in perpetual motion or acting motor driven
often talks too much
often responds to questions before they're completely asked
often has a hard time waiting
often butts in or interrupts others

In order for these behaviors to be considered symptoms of ADHD, they have to meet other conditions. They have to

1. be present for at least six months
2. cause problems in two or more areas, such as social, school, or work
3. be inappropriate for the person's age
4. cause some difficulty prior to age seven (although troubles that occurred may not be recognized until a later time)

For a diagnosis of ADHD-Inattentive type, the person must have at least six inattentive symptoms. For a diagnosis of Hyperactive-Impulsive type, six or more of these symptoms must be present. For the Combined type, the individual must have six or more symptoms from each category, for a minimum of twelve symptoms. Some older adolescents and adults may show improvement in some areas and thus have fewer than twelve symptoms. They would be considered to be in partial remission.

These inattentive and hyperactive-impulsive behaviors are generally not considered symptoms of ADHD if they are part of pervasive developmental disorder, schizophrenia, or other forms of psychosis. As children with ADHD get older and their lives become complex, sometimes the symptoms get buried under behaviors that clearly look as though they are something else, or as if they have a different source as happened with Lucy.

Peter Jensen, M.D., former associate director for child and adolescent development at the National Institute of Mental Health, says, "Parents should understand that ADHD is a pattern of behavior that we know can have a bad outcome. If their child meets all the criteria for ADHD, what they have identified now is a pattern of behavior." The clinician's job is to make a *differential diagnosis,* that is, to rule out the presence of other disorders. Self-diagnosis is not a good idea. Nor should the *DSM* list be treated as a grocery list—taken this way, the list would suggest that most of us have ADHD. We do not. Notice the word *often* before each symptom—and the other criteria.

You Can't Be a Little Bit Pregnant

You can't be a little bit pregnant, but you can be a little bit ADHD. Unlike certain medical conditions, which you either have or do not have, such as pregnancy, ADHD is considered a dimensional disorder. It consists of a range of human behaviors that all people exhibit from time to time. In the case of ADHD, those behaviors tend toward the extreme end of the spectrum.

- They are maladaptive (causing significant difficulties).
- They are age-inappropriate, meaning they are not typical for the developmental level.

Adolescence requires complex thinking and doing. As Lisa Freund, Ph.D., a researcher at the National Institute of Child Health and Development, explains, "We have some indication from research that the areas of the brain that are developing more during adolescence have to do with the frontal lobes. These are what we call the executive function skills and are associated with planning and organization. If you lay ADHD on top of what is already occurring at this stage—in other words, when there are deficits in the very areas of the brain that appear to be attempting to mature—then we have kind of a double whammy." The developmental nature of behavior may partially explain why we see a shift in the types of problems people with ADHD experience as they mature. For instance, the ability to sustain attention differs markedly between preschoolers and middle school students, including those with ADHD.

What makes ADHD a disorder? Well, like all medical conditions that are dimensional in nature, its measure has to do with the number of symptoms present and, perhaps more important, the extent of the difficulty these cause. For example, we all have blood pressure. Clinically significant high blood pressure means we have crossed the realm of normal, acceptable, and functional into the dimension of problematic, potentially dangerous, or life-threatening. In order for a person to be diagnosed with ADHD, the symptoms present have to cause problems.

It's important to note that the number of symptoms a person has and the severity of the problems they cause may change across the life span. Some people see a significant decline in symptoms. For some, that decline makes life much easier. Others continue to struggle and have high levels of dysfunction. The main concern is not so much the quantity of symptoms, but rather the degree of difficulty they cause.

What You Might See

Dr. Peter Jensen explains, "ADHD is not any single thing. We haven't gotten to the state of knowledge yet where we can say that it is principally driven by genetics under one set of circumstances, or anxiety under another." Dr. Jensen makes the point that ADHD is a very complex disorder with multiple pathways and causes. Therein lies one main reason why symptoms of ADHD vary among individuals.

Consider the various descriptions of problems given by parents and teens.

Having ADHD is like popping the clutch and staying a tenth of a second after you do it. Your body is always ahead of your mind. You can make some pretty stupid decisions.

Not turning in assignments, being late for things, being rushed, being disorganized, not meeting commitments with friends on time—having people upset with her about that.

My son doesn't go through anything to the end. He's very bright, and so I think he gets bored easily.

I have trouble staying focused. It's frustrating because I don't understand things that everyone else does.

It's ready, fire, aim. He does something, then he realizes it is wrong.

She wants what she wants and she wants it easy, and everything else is ignored.

He is physically aggressive, but not in a fighting way.

He has problems with organization, planning, grades, keeping all of his materials in order, not taking on more responsibility for what he needs to do.

By adolescence, the typical ADHD pattern of behavior mixes with enough life experience and challenging developmental tasks to muddy the diagnostic waters. Symptoms considered *DSM* criteria may get lost in the range of behaviors and characterizations that you see. Adolescents with ADHD are often described as lacking self-control and being "managed by the moment," a phrase coined by expert Russell Barkley, Ph.D. They may have trouble with planning and organization. They may reach frustration overload easily. They have been known to be insensitive to the needs of others. Yet they can be overly sensitive when it comes to criticism in their direction.

ADHD symptoms seem to fall into two patterns: problems stemming from attention difficulties and problems with behavioral disinhibition, that is, impulse and motor control. Between 50 and 70 percent of teens with ADHD have a combination of both patterns. If you review those descriptions given in the parent quotes above, I'm sure you can readily identify which problems fall into which pattern. These behavioral groupings are considered subtypes. ADHD has most recently been viewed as a disorder with three subtypes:

- Predominantly inattentive type
- Predominantly hyperactive/impulsive type
- Combined type (inattentive, hyperactive, impulsive)

ADHD in the Twenty-First Century

Inconsistent behavior is a hallmark of ADHD. It perplexes parents, teachers, clinicians, and even those who suffer with the disorder. People with ADHD are not always inattentive, unable to complete tasks, or poor self-regulators of behavior. Sometimes they do quite well taking care of business, so to speak. Think about the 15-year-old who spends two hours in line for concert tickets but can't stay focused long enough to complete a simple homework task because "this is taking too long," as many a teen with ADHD has been heard to say. Or consider the kid in the classroom who stares blankly into space and then suddenly perks up when a fellow student comes late to class. It's hard to understand that the same underlying neurological issues may be driving what appear to be conflicting

Q   RESEARCH LINK

For an in-depth, scholarly review and discussion about these three mental control processes (attention, memory, and executive function), read the book coedited by G. Reid Lyon, Ph.D., and Norman A. Krasnegor, Ph.D.: *Attention, Memory and Executive Function,* Paul H. Brooks Publishing Co., Baltimore, 1996.

behaviors. New ways of looking at ADHD and new research may help to make better sense of this seemingly contradictory behavior.

Dr. Thomas Brown of Yale University notes, "The *DSM* is the framework we are working in now," but he points out that the study and treatment of ADHD is in the beginning of a paradigm shift. Science is in the midst of seeing this disorder with new, improved glasses. Researchers are now looking into three mental control processes that seem to have a lot to do with ADHD difficulties: attention, memory, and executive function. Dr. G. Reid Lyon, chief of the Child Development and Behavior Branch of the National Institute of Mental Health, writes, "Without these abilities we could not plan, solve problems, or use language."

You don't have to have ADHD to have a problem with these processes, but such problems are highly associated with ADHD. They allow us to pay attention, remember, and organize and structure information. According to Dr. Lyon, without that ability we would not be able to alter our behavior in new situations. People with ADHD seem to have this problem. They don't generalize information and use what they know across situations.

When thinking about these mental processes, it's important to realize that the brain operates as a series of systems and subsystems. Attention, memory, and executive function are separate systems that operate alone as well as with other systems. If somebody is having difficulty figuring out what the main idea in a story is, for example, no one can point to any one area of the brain and say, "Well, there's the root of that problem." Broadly, the person could have a problem with attention, memory, executive function, two of these, or all three.

Furthermore, each of these systems mentioned (there are many others) has no central location and, as far as scientists know, no "ground control" center, either. Major brain systems also interact with each other. When it comes to determining what is actually going on in the constellation of symptoms that make up ADHD, given the depth of the brain systems involved, you can see why the answers are not so readily available.

As researcher Joseph Sergeant, from Vrije University in the Netherlands, explains, "You see, it is not just one part but various parts of the brain involved in the disorder. When we do certain types of study on children, we find not only the frontal lobes but the basal ganglia, the corpus callosum, and the cerebellum show deviations." Other brain regions implicated are the nucleus accumbens, the dorsolateral prefrontal area, and the locus coeruleus.

The brain research tells us that people with ADHD *do not* have brain damage or brains different from anyone else's. Nor are they less or more intelligent than the general population. Research using brain-study technologies show that certain brain areas have less activity and blood flow. Some brain structures are also slightly smaller. Many of these areas are rich in the neurotransmitter dopamine. Neurotransmitters are brain chemicals that help brain cells and systems communicate with each other. The neurotransmitter that seems to be most involved with ADHD is dopamine. It is widely used throughout the brain. Scientists have discovered a genetic basis for part of the dopamine problem in some individuals. Other neurotransmitters are implicated and being studied, too.

When neurotransmitters don't work as they are supposed to, the brain systems function inefficiently. Thus in ADHD, how the brain systems function, both alone and with each other, seems to be the main issue. Since these systems are diverse and extremely complicated, we can understand why we see the variations on the basic themes of ADHD, why

Q   RESEARCH LINK

For in-depth information about current brain research, see J. Swanson, F. X. Castellanos, M. Murias, G. LaHoste, and J. Kennedy. "Cognitive Neuroscience of Attention Deficit Hyperactivity Disorder and Hyperkinetic Disorder," *Current Opinion in Neurobiology* 8 (1998): pp. 263–271.

some people with ADHD have far more severe cases, and why they experience a wide variety of problems. It may also explain why everyone sometimes *appears* to have "a touch of ADHD."

Let's look closer at the current wisdom regarding these mental control processes and how they are connected to ADHD. While these don't tell the entire ADHD story, they do shed some light on the problems teens with the disorder have. This information may help develop an appreciation for the complexity of this disorder that may in turn change the thinking that ADHD is simply a matter of being too active or spacey.

Attention

Difficulty with attention is often seen as distractibility or not following through. Yet teens with ADHD can be stubborn in their focus on something they find interesting. At times, you can't distract them no matter how hard you try. At other times, they find tasks too tedious or boring. They tune out when things are dull and uninteresting to them.

Attention is somewhat of an umbrella term that covers a variety of mental control processes. Attention researchers believe that the brain has distinct networks involved with attention. Each network seems to be located in a different part of the brain and to be responsible for certain types of attention, such as beginning and seeing things through to the end, or paying sufficient attention.

Clearly, ADHD is not a problem of a complete lack of attention. Rather, it appears to be a problem of how much, how long, and under what circumstances.

Q　RESEARCH LINK

For a thorough discussion of the theory on attention and how it relates to ADHD, see Chapter 20 in Raja Parasuraman, ed., *The Attentive Brain*. MIT Press, Cambridge, 1998, pp. 448–460.

For more information on attention see M. I. Posner and M. E. Raichle, *Images of the Mind,* Scientific American Library, New York, 1994.

Memory

People with ADHD mainly have trouble with working memory. In turn, working memory problems lead to retrieval problems. Simply defined, working memory is an active part of memory that allows us to keep something in mind and use it to do something else. For instance, when we do mental arithmetic, we must keep numbers in mind, remember their products, and recombine those with more numbers to make new products. When 24-year-old Tyler Winston tells me that he studies very hard for his tests and knows all the answers but can't remember them when he gets to class, he's talking about a working memory/retrieval problem. In this case, he can't hold in mind what he needs to know in order to complete the task. It's as if he's trying to make an Internet link but is getting the "this page cannot be displayed" message.

While not listed as part of the *DSM* symptom list, teens with ADHD usually have complaints about aspects of working memory. In fact, working memory difficulties may sometimes be the reason people with ADHD blurt out or interrupt. As they are often heard to say, "If I don't say it now, I won't remember."

Executive Function

"The story of growing up is the story of increasing ability to manage oneself," says Dr. Thomas Brown. Brain functions that have to do with self-regulation are called executive functions. Basically, these brain functions manage other brain functions. They help mobilize, organize, coordinate, and oversee them. They also help regulate behavior. They help us size up situations so that we can act appropriately. As with the other mental control processes—attention and memory—no one knows for sure how these executive functions operate. We can sure see the effects when they do not work efficiently.

Many of these executive function problems fall under the heading of poor self-control. Teens, in general, have poor self-control on occasion. However, for teens with ADHD, poor self-control stands out almost as a constant. Noted researcher Russell Barkley has developed a new theory. He thinks ADHD is mainly a self-control problem, which he sees as the ability to inhibit and regulate behavior. People with self-control behave in

CLASSIC EXECUTIVE FUNCTION PROBLEMS

Poor executive functions lead to many difficulties. These problems don't occur all the time, nor do they always occur to the same degree.

poor planning
disorganization
being off task
poor problem solving
difficulty delaying today's pleasure for tomorrow's gain
problems working toward a goal
trouble seeing the big picture
having a poor sense of time/poor timing
poor handling of minor and major frustration
difficulty with motor control

a way that is in their long-term best interests. They can delay gratification and postpone today's desires for a better tomorrow. They can use the wisdom gained from experience to guide present-day decision making. They plan, organize, and problem solve.

People with ADHD, on the other hand, usually have trouble delaying and planning for the future. ADHD also causes difficulty in waiting, postponing, and thinking first before acting. That may explain the difficulties handling frustration. Many people with ADHD are hyperresponsive. Their brains readily flip into the reaction mode rather than pausing a moment to reflect before responding.

Dr. Barkley sees these self-control difficulties as stemming from a "time sight" problem. "Time sight" is the ability to use information from past experience to delay present action until we can see what the future result will be. He notes that the interval between thought and action is crucial to guiding our behavior. It allows us to think about what's going to happen before we do it. That moment of delay can mean the difference between a wise choice and a poor one.

Consider this: Teens and adults with the disorder are often described as risk takers. I take issue with this characterization. In actuality, taking risks

<table>
<tr><td>🔍   RESEARCH LINK</td></tr>
</table>

> Dr. Barkley has written a scholarly book about his theory,
> *ADHD and the Nature of Self-Control,* Guilford Publications,
> New York, 1997.
> He also gives a good description of it in his 1995 book for
> parents, *Taking Charge of ADHD,* Guilford Publications,
> New York.

means carefully sizing up a potential action and deciding to go ahead despite the potential downside. That's a far cry from going into something blindly or with a minimum of consideration, which is often the case in ADHD.

One of the exasperating aspects of poor self-control has to do with the difference between knowing what to do or not to do and then acting accordingly. Teens with ADHD know what to do and what not to do. However, they run into difficulty at the *point of performance*—that critical moment in time when they must inhibit or regulate behavior to act or think in their best interests and according to the situation at hand, be it a social moment or a school task. It is this point of performance problem that has led Dr. Barkley to make this important observation: "ADHD is not a problem of knowing what to do. It's a problem of doing what you know."

The world for teens with this disorder would be a much kinder place if attention, memory, and executive function problems were seen by everyone, including those with ADHD, as the result of neurobiological events rather than deliberate choices or stupidity.

Gender Similarities and Differences

Another reason why Lucy Lovitch did not get diagnosed until age 22 probably has to do with her gender. Until the last decade or so, most people viewed ADHD as a predominantly male disorder. The reason is simple: The telltale symptoms of hyperactivity and impulsivity, which are usually accompanied by aggression, captured attention more than spaciness did. Most females with ADHD do not stand out as the males do. Many are inattentive and disorganized. They may come across as "ditzy." Thus they get overlooked. As Patricia Quinn, M.D., has observed, "Through cultural and societal expectations, girls have learned to look at the teacher. They may not be paying attention, but nobody knows it." Fifteen years ago, those females who did get noticed tended to be quite hyper and aggressive.

Researchers are now studying ADHD specifically in females. Stephen Hinshaw, Ph.D., a University of California, Berkeley, scientist, is one of the principal investigators in a large, long-term study of preadolescent girls. None of the girls in his study is receiving medication as a treatment. To date, the team has noted the following results:

- Boys outnumber girls in the inattentive, hyperactive-impulsive type by 3 or 4 to 1.
- More girls have the inattentive type; the ratio of boys to girls is 1.6 to 1.
- It's probable that a significant number of girls have not been diagnosed.
- Like boys, girls have some serious difficulties in key life areas:
  1. peers' rejection
  2. academic deficits
  3. neuropsychological deficits (planning, allocating attention, preventing interference from coming into play)

Interestingly, Dr. Hinshaw did not find girls to be more anxious than boys. However, he notes that aggression and how it differs between girls and boys with ADHD is an area that needs to be looked into: "Girls show lower rates of physical and verbal aggression than boys. But girls tend to show a higher rate of aggression that is indirect and focused on a social relationship."

What do girls do? Well, they act "bitchy." They may exclude another female from a social activity by not extending an invitation. Or they may talk behind another girl's back. "For boys, aggression is a greater predictor of later delinquency and problems. For girls, very high rates of that kind of relational aggression are just as predictable of negative long-term outcomes," Dr. Hinshaw says.

Other studies have found girls to have poor language development and skills. Since females have a verbal culture, Dr. Hinshaw points out, these problems can cause them added difficulty. They might have subtle problems with articulation or difficulty being able to speak fluently. They may not understand multipart directions too well. Dr. Hinshaw suggests that evaluations of girls with ADHD screen for language difficulties that might stem from how the girl processes what is heard or from self-expression.

Another feature seemingly more apparent in adolescent girls is hyperreactivity. Many physicians have come to believe that emotionality and unstable mood are key features in females. Dr. Quinn believes girls have more internalizing symptoms and a lot of self-esteem issues. She has observed that when a boy doesn't do well on a test, he says, "It was a stupid test," whereas the girl will say, "I'm stupid."

Males and females tend to react differently, too. Dr. Quinn finds that boys tend to "blow off" school. The boys I've seen in school feel defeated, and then they cop an attitude of "Screw this."

"Girls," Dr. Quinn observes, "will work harder. They tend toward overcompensation and perfectionism." These traits appear to be good coping mechanisms. But, says Dr. Quinn, "it's to the girls' detriment, because then they don't get the diagnosis of ADHD."

Premenstrual syndrome (PMS) presents additional problems. In fact, the inattentive-type females who are not necessarily hyperactive or impulsive often remain fairly well hidden until puberty—as happened in Lucy Lovitch's case. PMS symptoms worsen ADHD symptomatology by adding to disorganization and emotionality. "The hormonal piece, the overcompensation piece, and the peer rejection piece are unique to girls," says Dr. Quinn.

Regarding eating disorders, to date no studies have been done specifically on females diagnosed with ADHD. In an informal survey with eighty-seven respondents, Dr. Quinn found bulimia to be much more common than anorexia. She thinks anorexia, or self-starvation, requires a great deal

INFORMATION LINK

To read more about girls with ADHD, see Kathleen Nadeau, Ellen Littman, and Patricia Quinn, *Understanding ADHD and Girls*, Advantage Books, Silver Spring, Maryland, 1999.

of control, whereas bulimia allows the females with ADHD to eat impulsively as much as they want and then purge. The most common eating issue of the respondents in Dr. Quinn's survey was eating to feel better.

Diagnosis: When and How

When You Need Professional Help

If you (or someone else) thinks your son or daughter has ADHD because you see the telltale signs, you may be correct. But remember, the signs are just an indication that something is amiss. When you see a sign, you need to investigate. Seek input from qualified health care professionals, such as psychiatrists, clinical psychologists, clinical social workers, pediatricians, family practitioners, or specially trained school psychologists. Because ADHD often coexists with other problem-causing conditions, and because other disorders can masquerade as ADHD, you want someone who knows about a wide range of health problems, both mental and physical.

Some parent guidelines:

- For referral sources, look to parent support groups, community mental health centers, local hospitals, your primary-care physician, and possibly school counselors.
- Interview your prospective therapist. Be sure you are comfortable with him or her.
- Don't be afraid to ask for referrals if problems go beyond his or her area of expertise.
- Avoid anyone who offers a total cure or a quick solution.
- Feel free to discuss fees. Some clinicians will help in severe financial circumstances.
- Use the Internet for information, but be cautious.

Diagnostic Protocol

Around tenth grade, Maria Lopez's son Joey began failing classes and missing school. The school did a preliminary evaluation that pointed to

INFORMATION LINK

For information and support, contact:

CHADD (Children and Adults with Attention Deficit Hyperactivity Disorder) at the ADHD National Call Center, (800) 233-4050, or www.chadd.org.

ADDA—The Attention Deficit Disorder Association (847) 432-2332 or www.add.org.

The American Psychological Association publishes *Talk to Someone Who Can Help,* a pamphlet to guide the public in selecting a mental health professional. Call (800) 964-2000 or visit www.helping.apa.org.

ADHD. Maria then took her son to her primary-care physician. "He just felt Joey had an attitude problem," she remembers. With that, the doctor sent them on their way. She also took him to a pediatrician. Despite a family history of ADHD, he did not diagnose Joey, either.

In this case, neither doctor used any of the recommended diagnostic procedures. Physicians should not be quick to judge, nor should they dismiss parental concerns. The American Academy of Child and Adolescent Psychiatry and the American Academy of Pediatricians have assessment guidelines. This diagnosis cannot be made competently in a twenty-minute office visit, especially with an adolescent patient. Nor should it ever be made based on your brief explanation of the problems that are occurring. Parents, be wary of any doctor who diagnoses your son or daughter without following the guidelines recommended by their professional organizations. These are listed below.

Diagnosis: Key Features

✓ **Initial Evaluation**

Adolescent's History

- Parents and patient interviews for developmental history, a review of school records (i.e., report cards and standardized test results), presence or absence of symptoms (which may be done with a checklist), how the symptoms developed over time, and what life areas they are affecting

Q RESEARCH LINK

For a thorough discussion of the recommended guidelines, see:
"Practice Parameters for the Assessment and Treatment of
    Children, Adolescents, and Adults with Attention-Deficit/
    Hyperactivity Disorder," *Journal of the American Academy of
    Child and Adolescent Psychiatry* 36:10, October 1997
"Diagnosis and Evaluation of Children with Attention-Deficit/
    Hyperactivity Disorder." *Pediatrics.* May 2000; www.aap.org
    /advocacy/archives/mayADHD.htm.

- Presence of symptoms of other disorders listed in the *DSM*
- Prior history of diagnosis and treatment for ADHD
- Areas of relative strength (e.g., talents and abilities)
- History of any medical conditions or neurological problems,
  e.g., lead poisoning, head trauma, seizures, primary sleep
  disorders, fetal alcohol syndrome. Any medications that could
  cause symptoms, e.g., phenobarbital, antihistamines, steroids,
  or alcohol or illegal drug use

Family History
- If other members' history of psychiatric disorders, e.g., tic,
  mood, substance use, personality, anxiety, developmental or
  learning disorders, or ADHD or schizophrenia
- Family coping style, organization, and resources
- Past or present stressors or crises, such as death, divorce, or
  severe illness
- Abuse or neglect

✓ **Standardized Rating Scales**

These are questionnaires filled out by parents, teachers, and the
adolescent, when appropriate. Some scales are ADHD-specific,
meaning they list only behaviors seen in the disorder. These help
the diagnostician determine the presence or absence of ADHD,
and the type. Other scales contain items covering a wide range of
problems, some specific to ADHD, some associated with other

disorders. These broadband scales help suggest or rule out ADHD and determine if the adolescent has more than one disorder. Clinicians recommend the use of both types of scales for all adolescents being evaluated for ADHD.

Remember that rating scales are only one part of the diagnostic process. The rule in diagnosis is to have *multiple sources of information*.

✓ **School Information**

It's advisable to get information from as many current and past teachers as possible. Kids get older, their thinking abilities change, and certain courses have greater demands for efficiency in attention, memory, and executive function. If a student is doing well in one class and not another, do not make the assumption that it's a matter of choice or preference.

In addition to rating scales filled out by teachers, the following information from the school should be assessed:

- Verbal reports of learning, academic performance, and behavior
- Reports from standardized tests and individual evaluations
- Grades and attendance records
- Special education or basic skills information
- School observations whenever possible

✓ **Adolescent Diagnostic Interview**

Here the examiner is looking to determine the history and the patient's mental status—for instance, speech and language abilities, aggressive behavior, etc.

✓ **Family Diagnostic Interview**

The purpose is to determine how the adolescent behaves with the parents and siblings, and what problem-solving efforts parents have tried, along with the results.

✓ **Physical Evaluation**

Examiners are looking for any medical conditions that may explain the problems.

You need to know that at present, no laboratory test or fancy technology exists to diagnose ADHD. You may hear about new brain imaging technologies such as the fMRI and the SPECT scan—simply wonderful tools. Dr. Freund, from the National Institute of Child Health and Development, echoes what every researcher I spoke with told me regarding the use of these new technologies for ADHD diagnostic purposes: "I think they'll be ready in about five to ten years, which is a long time if you are a parent wanting to make decisions about treatment. But in the scope of science, that's not so long." The bottom line is let the buyer beware. For a routine assessment of ADHD, these tests have not yet been perfected. They're great for research.

✓ **Further testing**

The AACAP guidelines underscore the importance of obtaining information about school performance, including behavior, learning, attendance, grades, and test scores. Furthermore, they recommend psychoeducational testing to assess IQ and to search for any learning disabilities that coexist with or look like ADHD symptoms.

Reevaluation

Adolescence brings about so many changes that for kids diagnosed with ADHD early in their lives, it's a good idea to update evaluations throughout the years. As Arthur Robin, an author and a practicing clinician for over twenty-five years, says, "I get a lot of parents where the kids were either fully or partially diagnosed when they were younger and treated with a little bit of medicine. Then not much was done for a while. Now, at 13, 14, 15, the parent wants to find out if the youngster still has ADHD and what to do."

Dr. John Curry, director of clinical training in Duke University's Department of Psychology, advises parents to seek reevaluation if a new problem arises. "If the child has ADHD at age 6 and then turns oppositional or moody at age 12 or 13, that would be cause for another evaluation," Dr. Curry explains.

We parents should also seek help if we have been unsuccessful in our attempts to solve problems. Of course, it's always a good idea to get help during times of family stress, particularly when one or more of the members has ADHD.

In Search of the Golden Stone

When Maggie Prescott looks at her 17-year-old son, Mark, sometimes she thinks, "Oh, I would have wished it easier for you." She tells me this with some pain in her voice. Mark's mom, like so many parents, is experiencing what author Pauline Boss terms "ambiguous loss." These are feelings of loss that are vague and don't go away. One of the first things that parents and teens with ADHD have to do after diagnosis is change the relationship we have with the feeling of loss.

Psychologist Drew Yellen finds that patient and family education is a cornerstone for putting the loss into perspective. "If I can get my patients to understand that they are not stupid or lazy, that they have a condition that's relatively easy to compensate for once they understand it, then that's 90 percent of the battle," he comments.

Notice the word *compensate*. I have a confession to make. Though I know better, I still believe at times that if only I could get the right combination of this and that for whatever, ADHD would in essence go away. Maybe you have similar magical thinking.

Bad feelings are one by-product of ADHD. To have them is to be human. To ignore them is to give them hidden power. Our perceptions, our ghosts, and what we do to deal with an ongoing problem has a great impact on our ability to adapt, to solve problems, to come to peace, and to find joy.

While speaking with researcher Joseph Sergeant, I realized that I had been empowering a harmful belief. I told Dr. Sergeant that I, along with many of the parents I knew and wrote about in my first book, thought that if we learned all we could about ADHD and got really good at using the recommended treatments as they were growing up, our kids would have great outcomes. Dr. Sergeant replied, "We always have the secret hope, researchers particularly, that we will find the golden stone. I think we should be very content with modification."

At first, I found his advice less than satisfactory, and I told him so.

"It depends on what your objectives are, Mary," he answered. "If your objective is to make the person perfect—the most amiable, the most highly intellectual, a career-driven individual—I think you have given yourself an impossible task. On the other hand, if you have, for example, prevented the child from leaving school early so that the basic skills are there, I think you've done a great job. If treatment keeps the child from drugs or out of jail, that's a huge success. I think we should be happy about the smaller things—if the family is still intact, if the child is able to drive a car without too many traffic accidents."

Dr. Sergeant reminds us to look at the criteria we have for determining failure and success. Those things that we can do to manage the ADHD symptoms are the bricks and mortar you will find in the following chapters. But the cornerstones—understanding, acceptance, motivation to change, and changing our belief systems—are things we have to find within ourselves. There is no cure for ADHD—no golden stone, as Dr. Sergeant would say. What we are talking about is improving the quality of life.

CHAPTER THREE

Teen Stew

Many mental health disorders have symptoms in common. During adolescence, many teens develop new symptoms or conditions. Problems may change or increase. This chapter describes conditions that cause confusion: the ones that look like ADHD and the ones with which ADHD frequently co-occurs. Should your teen seem different or if matters have become more complex, take these changes as an indication that a visit to a treatment professional is in order. He or she will rule in or rule out the presence of other disorders. Do know that sorting through mental health symptoms can be quite confusing.

I t can be a frustrating paradox. The more you know, the less you know. Some teens have ADHD; others have additional disorders. Add to these an assortment of ingredients including peer and parent influences, individual personality traits, genetics, and life experience, plus the physical, social, emotional, and intellectual changes that accompany adolescence, and you wind up with teen stew. It may be hard to figure out what's in the pot.

About one-fifth of American teens have sufficient troubles and are disruptive enough to require professional mental health intervention. Fifty percent of youth with ADHD also have one or more other psychiatric disorders. Though early signs may have been present, these other disorders often erupt during the teenage years. Many parents feel guilty and confused. They wonder how they could have missed something so important as a mental health issue.

Whether one disorder or many are present, teens with troubles may act in ways that camouflage their underlying problems. For instance, they may seem to not give a damn, or they may cry at the drop of a hat. They may scream when spoken to or withdraw in angry silence. They may cause disruption whenever they can. They may create trouble in classes or stop showing up for school. They may spend hours alone in their rooms or run away from home. Frequent verbal or physical fights, promiscuous sexual activity, and sudden changes in friends and activities as well as in moods and temper can all appear as if out of nowhere. When actions such as these first arise, parents, teachers, and other adults in the teen's life may be inclined to see the teen as "bad" rather than troubled. In reality, such actions are usually warning signs of emotional problems that may be caused by underlying mental health disorders. It can be difficult even for a trained clinician to sort out whether or not the teen's behavior is due to ADHD. The clinician must consider the following possibilities:

- It looks like ADHD but is something else.
- It may be a combination of ADHD and another disorder.
- It may be the result of untreated ADHD or other disorders.

Sizing Up the Complicated Kid

Few parents will have a teen as tough to figure out as 17-year-old Carrie Herr. She's been diagnosed with ADHD, bulimia, major depressive disorder, bipolar disorder, obsessive-compulsive disorder, generalized anxiety disorder, panic disorder, posttraumatic stress disorder, central auditory processing disorder, and most recently substance use disorder. "I have three file drawers of tests and notes on her. It feels like a game of connect-the-dots," her mother, Marsha, says with amazing calm.

From her earliest days, Carrie has been hard to handle. She is moody, temperamental, and a perfectionist. She's also exceptionally intelligent and a talented singer, dancer, and swimmer. When she didn't outgrow her inflexible behavior, sudden outbursts, and moodiness by the age of 9,

Carrie's parents sought an outside evaluation. The clinician diagnosed her with ADHD. Her parents chose not to use medication, but instead made some minor adjustments.

Just as she reached puberty, Carrie and her family got hit with a number of stresses. Her parents, both well-educated intellectuals and entrepreneurs, had another child through a surrogate mother when Carrie was 11. A year later, Carrie's father left and moved three thousand miles away. Within the next year and a half, all four of her grandparents died. Her mother tried to manage as best she could with the divorce, the deaths, a toddler with a very difficult temperament, and a financial need to return to work.

And there was Carrie's ever-worsening behavior to deal with, too. Breaking rules, missing curfew, and lying about her whereabouts happened almost daily. In ninth grade her honor roll grades plummeted. She became sexually active with an older boy who had a reputation for being wild. Carrie developed a reputation of her own—wild and crazy. Marsha figured her daughter's behavior to be mainly a reaction to the family troubles, and partly due to the fact that Carrie had started a new school that year.

The only life area going well was swimming. Carrie won meet after meet. The team considered her a star. Then days before a key meet, Carrie got disqualified due to a school disciplinary action. Marsha thought that Carrie's behavior might have been a response to being dumped by her boyfriend. A lot more was going on. By the state championship two months later, this once strong swimmer had dropped twenty pounds. She did miserably, quit the team, and vowed never to swim again. Shortly thereafter, Marsha discovered that her daughter had bulimia. During the next two years, Carrie's behavior managed to go from bad to worse.

Given the wide range of symptoms that Carrie presents, her mother has had to take her to numerous specialists. When the symptoms of one disorder get somewhat under control, those of another break out, often prompting a shift in medications and treatment approach.

As Carrie's story illustrates, it may not be so easy to sort through the problems of teens who have complications. Psychiatrist Peter Jensen says, "Parents should make sure they have an expert diagnostician. And they shouldn't be surprised if even really expert diagnosticians disagree." Diagnosticians might disagree because a teen shows a pattern of symptoms one week that isn't there another, as is the case with Carrie. As Dr. Jensen explains, "There may be an underlying process going on. We get more information over time to understand what we *think* are the underlying processes."

That being said, Dr. Jensen also notes with great honesty that sometimes "we have to bubble-gum-and-string it together." If you are at all like me, you want immediate answers. Guesswork and trial-and-error approaches can be frustrating and upsetting. But medicine is not an exact science. And the science of mental health issues is a fairly recent frontier. Until we unlock the brain's secrets, most mental health conditions must be diagnosed on the basis of observable symptoms. Given the volatility of the teen years and the elusive nature of symptoms, it's easy to see why the picture changes.

Parents of complicated kids have to slog through the stew. As Carrie's mom says, "I learned that I need to be a student of her total illness so I can help her." Though Carrie's situation is far from stable, Marsha's efforts are bearing some results. Carrie is now a senior, and it looks as though she will graduate with her class. Last marking period, she even made the high honor roll. She's also back swimming. "I don't know if that's because of her treatments or because I'm learning to handle her better. I've learned to pay attention in the places where I can make a difference: helping her to keep her medical appointments and take her medications, and choosing what battles to let go. I know I'll be ineffective trying to help if I don't keep good communication, trust, and rapport with her," her mom says.

If you are unsure about your teen's problem(s), the following information about commonly comorbid and look-alike disorders might help you target a physician and a treatment plan.

Disruptive Behavior Disorders

ADHD appears in this *DSM-IV* category along with oppositional defiant disorder (ODD) and conduct disorder (CD). These two disorders most frequently co-occur with ADHD. That's particularly the case with the kids who are hyper and aggressive at young ages. Personally, I dislike the labels

INFORMATION LINK

For more information about ADHD and comorbid or look-alike
  disorders, see:

Russell Barkley, *Attention-Deficit Hyperactivity Disorder: A Handbook of Diagnosis and Treatment,* Second Edition, Guilford
  Publications, New York, 1998 (intended for professionals).

Arthur Robin, *ADHD in Adolescents: Diagnosis and Treatment,*
  Guilford Publications, New York, 1998 (intended for
  professionals).

Steven Pliszka, Caryn Carlson, and James Swanson, *ADHD with
  Comorbid Disorders,* Guilford Publications, New York, 1999
  (intended for professionals).

"Mental Health: A Report of the Surgeon General" (a very
  readable report that explains and describes all major
  psychiatric conditions), www.nimh.gov/mhsgrpt

ODD and CD. While they may be apt descriptions of behavior patterns
clinicians see, the public's translation is "bad kid." For now, it appears we
have to live with these terms. We need to be mindful that children do not
set out to become defiant and hard to manage, and that such problems
may in part have a neurological base.

Oppositional Defiant Disorder (ODD)

Approximately 59 percent of youth with ADHD compared to 11 percent
in the general population will meet the criteria for the ODD diagnosis at
some point in time. It is by far the most common co-occurring condition.
About 25 percent of youth with ADHD will have this diagnosis for a limited time, usually about three years. Another 25 percent will go on to
develop conduct disorder, which is far more severe.

The *DSM* describes ODD as "a recurrent pattern of negativistic,
defiant, disobedient, and hostile behavior toward authority figures" that
lasts at least six months. Four or more of the following behaviors must be
present, occur often, and cause clinically significant impairment:

- loses temper
- argues with adults
- defies or refuses to do what adults ask
- deliberately annoys people
- blames others
- easily annoyed or touchy
- angry and resentful
- spiteful or vindictive

Clearly, a teen who behaves this way is going to get a lot of negative attention. But by drawing attention to him- or herself, kids with ODD tend to get diagnosed earlier. These criteria don't take into account female forms of negative, hostile behavior. Thus boys get identified earlier than girls. Dr. Barkley cautions clinicians to look for this bias. Psychologist Arthur Robin notes that defiant behavior is higher in early adolescence (ages 12 to 14) than in middle (15 to 17) and late adolescence (18 to 20). The good news for parents is that the hair-raising behavior of the early adolescent years may improve with age.

Conduct Disorder (CD)

This disorder is the most extreme form of child and adolescent defiant behavior. Approximately 25 percent of the teens with ADHD will develop conduct disorder. Teens who have this problem will basically have a pattern of behavior that society terms "delinquency." Expert Russell Barkley explains, "CD is that greater level of irresponsibility, violation of the rights of others, disregard of societal norms, confrontation with victims, lying, stealing, running away from home, and truancy." Parents of teens who have conduct disorder have a terrifically hard road, as do these unfortunate kids.

Teens who develop CD after age 12 have a better outcome because they are less prone to physical aggression and disturbed peer relations. Though generally thought of as a male disorder, during adolescence females "catch up" to males in terms of conduct disorder rates.

When ADHD, ODD, and CD Are Present

Youth who have this triple combination face the following risks: greater family conflict, substance abuse, school expulsion, higher dropout rates, and trouble with the law. Why such terrible outcomes? Part of the problem has to do with treatment. As Dr. Sergeant explains, "We can successfully treat many anxiety disorders and many types of depression. We are less successful in treating conduct disorder and aggression because we don't have a drug for it." Social and family factors plus peer supports significantly enter into the picture. These contributing factors and complications are hard to control. Treatment is not simply a matter of altering biology with medication. People, places, and things need significant attention and change.

Mood Disorders

When Kevin Gillingham was in fifth grade, he became severely depressed. "It was horrible. All he did was watch television," his mother says, shaking her head. Jill knew if she turned off the television, Kevin would become hysterical. At times she took to standing in front of the set and acting like a television to get his attention.

Kevin is one of an estimated 30 percent of individuals who have a mood disorder along with ADHD. There are different types of mood disorders. Two most commonly found to coexist with ADHD are depression and dysthymia. Bipolar disorder, too, can coexist in ADHD. Symptoms of ADHD and bipolar disorder may also be mistaken for each other. Let's look at each of these disorders.

Depression

It's normal for people sometimes to feel sad, apathetic, or a bit blue. But when these emotions overcome the person or become the person's usual mood, or when they exist for a prolonged period of time, then they may signal depression. Symptoms of depression include:

- sadness
- loss of interest in previously enjoyable activities
- sudden changes in weight
- sleep disturbances (too much or too little)
- energy loss
- obvious physical agitation, jitteriness
- difficulty thinking, concentrating, or making decisions
- recurring thoughts about death or suicide

Signs of depression are not to be taken lightly. Major depressive disorder, also known as unipolar major depression, is diagnosed when a person has five or more of the symptoms listed above. These have to cause significant problems in daily function and exist for at least two weeks. When Kevin stopped functioning, he had major depressive disorder. This type of depression can reoccur, and occur along with ADHD. Dysthymia, a common and less severe form of depression, consists of a predominant depressed mood that lasts for at least one or two years. People with dysthymia usually feel blue most of the time, although youth may express low mood as irritability. Dysthymia is also accompanied by two or more of the following: appetite problems, sleep disturbances, energy loss, low self-esteem, poor concentration, decision-making problems, or a sense of hopelessness.

Depressions range in severity from mild to severe. Furthermore, depressions are more common in women. Dr. Hinshaw, who has been studying females with ADHD, notes that in every culture, the ratio of severe depression in women to that in men is 2 to 1. Interestingly, Dr. Hinshaw reports, "Before puberty, boys have somewhat higher rates than girls. By about ages 13, 14, 15, the girls' graph starts to go way up and the boys' graph starts to go down." Depression frequently gets masked behind aggression and self-destructive behaviors such as reckless driving and substance abuse.

Depression may arise for a variety of reasons. First of all, the teen may have a genetic predisposition—depression tends to run in families. Second, dealing with the ADHD rejections—the negative feedback, the low self-esteem, the constant put-downs, the inability to get it together when needed—would wear any person down.

For some reason, our society tends to think that adolescents and even children who are depressed will snap out of it. Some kids do, but depression is an illness. Just like the flu, some people who are healthy get hit with the bug. Others get the flu because they are run down and more susceptible. If you ignore the flu, you can wind up dead. Depressed kids seldom snap out of it. Despite the cause of the depression, the symptoms warrant attention. By the way, most experts agree that adolescents have a better grip on their internalizing symptoms of depression and anxiety. Thus, their self-reports are reliable. These should be a part of the assessment.

Bipolar Disorder (BPD)

Also known as manic-depressive illness, bipolar disorder can be a severe and often lifelong illness that may seriously disrupt a person's life and cause great suffering. Most causes of bipolar disorder develop between the ages of 15 and 19, but experts now recognize a juvenile-onset form. Since bipolar disorder (BPD) and ADHD plus ODD share some symptoms, BPD may be mistaken for ADHD, especially in the early years. According to Dr. Barkley, "Maybe 1 to 6 percent of ADHD turns out to be bipolar. That estimate is not as high as initial studies thought it was going to be." The incidence of BPD in the general population is quite small—1 percent.

Just what is BPD? The Surgeon General's Report on Mental Health defines bipolar disorder as a "serious brain disease that causes extreme shifts in mood, energy, and functioning." Bipolar disorder tends to run in families. People with it have periods where it flares up and disrupts work, family, and social life. As its name suggests, bipolar disorder has symptoms consisting of extreme highs (manic episodes) and extreme lows (depressive episodes).

Sometimes the mania can be mild, but even so, it is noticeable to others. Mild mania episodes may take the form of increased energy, elevated mood, irritability, or intrusiveness. Hallucinations or delusions may also be present during a bipolar episode.

The frequency of bipolar episodes tends to increase with age. This disorder is mainly treated with medications that fall into the class of drugs called mood stabilizers. Recently, some anticonvulsant medications have shown promise. Individual and family psychotherapy may also help, as might patient/family education.

DEPRESSION EPISODES	MANIA EPISODES
Persistent sad mood	Abnormal and persistent elevated
Loss of interest in once-	mood or irritability,
pleasurable activities	*Plus 3 or more of the following:*
Significant changes in appearance	Grandiosity
Sleep disturbances	Decreased need for sleep
Physical slowing or agitation	Increased talkativeness
Loss of energy	Racing thoughts
Feelings of worthlessness or	Distractibility
inappropriate guilt	Excessive goal-directed activity,
Difficulty thinking or	e.g., spending money
concentrating	Physical agitation
Recurrent thoughts of death	Risky behaviors
or suicide	

ADHD, BPD, or Both?

At present, the child psychiatry field seems to be in a bit of a debate over ADHD and BPD. When presented with a child or adolescent who has violent, intense temper outbursts, aggression, irritability, extreme hyperactivity including talkativeness, and high distractibility, the picture is not so clear. Is it severe ADHD (meaning ODD as well), or ADHD plus depression or mood problems, or BPD, or both? To distinguish between the disorders, Dr. Barkley suggests that diagnosticians discount the signs already mentioned in this paragraph. Then he advises looking for the more classic symptoms of BPD: mood swings, mood instability, severe irritability accompanied by rage attacks, destructive outbursts, and a family history. In fact, he says, "The family history is often the best tip-off that an individual is bipolar rather than ADHD." When there is no family history present, Dr. Thomas Brown leans toward first treating the patient as having a severe case of ADHD with accompanying mood problems.

Dr. Barkley also mentions that a great many people who eventually wind up with the diagnosis of BPD start out with an ADHD diagnosis. Why? "The first symptoms people recognize are the hyperactivity and dis-

INFORMATION LINK

> To learn more about bipolar disorder in children and adolescents,
>   read:
> Demitri and Janice Papolos, *The Bipolar Child,* Broadway Books,
>   New York, 1999.
> Mitzi Waltz, *Bipolar Disorders: A Guide to Helping Children
>   and Adolescents,* O'Reilly Press, Sebastopol, CA, 1999.
> For a moving and hopeful autobiography read:
> Kay Redfield Jamison, *An Unquiet Mind,* Random House,
>   New York, 1997.

tractibility, and even the irritability. Then it starts to progress to something much more serious and explosive than ADHD," he explains.

Author and clinician Dr. Patricia Quinn believes that women frequently get misdiagnosed with BPD. She finds that some therapists misinterpret women's hyperactivity and reactivity as mania or hypomania. Because women with ADHD often have depression, too, Dr. Quinn believes the combination is what makes them look more like they have BPD. Before accepting a diagnosis of BPD, Dr. Quinn advises women to bring the *DSM* bipolar criteria to the therapist and ask, "How do I meet these criteria, or do I have ADHD symptomatology and depression?"

ADHD and BPD do co-occur. When both disorders are present, the unstable mood of bipolar must be treated first, and with good reason: Stimulant medications and antidepressant medications may make the mood symptoms worse. However, physicians may use a combination of medications, including stimulants, to treat the symptoms of both conditions with good effects.

Anxiety Disorders

Anxiety disorders are the most frequently occurring mental health disorders. People who have them show disturbances in mood as well as thinking, behavior, and physiological activity. Anxiety disorders come in various forms. Approximately 25 to 40 percent of adolescents with ADHD will also have some form of anxiety disorder. The most frequently co-occurring forms are these:

Panic disorder has symptoms that range from intense fear to discomfort, and often includes physical symptoms such as sweats, heart palpitations, and nausea.

Social phobia leads people to avoid social situations.

Obsessive-compulsive disorder (OCD) consists of recurrent and unwanted thoughts or rituals and doing things over and over in a compulsive way.

Hallie Banks has ADHD and OCD. "I'm always freaking out because things aren't perfect," she says. Hallie has many obsessions and compulsions. One has to do with always looking down. "I look at the cracks on the floor or the sidewalk. If I step on one of them, I have to step on another because I have to be even with my footing."

Some experts believe there is an anxious subtype of ADHD. In determining if a child has ADHD or an anxiety disorder, Dr. Robin notes that these are easy to distinguish. "Most children with ADHD do not classically manifest a great deal of anxiety about their performance," he writes. In fact, he points out something that many of us parents find astonishing: Youth with ADHD don't seem to get upset at all about the impact their actions have on themselves and others, although they do get upset by the responses they receive from others due to their actions.

ADHD, Generalized Anxiety Disorder, and Posttraumatic Stress Disorder (PTSD)

Generalized anxiety disorder and posttraumatic stress disorder both can be mistaken for ADHD. When you look only at the symptom lists, the similarity between symptoms explains why.

One quick way to distinguish between ADHD and these two anxiety disorders in adolescents is to ask these questions: When did this start? How

GENERALIZED ANXIETY DISORDER	PTSD
Restlessness or feeling keyed up or on edge Being easily fatigued Difficulty concentrating and mind going blank Irritability Muscle tension Sleep disturbance	Exposure to a traumatic event that involves actual or threatened physical or emotional harm, followed by some or all of the symptoms listed below: Difficulty falling or staying asleep Irritability or anger outbursts Difficulty concentrating Hypervigilance Exaggerated startle response

long has it been going on? Has anything major happened? If the symptoms suddenly appeared, beware. There is no such condition as sudden-onset ADHD. Any of us who have experienced major life stressors or a traumatic event can report difficulties with concentration, restlessness, and perhaps doing things that are not thought out. Of course, it is possible for youth with ADHD to also have one of these two forms of anxiety as a result of some major life event. The point is, do not rush to conclusions.

It seems logical to think ADHD behaviors could make a teen more likely to experience some kind of trauma, but as reported by Dr. Barkley, ADHD alone does not lead to posttraumatic stress disorder, although if someone with ADHD has a trauma, ADHD symptoms may be aggravated. PTSD is more likely to occur in teens who have ODD or CD. There are two types of trauma. Victimization trauma results from assault, mugging, community violence, family violence, and sexual molestation. The other type, nonvictimization trauma, comes from accidents, disasters, or illness. "Accidental trauma is much more likely for ADHD," Dr. Barkley reports. He also notes that ODD may make a child prone to PTSD, as 25 percent or more of youth with ODD will wind up in a situation that can be traumatizing.

Learning Disabilities (LD)

My switch from high school to middle school teaching came with an unexpected bonus: more opportunity to reach students who had lost motivation to learn. I see interest in learning and motivation to learn as two different things. I had plenty of poorly performing students who had an interest in learning. They just weren't motivated because they didn't think they could learn. Years of struggle and failure wore them down. They became convinced they were stupid and worthless. Many developed an attitude. I have an attitude, too. I don't believe there's any boy or girl who doesn't want to learn. Just look at little kids. They are naturally curious. They love to learn. Now, that doesn't mean they want to sit behind a desk. Some kids do, but others don't or can't without a lot of effort, especially when they have ADHD. A change in the learning conditions frequently gets a better result.

Adolescents with ADHD don't want to fail or look stupid in front of their peers. And they are highly practical. If they only succeed every once in a while, they move on. Often they move on to acting out or acting in (internalizing) behavior, performance anxiety, poor peer influences, and dropping out.

Multiple causes contribute to school failure. Two of the most common are learning disabilities and ADHD. Though these disorders usually share the same outcomes when left untreated, they are not the same. People with learning disabilities have a problem with the basics of getting data in, mentally working with the data that comes in, and getting data out. They have problems processing information at the point of entry, the point of operations, and/or the point of exit. People with ADHD have problems at the point of performance. They can get the data in—when their attention is focused. To get the right data in, they often need help figuring out what is the most important information versus what is most interesting. Once the data is in, they often have trouble working with the data due to problems with attention, memory, and executive function. If the data goes in inefficiently, students with ADHD will have difficulty outputting it. They may also have output difficulty due to executive function and working memory problems. Data consists of many types of information. It's not just facts and figures. It's social infor-

INFORMATION LINK

To learn more about learning disabilities, contact:

Learning Disabilities Association, 4156 Library Road, Pittsburgh,
    PA 15234, www.ldanatl.org.

ldonline.org, an interactive on-line site: www.ldonline.org.

National Center for Learning Disabilities, 381 Park Avenue
    South, Suite 1401, New York, NY 10016; (888) 575-7373 or
    www.ncld.org.

mation, emotional information, and bodily-kinesthetic information, for example.

Like students with LD, students with ADHD often have difficulty with reading, writing, and arithmetic. Researchers estimate that between 12 and 60 percent of students with ADHD also have learning disabilities. What explains such a wide range? I believe it has to do with the way the two problems are defined. Given the considerable overlap between these disorders, *all students with ADHD should be evaluated to determine whether or not they also have a learning disability.*

Tourette's Disorder

Over half the kids who have Tourette's Disorder have ADHD and/or OCD. That doesn't mean half of the kids with ADHD have Tourette's, though. Researchers think Tourette's may be inherited from a single, dominant gene. It's more common in males than females. People with Tourette's have tics, which are involuntary body movements and noises— for example, unintentional throat clearing, eye blinking, lip licking, hair chewing, barking, or spitting. The list goes on.

Hallie Banks also has Tourette's in addition to her ADHD and OCD. Over the years, she has received negative responses for noises and movements that she doesn't even know she's making. Now she blames herself, even to the point of believing she's deliberately trying to get everyone's goat. And maybe sometimes she is. Abuse from others has a way of making us angry. It leads to acting out and other socially inappropriate behavior. Tourette's can be treated with medications and psychological treatment.

Substance Use Disorders

Dan Primavera is a recovering alcoholic. He knows the signs of addiction and what can lead to abuse problems. Yet, when this father saw the hands on his 21-year-old son shake from tremors, Dan told himself, "He's just partying like other kids." Eventually Dan decided to talk to his son about drinking. Louie brushed off this father-and-son chat. "He tells me he knows everything about alcohol," Dan says, shaking his head because he fell for this line.

A few months after that talk, Louie got into some legal trouble and also barely passed the semester. The truth came out. Though Louie has ADHD, many of his functioning problems and much of his spaciness had to do with the fact that he had been getting stoned every day for three years.

A considerable percentage of teens with ADHD abuse substances. Some develop addiction problems. What's the difference between abuse and addiction? Abuse is a consistent pattern of use. It causes trouble with life functioning, such as poor school attendance or driving under the influence. It is a disorder. Dependence or addiction, which is more severe, also affects life functioning. In addition, addicted individuals need increasing amounts of a substance to get the same effect. They may use more frequently, go through withdrawal, switch substances in search of a better high, not be able to cut down, or spend a lot of time trying to get the substance. Abuse and addiction require intervention.

Teen substance problems can occur for various reasons. Dr. Sallie Montgomery, cosupervisor of the clinic at the Hazelden Center for Youth and Families, one of the leading assessment and treatment facilities, says, "Some teens start out by partying and wind up becoming hooked. Other teens wind up with a poor peer group, possibly because they do poorly with school and socially. Some may be self-medicating." It's fairly common for teens and adults with mental health issues to turn to substances such as alcohol, pot, or other drugs to feel good. ADHD is also a risk factor.

Why does ADHD create such a risk? No one knows for sure. As explained by Dr. Joseph Sergeant, European studies suggest that it's not necessarily which or how many disorders a person has that places a person at risk. Rather, the development of abuse and addiction problems seems to have to do with which areas of the brain are affected. Some areas of the brain and some neurotransmitters are associated with pleasure and reward. When these are impaired or malfunctioning, there's a strong possibility for substance use and abuse. It's not a matter of how many symptoms a person has that determines the degree of impairment. As Dr. Sergeant explains, "Some parts of the brain, when they are impaired or shown to be malfunctioning, may only cause a few symptoms, but those symptoms could be more important than having a whole batch of symptoms."

Dr. Sergeant further notes that the youth who is neurologically driven to seek rewards, as is usually the case with ADHD, will be more susceptible to the neurologically pleasurable rewards that recreational drugs, including alcohol and nicotine, can bring. Combine the search for reward with a loss of inhibition and you increase the probability of substance abuse. Also, as Dr. Montgomery explains, marijuana is known to affect the reuptake of the neurotransmitter dopamine in certain brain areas involved with rewards. As you know, dopamine imbalance is thought to be an underlying cause of ADHD.

Substance-abusing or addicted teens can be baffling creatures. Unfortunately, many parents don't find out their teens are doing more than minor experimentation until significant problems develop. Denial may come into play here. Some parents lull themselves into an "it's not that bad" mentality. And some teens are masters at hiding their use.

"When teens are using, they get into behaviors that are related to the use," Dr. Montgomery points out. She lists the following warning signs that parents should heed:

- sudden behavior changes
- changes at school, such as a rapid decline in grades, truancy, or nonattendance

- sudden changes in friends or peer group
- different sleep patterns—either great fatigue or boundless energy
- withdrawal from the family
- irritability
- appetite changes (the munchies, particularly late at night)
- changes in the way the teen keeps or decorates his or her bedroom—"druggie chic"

Sorting Through Symptoms

Staff at the Hazelden Clinic frequently see teens who come in with a string of diagnoses. Many do have multiple problems. "But all too often," says Dr. Montgomery, "people do not look at the whole picture." For instance, she has seen kids who have been diagnosed with ADHD who had no attention problems until they began smoking marijuana in early adolescence. Dr. Montgomery advises parents to find someone who is well rounded in working with adolescents, who knows substance abuse, and who is used to making dual diagnoses. "These things are very hard to tease apart," she observes.

When a teen's substance use problems become so severe that they need to be in an inpatient treatment center such as Hazelden, Dr. Montgomery says, parents should not be surprised if their son's or daughter's previous diagnoses change. For instance, after drinking alcohol, some kids who are normally mellow become quite aggressive and do things they wouldn't do if they weren't under the influence. Because they are using so frequently, they seem to be ODD or CD. The same is true for bipolar disorder. Chronic inflexibility, mood swings, and explosive outbursts can be related to substance use disorder.

One reason why misdiagnosis may occur has to do with taking the word of the substance-abusing teen. While teens are great at giving accurate self-reports when it comes to talking about anxiety or mood problems, their accuracy leaves a lot to be desired when it comes to substance use. Teens with abuse problems will often tell a physician that they smoke an occasional joint or have a drink once in a while. That response cannot be taken at face value, particularly when the warning signs of drug and alcohol abuse are present. I think some parents may get led astray because of trust. What parent wants to believe a son or daughter is lying? Yet when it comes to abuse and addiction, teens are no different from adults. They usually lie to others and themselves. In a state of denial, they may tell themselves, "I'm no druggie" or "That can't happen to me."

Early detection and treatment of substance use problems can save a youth a lifetime of pain. And it can a save a family, too. Substance abuse puts everybody through a living hell. Be a wise parent. Forget about guilt, or thinking you are the cause, or that it can't happen to your child. Regardless of whether the teen has ADHD, depression, or whatever, if your teen is having problems and you even slightly suspect your teen is using substances, seek an assessment.

With No Wish to Alarm

Parenting a teen can be really tough on the morale. We read, see, and hear so much bad news that we can lose sight of the joys of this stage, which are many. Yet I cannot in good conscience write about teens without addressing the issue of teen suicide. The rate is at an all-time high. The Centers for Disease Control estimate it to be the third leading cause of death for teens under the age of 19. Furthermore, a MSNBC broadcast reported that one-fifth of the teen population has seriously considered suicide. Dr. Andrew Slaby and Lili Frank Garfinkel write in *No One Saw My Pain* that five thousand youths under the age of 25 kill themselves in the United States every year. Two thousand of these are teenagers. They also state that for every completed suicide, three hundred serious attempts are made. When you consider the number of teens in the general population, the number of suicide deaths is not a lot, unless it's your son or daughter or the child of someone you know. Then the number is too high.

Dr. Barkley notes that having ADHD can increase the risk slightly. He also points out that the risk of a suicide attempt is much greater for youths who have CD and ADHD.

There are many signs that may indicate possible suicidal ideation or behavior. The most telling signs are listed below. If you see these or any signs that cause you discomfort or alarm, seek help from a trained professional immediately. Remember, most suicides and suicide attempts are really cries for help. Being alert allows the cries to be heard.

Common Warning Signs of Suicidal Behavior

These warning signs* are presented beginning with the most dangerous ones:

- direct and indirect suicide threats
- making final arrangements
- giving away prized possessions
- talking about death
- reading, writing, and/or creating artwork about death
- hopelessness or helplessness
- social withdrawal and isolation
- loss of involvement in interests and activities
- increased risk taking
- heavy use of alcohol and drugs
- abrupt changes in appearance, personality, or attitude

Where Do We Go From Here?

Whether or not your youth has ADHD only or ADHD in combination with one or more other disorders, I'm sure your main question is, "What do we do? How can we help our son or daughter?" Most of this book aims to provide guidance and answers to these questions. The following chapters approach the management of ADHD and related or comorbid

*Adopted from *Crisis Prevention and Responses: A Collection of NASP Resources*, "Suicidal Ideation and Behaviors," Table 1, "Common Warning Signs of Suicidal Behavior," p. 140. Copyright © 1999 by the National Association of School Psychologists. Reprinted by permission of the publisher.

difficulties strategically. Strategies range from the simple answer for the not-so-complicated kid to the tough calls for the very complicated kid.

Regardless of what type of stew you are in, stay as cool, calm, and collected as you can. These challenges require a parent who can problem-solve. While you may use a therapist or counselor for guidance along the way, no counselor can fill your shoes. You are on the front lines each and every day. Try to look at the tough situations as opportunities. That change in viewpoint can go a long way toward helping you be an effective manager with some measure of dignity.

CHAPTER FOUR

Medical Intervention

An interesting paradox of the teen years is the attempt to fit in and be unique simultaneously. Peer pressure powerfully motivates teen behavior. Not surprisingly, many adolescents, including those who have had serious troubles, such as school failure, conflict with authority, or legal problems, do not want to be seen as having a disability. Consequently, many parents face treatment resistance from their teens, even from those young people who as kids acknowledged their difficulties and accepted management strategies. The management method most often resisted is medication. This chapter explores the medication issue in depth.

"One day I just woke up and realized I was screwing up," 16-year-old Brian Ballard remembers. Before he came to realize that he could take charge of his life, Brian felt inadequate, sad, and on the outside of his world. Brian saw himself as "defective" and viewed his life through pessimistic glasses. During this gloomy period, "there were many times I cried," he says quietly.

It bothered Brian that his classmates were learning and he wasn't. Though he had hobbies, he didn't like sitting home alone while everyone else socialized. Football bugged him the most. Brian joined the team in ninth grade. Despite his love of the game and his motivation, Brian could not remember the plays, try as he might. Demoralized, he told his parents that he wanted to quit. That's when they suggested he think about trying something else he had quit—medication.

During grade school Brian had taken Ritalin to help manage his difficulties. It gave him headaches. Still, he remained on the medication. As puberty approached, Brian had other complaints. "I'd act differently on it. I wouldn't be my personality." The medication made him really quiet. He felt dull and worn out. On top of that, Brian had early adolescent issues with it, too. He felt he should be who he was. As young teens are apt to believe, that meant being like everyone else. "I saw medication as taking something to be advanced and better than I was—almost like cheating."

When Brian returned to medication at the beginning of tenth grade, he had a renaissance. "Everything started clicking," he explains. Not only could Brian remember the football plays, but "I started reacting faster to what was going on around me," he reports with great animation. His off-the-field performance skyrocketed, too. "People in the honor society were barely passing biology, and here I was, just having a ball because I was able to understand what was going on," he says, smiling. He savored the learning experience and stopped rushing through assignments.

Brian also made a great self-discovery: "I had a memory. I was able to give information back on tests. I never had a short-term [working] memory. It was like the greatest thing. When a friend gives me a phone number, I remember it." This change also led to reading improvement.

With regard to the role medication plays in his life, Brian has good perspective. He does not give it credit for his hard work. Brian is driven to succeed. He reminds us that ADHD may be tough, but it's not invincible. Medication gave him the change in biology he needed in order to allow his ambition and ability to be effective.

To what does Brian attribute his honor roll grades, his large circle of friends, and his football trophies, including MVP in the state finals? "You need to set goals and achieve them. Instead of setting goals, I used to set limitations," he says. The goals Brian sets aren't unrealistic. He also sets microgoals. He breaks dreams into small units and goes after them one at a time.

Brian gives another reason for his success. "Good fortune," he says, giving credit to the people who stood by and encouraged him, especially his parents. Today, he's outgrown that early-adolescent pack mentality. When asked what he'd like to tell the world about ADHD, Brian answers without hesitation: "Everyone's been given something in life. Whether it is good or bad, more than one thing or just one thing, you have to accept it. People with ADHD are just like everyone else. Just give them a chance."

I agree with Brian that everyone has something, be it a burden or a problem. Everyone should be given a chance, but many adolescents turn down chances when it comes to taking medication or using any of the recommended management strategies for ADHD. Denial becomes a problem during these teen years. So many parents tell me their teen says, "There's nothing wrong with me." That's true even for teens who have been diagnosed since their childhood days.

You might think that a diagnosis should come as a relief to a struggling teen. That's not readily the case. "Teens don't want to be pigeon-holed, labeled, or stereotyped," psychologist Drew Yellen remarks. "Teens really feel strongly that 'regardless of what I have, I am an individual.'"

By the teen years, a lot of defensive walls are up. Many have had to build fortresses around themselves because they suspect, as Brian did, that they are defective in some way. Dr. Yellen finds many of his new patients come in with a lot of rage: "It's a wonderful mechanism for them because it pushes everybody away." Why would a teen want to do that? Dr. Yellen thinks it helps them hide their deep, dark secret beliefs: "I'm stupid," "I'm dumb," "I'm lazy," "I'm crazy." Over time, these teens have had a lot of negative experiences to help them develop the idea that they are all of the horrible things they may secretly believe about themselves.

What they hear about ADHD might make matters worse, especially when it comes to taking medication, particularly Ritalin. You also may be shying away from using medication as part of the treatment package for your teen because of misinformation and sensational headlines. To manage ADHD, you need a bag of tricks and tools. Given that teen years do have a measure of storm and stress, it seems appropriate to begin a discussion about the various treatment techniques with the most controversial—medication.

Though medication is the subject of this chapter, I want to emphasize the need for parents and their teens to be involved in a total treatment program. Medication alters abnormal biology into a more normal state, but pills don't teach skills. As Brian Ballard knows, once ADHD symptoms are lessened, personal goals, effort, and know-how are still needed. Chapters 6 to 12 go into these other management tools and strategies in detail.

Whether you and your teen *with the guidance of a physician* decide to use or not use medication is a highly individual decision, and often a difficult one. The decision can be made easier when you have accurate information based on well-researched scientific findings. Sometimes school personnel may suggest that medication would be good for your teen. They may be right—so for that reason you might want to consider such recommendations. Still, the decision is up to the physician, the parents, and the patient.

Among the ADHD-related problems that improve with stimulant medications are

- inattention and poor working memory
- restlessness or fidgeting
- poor impulse control
- poor organizational skills
- difficulty setting and keeping priorities
- weak problem-solving strategies
- poor school performance
- low self-esteem
- poor peer relations
- poor driving practices
- uneven work performance
- sensitivity to criticism
- poor frustration tolerance and irritability
- inappropriate anger

Findings From the Multimodal Treatment Approach (MTA) Study

In 1999, the National Institute of Mental Health (NIMH) and the U.S. Department of Education Office of Special Education Programs (OSEP) reported the findings of a five-year, multisite study it funded on ADHD and treatment, which is the largest national study done so far. The purpose was to compare the effectiveness of the various treatment approaches recommended for ADHD. MTA stands for "multimodal treatment approach," which means to use more than one type of management technique. When a youth is diagnosed with ADHD, the recommended treatment approach consists of four core interventions, plus one other one on an as-needed basis:

- medication (usually stimulants)
- patient, parent, and teacher education about the disorder
- behavioral therapy
- environmental changes—including an appropriate school program
- as needed, supportive psychotherapy

The overall results of the MTA study have many implications that guide parents and clinicians. One of the most important findings has to do with the effectiveness of the various treatment approaches. According to Dr. Peter Jensen, NIMH's lead investigator, "Parents need to know that when done well, medication treatments are powerfully effective. Sometimes people turn to them as a last resort. The findings suggest we ought to be thinking differently about that. They are so powerful, so superior to the very best behavioral treatments we can do, that medication is probably a wise first step." Of course, Dr. Jensen doesn't mean to imply that medication is the right choice for every child. However, all things being equal, it's likely to be the most effective.

This finding seems particularly important in light of the comparison between medication and behavioral treatment. "I do think the behavioral approach used was the most intensive one ever put together on planet Earth," says Dr. Jensen. The researchers already knew from previous studies that behavioral approaches work for ADHD. The question was how effective they were when compared to another treatment. Researchers found that for kids with ADHD who were not anxious or depressed, medication got much better results than behavioral treatments. Kids with ADHD who also had anxiety did as well on the behavioral therapy approach as they did on medication in most cases. The take-home message for parents is not to rule out medication based on misinformation.

The second implication of the study had to do with the way medications are delivered to the patient. When compared to common practice in the community, the researchers found that their methods produced better results. What did they do differently? For one thing, Dr. Jensen says,

"We carefully picked the right dose for each child." Seemingly, pediatricians tend to prescribe lower doses than what is called for. Dr. Jensen believes that may have to do with parental request. "The parent may be so worried about this medication that they ask for a small dose. Or the pediatrician will sometimes decide to prescribe only a small dose."

The goal of therapy is to give enough medication to normalize the problems without causing side effects. "If you undermedicate a child, it's like having a bacterial infection that's only partly controlled. You've reduced him from being a nudge to half a nudge," Dr. Jensen explains. Researchers also gave their patients three doses a day as opposed to the customary morning and noon doses generally prescribed by community-based physicians. The third dose was given in the late afternoon to help the child during homework periods and the times when he or she would be interacting with siblings and parents. On a two-dose regimen, most families rarely get to see the positive effects of medication firsthand.

That's because the most common medications used for ADHD, the stimulants, are short-acting, meaning they are in and out of the body in a matter of hours. Thus, the ADHD symptoms return when the meds wear off—usually by the end of the school day. Without the late-day dose, teens and their families may have to contend with the ADHD symptoms, which frequently set the stage for home conflicts, often having to do with homework hassles and siblings.

In addition to using higher doses, the research teams also saw their patients far more frequently than is common practice in the community. They saw each patient every month, while community doctors averaged two visits a year. The more frequent visits allowed the research teams to work with parents, answer concerns about the medication, and give counsel and advice on other issues. Dr. Jensen describes the current community practices as "very poor, and probably unethical." However, he doesn't fault the physicians. He points to limited visits allowed by insurance companies as the reason why parents don't see their children's physicians on a regular basis.

Feedback

MTA researchers consider feedback about the effects of medication to be an extremely important part of the treatment. Interestingly, they found teachers did a better job assessing attention problems and oppositional behavior. Parents gave better information regarding side effects such as appetite loss, dulling of personality, and sleep problems. Ideally, teachers would be able to give feedback to doctors, but that doesn't happen as common practice.

"Lucky is the child who is able to have the parent who can finesse this with the doctor and the teacher, and get everyone cooperating and taking extra time for him or her," observes Dr. Jensen, who adds, "That child will have a lot of advantages." Clearly you need multiple reports to ensure an accurate picture. You don't just give a pill and assume all is well. Similarly, if side effects occur, they need to be assessed. Sometimes a dosage adjustment or a different medication is needed.

During the teen years, feedback can be hard to get. Many adolescents don't want anyone to know they are on medication. Dr. Jensen often encourages such patients to pick a teacher they really care about, know, and trust to provide feedback about how he or she is doing on medication. If the teen still resists teacher involvement, Dr. Jensen doesn't push it. "If I lose the adolescent's goodwill in the process, I've lost the battle and the war," he says. Eventually, older adolescents on medication can provide good feedback when given a structured form, such as a rating scale, to follow.

Another problem with medication feedback has to do with the amount of time middle and high school teachers spend with a student during a day. Like everything having to do with adolescence, the teacher's report becomes more complicated, too. Perhaps the student does great in a particular subject. The feedback may be atypically good, possibly because the teen has a special interest in that class. Or maybe the class is first thing in the morning or at a time when the medication is wearing off. Then the feedback might be poor.

Bias must also be taken into consideration. Some teachers and school personnel don't *believe* in ADHD. Others may acknowledge it but be against medication. Still others may be for medication and nothing else. If one or more of the school staff suggest the use or disuse of medication, take the comment as worthy of investigation. Contact your teen's physician or mental health professional. That professional may ask you to have teachers fill out a shortened version of a behavior rating scale or some other type of feedback form.

Using Medications Wisely

Let's say you bring your teen to the doctor. You tell the doctor about the problems your teen has. You say someone told you it sounds like ADHD. The doctor asks a few questions. You and your teen leave with a prescription. If this is your doctor's approach, consider finding a new doctor. Before recommending medication, a thorough evaluation as described in Chapter 2 should be done to make sure your teen has ADHD and to determine if medication might be helpful. The evaluation should also uncover information that might help a physician determine which type of medication would be best. Selecting the right medication can save a teen from unpleasant medication effects.

Consider the experience of Adam O'Leary. "I just got tired of waking up every day and taking a pill. But mostly, the effects annoyed me. I wasn't hungry. I felt like I couldn't smile. Even if something was funny, I wouldn't laugh. I'd frown and be depressed. That's another reason I hated to take the medication. It made me feel like shit."

Good psychopharmacology would have been able to help Adam. A well-trained physician would have known other medications to try, either separately or in combination. Sadly, Adam went off medication and refused to try it again for years. He eventually wound up with significant behavioral issues, including a substance-abuse problem. When I met him, he was trying to get his life back on track. Despite his poor experience with meds, he had this advice for other kids. "You should attempt to do better and do whatever it takes to treat your ADHD. If you've got to, take medication because you'll do a lot better. I realize that now."

Once your teen has been determined to have ADHD, then the next step is figuring out if medication is necessary. If it is, the questions become how much, how often, and what is the treatment goal? Following are answers to some frequently asked questions.

When Is Medication Necessary?

One of the points made in Brian Ballard's story is that he could hobble along through life up to a point without medication. But Brian experienced more than minor difficulties because of his ADHD problems.

Though a desire to do well in football motivated him to seek medication as a treatment, his main suffering came from his inability to perform well in school and with peers. The American Academy of Child and Adolescent Psychiatry (AACAP) recommends that medication be considered (1) when there is a diagnosis of ADHD and (2) when symptoms are persistent and severe enough to cause functional impairment at school, at home, or with peers.

The AACAP also recommends that medication be used in conjunction with an individual treatment plan that includes appropriate school placement and modifications.

How Should My Son or Daughter Be Involved in the Decision-Making Process?

Another point illustrated in Brian's story is that adolescents must be involved in the decision to take medication. A parent or a doctor cannot force a pill down an unwilling adolescent's throat. In fact, when medication is indicated, if the adolescent is unwilling to take it, the best you can do is hope he or she will come around, as Brian did. If you make it an issue, you'll probably find yourself in constant battle with a teen who may dig his or her heels in even more.

When adolescents are not involved in the treatment process, they generally find ways to thwart it. One family I know well did not find out until their son was in his early 20s why the medication stopped working once their teen had become an adolescent: He had kept the pill under his tongue until he could safely spit it out. Wise are the physician and parents who look beneath the surface when something that once worked stops being effective.

Principles for Adolescents and Medication Treatment

Eventually teens will have to assume responsibility for managing their disorder. Adolescents need to be treated respectfully and as full participants in treatment decisions. Following are some guidelines for the safe and effective use of medication. These encourage adults to listen to teen concerns, which in turn tells teens that their thoughts and feelings count.

- *Involve the teen in a discussion about the proposed medication before it is prescribed.* Give the reasons why it's recommended, an overview of how it works, and information about any potential side effects. With more information, teens are less likely to think "creatively" and draw the wrong conclusions. Though they use denial as a defense, teens may suspect they have serious problems. It's important to educate them about ADHD and demystify their behavior. It's a good idea to explain what is known about the neurobiology of ADHD. Honesty about what is not known is important, too.

- *Allow the teen to communicate directly with the health care provider.* The teen should be able to discuss with the physician how the medication is working, and review the feedback being given to the doctor by parents and teachers.

- *Encourage the teen to ask questions.* Teens with ADHD may have trouble thinking about their questions ahead of time, remembering them when they see the physician, or responding when on the spot. Periodically make a list of concerns. Also, providing a side-effects questionnaire from the physician may be a good way to prompt questions and concerns.

- *Provide instruction to the teen about the safe use of medication.* Adolescents need information that will enable them to avoid the misuse of medicines. Such information might include overdosing, sharing, using the medication in a manner other than prescribed, or taking it with alcohol, marijuana, or other drugs. Since teens experiment with alcohol and other substances, they should be given the privacy to discuss the safety of taking medication under these circumstances with their physician.

- *Practice the safe use of medication.* The actions of parents and other caregivers should show the appropriate use of medicines. Read the instructions on the bottle. Take as directed. Parents or teens should not adjust doses without physician approval.

- *Gradually transfer responsibility for taking medication.* The AACAP does not recommend that parents give children and adolescents responsibility for taking their medications. Because of impulsivity and disorganization, and the general dislike of taking medication, teens may avoid or forget to take it. Dr. Freund suggest that parents stand by and monitor as teens take their medications. In late adolescence that transfer of responsibility should begin to the extent that the teen shows maturity and appropriate responsibility. Perhaps a reminder or a daily pill dispenser can be used. Also, college students might keep their medications locked up or in a hidden cupboard while at college.

- *Avoid giving credit or blame to the medication.* Thinking or saying a teen's behavior, good or poor, is seen as a result of medication robs the teen of his or her independence and self-respect. Avoid statements such as "You're not doing too well today. You must have forgotten your pill" or "You're really doing great. Those pills must be working." Such statements tell the teen that the medication is in charge. It's not.

Medication Resistance

Some adolescents, no matter how much information they have, will continue to resist taking medication. Often their resistance has to do with one or more of the following reasons:

- denial
- embarrassment—fear of peer response
- loss of control (medication is seen as another way for parents and teachers to control the teen)
- loss of identity (basically the fear that something external is manipulating personality and behavior)
- annoying side effects
- dislike of the way the medication makes them feel (dulling of their personality)

Clinical psychologist Arthur Robin has seen a fair number of adolescents over the years he has been in practice. He finds that teens resist medication because "it makes them feel weird." That means it mellows them out too much. "They don't have as much fun, and they're not as outgoing and extroverted. They think their friends will perceive them as less fun." Dr. Robin has found through experience that a good number of his clients will compromise once they know the following information: It is the ADHD symptoms that the medication is effecting, and that life is a series of compromises. He says they respond when he tells them that they can give up a little bit of wildness for a few hours to get a little better school performance, and that they can be wild at night and on the weekends.

As we saw with Brian Ballard, when he had a goal he wanted to reach, he had no problem making that compromise. As Dr. Freund points out, "I've always felt medication helps the child become more who they really are as opposed to changing who they really are. That message needs to be sent over and over."

When a teen adamantly refuses medication, there isn't much a parent can do. The clinician, however, can be very helpful. "First of all, the doctor has to have a relationship with that kid. I never prescribe medication for a kid who doesn't want to take it," Dr. Jensen explains. Furthermore, if the teen doesn't like his or her personality on the medication—whether the change is real or perceived—or if he or she complains about side effects, "we look for another medication," Dr. Jensen says. Why? "Because I want the teen working with me totally on this medicine issue," he states emphatically. He has a strategy he sometimes uses. "I put the teen right smack dab in the driver's seat." The vehicle he gives them is a clinical trial. He and the teen agree to do an experiment.

He tells the teen, "I'll set something up with the pharmacy so that for three weeks you will be taking pills. All of them will look the same. But one week they'll be a usual dose of medicine. Another week they'll be placebo, which means they'll have no medication. Another week will be a partial dose. I won't know which week is which. You won't know, either. Only the pharmacist will know." Each week of the trial, Dr. Jensen gives the teen's parents and teachers rating scales to fill out. Then at the end of the trial, they look at the reports and find out if there's a big difference. "If we think one week is really good," he tells the teen, "then we'll find out which pill it was. If it's placebo, you're the grand-prize winner. If it's not, then you can decide."

Notice that either way, the teen decides. Making him or her "a little bit of a junior scientist" removes the emotional charge and keeps the teen talking with the clinician. Dr. Jensen also tries to get the teen talking about the medication in the third person, as something separate and apart from the teen. This type of approach may be difficult for a primary-care physician to do given the nature of this type of medical practice, but a community or private mental health professional could set it up.

Clinical psychologist Dr. Richard Zakreski finds it quite common that teens he has seen since childhood come into his office and say, "I'm not ADD. I don't need to take medication anymore." If they are really adamant, he allows that sometimes the teen has to learn from experience. Though the teen may stop medication, he hopes that the teen trusts him and his or her parents enough to keep the lines of communication open. Dr. Zakreski also tries to put other systems in place to monitor the teen's progress. "A lot of kids who have a period of resistance to treatment come back around."

Teens may also become totally unwilling to see the doctor or mental health professional. While parents would be hard pressed to simply pick the teen up and bring him or her to the doctor, they may have some leverage. First, though, Dr. Jensen thinks parents need to be clear in their own minds about the importance of going for help. He often asks the parents what they would do if their teen had a problem with his or her appendix and didn't want to see the doctor. "What I'm doing is helping the parent figure out what their bottom line is," he says, and adds, "Sometimes they back off too quickly." Some of the negotiation techniques explained in Chapter 6 might help.

Sometimes teens need to be rescued from themselves. Sometimes they need to reap what they sow. With early and middle adolescents, while you still have a lot of leverage, you'll usually want to use it to get your teen to simply talk to a professional. Where treatment goes from there is between you and the teen and the practitioner.

Commonly Used Medications

There are different types of medications that may be used to treat ADHD. Which one is used and how much depends upon the individual. For edu-

INFORMATION LINK

A very useful book written for parents, and one of my favorite references, is by Timothy Wilens, *Straight Talk About Psychiatric Medications for Kids,* Guilford Publications, New York, 1999. Mitzi Waltz, *Bipolar Disorder*, O'Reilly Press, Sebastopol, CA, 2000, has an excellent chapter profiling many different medications.

cational purposes, I describe various types and how they work. But in no way should the information herein replace wise medical counsel.

The Stimulants

These types of medicines are the medicines of first choice in the treatment of ADHD. The stimulants mimic brain neurotransmitters, especially dopamine and norepinephrine. They increase the level of activity, arousal, and alertness. As previously stated, ADHD appears to be the result of a problem with the dopamine system, and possibly the norepinephrine system (both neurotransmitters are widely distributed throughout the brain). The areas of the brain responsible for inhibition and planning have abundant dopamine and norepinephrine receptor sites. However, other brain areas seem to be involved as well. Some stimulant medications block dopamine reuptake, thus increasing the amount of dopamine in the synaptic cleft, the gap between one neuron and another.

How does this happen? Remember, neurons communicate with one another through neurotransmitters. One neuron will send its chemical messenger into the synaptic cleft, where the receiving neuron will accept some or all of the neurotransmitter. The sending neuron then reabsorbs the excess neurotransmitter not taken by the receiving neuron. Sometimes problems arise because the sending neuron takes back too much and the receiving neuron takes in too little, which, in turn, can affect the release or reuptake of neurotransmitters. Also, there are other neurotransmitters at work, so a change in one neurotransmitter system may result in changes to the others.

Q   RESEARCH LINK

Timothy Wilens, Thomas Spencer, and Joseph Biederman.
"Pharmacotherapy of Attention Deficit Hyperactivity
Disorder," *Current Opinion in CPNS Investigational Drugs*,
1, 4 (1999): 453–465. This article, which is a bit technical,
gives a great overview of the medications used with ADHD
and comorbid conditions.

Knowing a bit about how the medications work allows us to understand what might seem contradictory or confusing. For instance, many
medications are given on the basis of a person's weight. That's not so with
the stimulants. In fact, a fairly common assumption is that an adolescent
will need a higher dose of medication because of growth spurts. Actually,
an adult might need a proportionally lower dose of medication than a
child. How much medication an individual might require to get the
desired effect depends on what neurons and neurotransmitters are working inefficiently. Obviously, that varies between individuals.

When medication is first given, the physician normally starts the teen
on a trial dose beginning with a small amount. Doses are raised in incre-
ments until the patient has relief from the symptoms. For instance, Brian
Ballard found that on his optimal dose he had an improved working memory, which, in turn, allowed other aspects of his schoolwork to improve.

With stimulant medications, doses may need to be adjusted from
time to time. For instance, many parents note a huge change in their
child's medication response as puberty hits. Think about what is happening. At this stage, the teen's entire body is undergoing dramatic hormonal
changes as well as brain changes. Your teen may have been taking medication with great results for a few years. Then, as if out of nowhere, you
begin to hear from the school. You see changes at home. Your teen has hit
a glitch. Don't be alarmed or disheartened. It's par for the course, and it
means it's time to problem-solve. Usually you begin with a trip to the doctor. In these cases, the doctor will often make a dosage change or prescribe
other medications. In some cases, medication may have to be stopped for
a long period of time. The point is to look, listen, and respond.

Is One Stimulant Medication Better than Another?

Yes and no. The only way to tell which stimulant is better for your teen is to try the medications. Each has its benefits and drawbacks. When I say "try the medications," I don't mean haphazard experimentation. Your physician should evaluate your adolescent's symptoms and weigh the pros and cons of each medication for the individual patient. If your teen has been on medication that stops being effective, the doctor may switch to another stimulant. If other problems become apparent, such as depression, the doctor may try a different class of medications. Don't be afraid to ask questions. You are a valuable member of the treatment team.

Sometimes a medication is chosen because of its duration. Your adolescent may need a long-acting medication or a short-acting one. It depends, again, on individual circumstance.

Presently, there are six brand names of stimulant medications, plus their generic forms: Ritalin, Dexedrine, Cylert, Adderall, Concerta, and Metadate. Stimulants do not cure ADHD. Rather, they reduce the symptoms by mimicking the neurotransmitters. The result is more efficient brain function. Because stimulants are out of the body in a matter of hours, brain function quickly returns to its premedicated state and the patient will have a return of the basic ADHD symptoms. However, the medicines may indirectly have a longer-lasting effect: Because the adolescent has less trouble with ADHD symptoms, he or she will most likely do better at home, in school, and with peers. Thus, some of the secondary problems that result from ADHD—worrying, sadness, poor self-esteem—will likely be lessened.

What's the Difference Between the Different Stimulants?

Ritalin, the most widely researched of all psychiatric medications given to youth, is a brand-name form of the compound methylphenidate. Many doctors do not like to prescribe generic methylphenidate because they don't find it to be as effective as the brand-name drug. Ritalin has been on the market for a number of decades. It comes in both short-acting and sustained-release forms. Because the short-acting form of this medication is in and out of the system quickly, patients usually need to take additional doses throughout the day. Its short-acting properties can be advantageous; it depends on the treatment goal. For instance, a college student may need medication primarily during classes.

Concerta, also a methylphenidate compound, is a relatively new medication that lasts all day—about ten to twelve hours. Each tablet has a medication coating that begins working about fifteen minutes after the tablet is swallowed. Then, throughout the day, the methylphenidate within the tablet shell is gradually and evenly released so that the patient receives a smooth, continuous flow of medication. This unique delivery system alleviates the ups and downs that sometimes occur with other stimulants. Some patients need to take a dose of a short-acting stimulant, like Ritalin, for early evening coverage.

Metadate® CD Extended Release capsule is the newest form of methylphenidate medication. The capsule uses a two-phase release system. When the patient takes the capsule, an initial dose of the medication is released. This first phase is followed by a second release about four and a half hours later. Coverage lasts the length of a school day.

Adderall, an amphetamine compound, has been shown to work well for many patients. It is often used as an alternative to methylphenidate. Its amphetamine compounds are time-released, so it lasts about six hours. Dexedrine, dextroamphetamine sulfate, has also been used for many years, but not as widely as other stimulants. Cylert, pemoline magnesium, is the only stimulant that builds up in the body over time—usually in three weeks. There have been reports of liver effects, so doctors generally do not prescribe it as a first choice, although it has been shown to be effective.

What About Side Effects?

The stimulant medications have similar side effects: insomnia, decreased appetite, weight loss, dysphoria, and rebound (which means the symptoms actually worsen for a short period of time as the medication wears off).

Two areas of concern with the stimulants are blood pressure and tics. The doctor should check blood pressure before prescribing a stimulant. "Stimulants don't cause hypertension," Dr. Barkley says, but he notes that "African-American male teenagers need to be screened more vigilantly because they are prone to hypertension." Stimulants can aggravate an underlying cardiac abnormality.

Tics, which are involuntary motor movements such as eye twitches or lip licking, can be aggravated by stimulant medications. As you know, tics are the predominant feature of Tourette's disorder. Stimulant medications do not cause Tourette's. They may aggravate the tics, but when tics are present, the medications can be used with caution and careful monitoring by the physician.

Though quite rare, other, more serious side effects can arise. Discuss all potential side effects with your doctor. Your doctor will prescribe the medication that seems best suited to your adolescent's clinical picture, especially any comorbid conditions. For ADHD, they generally begin with one of the stimulant medications mentioned in the previous section, as these are quite effective and tend to have mainly nuisance side effects, such as dry mouth, appetite suppression, headaches, and stomachaches.

Monitoring Medication

Medication should be monitored for two reasons: side effects and effectiveness. Dr. Barkley recommends using school-based information. To do so, teachers should complete rating scales, which he recommends be done at least two times before medication begins. Because there is often a decline in scores from the first to the second rating, he suggests the second one be used as the baseline. He also finds it helpful to have parents and teachers complete a weekly side-effects questionnaire. There should also be monthly contact between the parent, the prescribing physician, and the teen. Teacher feedback can be obtained by using a rating scale.

A common practice is to reassess the drug's effectiveness by taking the adolescent off the medication at the beginning of each school year to see if it is still needed. Dr. Barkley believes it's best to take the teen off later in the school year to make a reassessment, and I agree. I can tell you from my classroom experience that most kids begin the year with their best foot forward. Many have promised themselves that this year will be different. They come in with great resolve. They often do well until the end of the first marking period. That would be one reason not to stop medication to assess the need to continue its use until later in the school year.

This first marking period honeymoon effect seems to be true for many kids who aren't on medication, too. In his clinical practice, Dr. Richard Zakreski finds that "once the second marking period report card gets out, referrals really pick up. The parents, either on their own or with the teacher's cooperation, have tried to get the problems under control. When it doesn't work, they get outside help."

When the Stimulants Don't Work

Other medications can be used. Tricyclic antidepressants, such as Norpramin (desipramine), Tofranil (imipramine), and Pamelor (nortriptyline), seem to be less effective than the stimulants on executive function problems, but they tend to work well on mood and impulse control.

Catapres (clonidine) and Tenex (guanfacine) are antihypertensive medications used, sometimes in conjunction with a stimulant. These help with hyperactivity, impulsivity, and aggression. They also have been shown to be useful with sleep problems.

Wellbutrin (bupropion), another antidepressant, has also been shown to be somewhat effective. It's helpful for teens with comorbid bipolar disorder, mood problems, or with substance use disorders. However, it should not be used when eating disorders are present.

The list of medications that can be used goes on. The complicated

 INFORMATION LINK

The following Web sites offer quality information based upon reliable research. There are many others, but these will get you started. For information about specific medications, you can access most pharmaceutical companies by typing in www. and the company name.

www.nlm.nih.gov/medlineplus (from the National Library of Medicine)

www.healthfinder.gov

www.MayoClinic.com

For information about precautions to use when contacting mental health sites, see the pamphlet, "dotCOMSENSE" published by the American Psychological Association. Call (800) 964-2000, or visit www.helping.apa.org or www.dotcomsense.com.

decision of which to use and when is best left to your in-depth discussion with your teen's physician and your own research. I encourage you to read about medications from dependable medical Web sites. Stay informed.

Multiple Medications

Sometimes more than one medication may be necessary. As Dr. Jensen explains, "Parents have to understand. It's like allergies. Shots may do very well for suppressing my allergies to pollens, but I still wheeze a lot because of cockroach droppings. So I'm going to have to add Claritin. And in addition, I may need an inhaler. I may have to take three or four medications to get control of the symptoms." Whether your teen takes one medication or more, keeping a daily chart or log of the medications taken, the results, and any adverse effects will be good feedback for the doctor. It may also help you feel a bit more in control.

What About Medications and Substance Abuse?

Three questions come to mind.

1. Does treatment with stimulants lead to substance use disorders?
2. Do teens abuse stimulants?
3. What happens if my teen uses substances recreationally while on a stimulant?

Does Stimulant Use Lead to Substance Abuse?

Teens with ADHD, especially those with comorbid conduct disorder, are at higher risk for substance use disorders, which is the chronic misuse of or addiction to drugs or alcohol. Apparently, prior treatment with stimulants

 INFORMATION LINK

For a sample medication log, see Timothy Wilens, *Straight Talk About Psychiatric Medications for Kids,* Guilford Publications, New York, 1999, p. 107.

doesn't raise that risk. A study done by the ADHD research group at Massachusetts General Hospital found that Ritalin treatment actually reduced substance abuse. The authors concluded that treatment with medication may *protect* teens from developing abuse and addiction problems.

These results make sense. We've known for a long time that certain risk factors accompany substance use problems. These are mentioned in Chapter 3 under the heading "Substance Use Disorders." Not treating ADHD generally leads to school problems, social maladjustment, and family conflict, not to mention negative feedback and low self-esteem. These are setups for self-medicating behavior. If you feel bad, you'll find a way to feel good. It stands to reason that treated teens will feel better and then have less need to self-medicate.

Do Teens Abuse Stimulants?

Yes, they do. I don't wish to alarm you. I do want to alert you. Anybody can misuse any substance, including the can of whipped cream in your refrigerator—teens have been known to inhale the propellant. As noted in the *Journal of the American Medical Association,* "There is little disagreement that stimulants as a class have a marked abuse potential. Their misuse can have severe adverse medical and social consequences. However, stimulants differ in their ability to induce euphoria and thus liability to abuse."

Dr. Sallie Montgomery, from the Hazelden substance abuse treatment facility, sees a lot of adolescents with SUD problems. She is quite familiar with their use of stimulants. Based on her clinical experience, she reports, "Kids will work with the delivery system. They will crush and snort rather than take their medication as they are supposed to. Psychostimulants are pretty fast-acting. The more fast-acting a medication is, the more addictive it is." Parents of teens, even those without ADHD, need wide-open eyes.

Clearly, abuse issues of stimulants can be avoided when parents carefully monitor their teen's medication.

- Keep count of the pills in the bottle.
- Watch as your teen takes his or her medication.
- Don't give your teen ready access to any medications.

These guidelines may seem to be suggesting that you take control away from your teen at the age when he or she is becoming more responsible. In a way, they do. If you have the primary responsibility for monitoring the taking of medication, your teen stays off the hook when friends ask them to share their medication. "Oh, just let me try one of your pills" becomes a nonissue when the pill is very hard to come by. As stated in the *Journal of American Academy of Child and Adolescent Psychiatry,* "Giving or selling medication to peers is more common than abuse by the patients themselves."

Let's say the teen with ADHD does cross the line into substance abuse or addiction. At Hazelden, when a teen with ADHD is in treatment, the staff is very selective about what they prescribe. As Dr. Montgomery told me, "We certainly do not encourage the use of the psychostimulants. We will try patients on a nonaddictive substance such as Wellbutrin. After they are stabilized on the Wellbutrin, if they are not doing well, then we will, in fact, do a trial on the psychostimulants to see if there is a change." Dr. Thomas Spencer, a leading ADHD psychopharmacology research expert, also counsels the cautious use of psychostimulant medications until the appropriate addiction treatment has been undertaken and the person has remained drug- and alcohol-free for a period of time. Dr. Spencer notes that other disorders should be ruled out as well.

Alcohol and marijuana are the substances most frequently abused. You should know that teens with ADHD do report that marijuana helps them concentrate better. As explained by Dr. Montgomery, "Marijuana prevents the reuptake of dopamine in the frontal parts of the brain." Despite what the teen might say, marijuana is not an herbal remedy. Dr. Montgomery notes that the problem with marijuana, aside from its illegal status, is that it's far more potent these days. It is also frequently mixed with other drugs, so the user really doesn't know ahead of time what he or she is smoking.

What About Use of Alcohol or Pot When My Teen Is Taking Medication?

No one condones underage drinking. And pot is illegal for any age. But we do know that some teens on stimulant medications drink and smoke pot. Of course, such behavior concerns most parents. While Dr. Barkley is not endorsing substance abuse, he does say, "Parents don't have to worry if their child is taking one of the stimulants and has something at a party. You are not placing his or her life in danger. There won't be any serious, life-threatening interactions if your child takes Ritalin and has a beer or smokes a joint." He adds that the more serious cause for concern is when crack or cocaine is taken, because they are stimulants. Since Ritalin is also a stimulant, these drugs will compound each other's effects. It is important to note that Dr. Barkley's comments do not apply to medications other than stimulants. Nor do they apply to the kid who's drinking or smoking pot heavily, on either one occasion or multiple occasions. Certainly, he's not encouraging parents to look the other way.

Dr. Jensen has a similar point of view when it comes to alcohol. "I don't condone its use," he says, "but I also am smart enough to know it happens. Basically, if I were to tell a teenager that if they used alcohol, they couldn't be treated with medication, nine-tenths of them wouldn't be given any treatment." He will not treat if he has a kid actively abusing any other substances, including marijuana. And with regard to alcohol, he says, "If I have a kid drinking regularly—daily or every weekend—I'm going to take that very seriously. As with the use of cocaine or marijuana, I'll get very exercised and concerned about the potential for interactions even though I can't say I know this interaction is likely to occur, because we don't. There are no studies we can point to." In case you wonder why there are no studies, Dr. Jensen explains, "You don't give a kid a six-pack and then 20 mg of Ritalin. We just don't do those kinds of studies."

The bigger concern parents should have if they know their teen is taking Ritalin and drinking intermittently really has to do with the alcohol. As Dr. Jensen says, "They may get hurt from driving under the influence of alcohol. That's the biggest worry, not the interaction of the two."

What About Cigarettes?

"I used to smoke cigarettes a lot," says 16-year-old Kevin Gillingham. "It started as a peer pressure thing. Then it was an outlet for my stress." Youths with ADHD are at greater risk to become smokers. Nicotine boosts dopamine levels. That may be a reason why many teens with ADHD smoke. What might start out as Joe Cool becomes a realization that "I focus better when I smoke." Without the teen's knowing why, nicotine becomes a drug of choice.

Finding the Right Help

I gave guidelines for selecting a practitioner in Chapter 2. Now I want to give a pep talk. Sometimes complications arise. And sometimes a therapist who may have served you well in earlier days may not be the right person as time goes on. Only you will know what's working. If your son, daughter, or family continues to struggle after a good amount of time, it may be time for a change. Don't be disheartened.

Therapists generally have individual points of view they bring to the treatment table. Many specialize in a specific type of therapy. Psychopharmacologists, for instance, use medications. In addition to this approach, cognitive-behavioral therapy is usually recommended for the treatment of ADHD. Therapists with this type of practice educate the parent and the teen about the disorder. They work to identify key areas of concern. This approach mainly uses a problem-solution base. The patients learn to see what needs to be done and change their behavior accordingly. This approach also works well with people who are anxious or depressed. It helps them identify the streams that feed their emotional states; changing what they do changes their viewpoint.

People with ADHD don't tend to respond to talk therapy very well. So as a treatment for this problem, psychoanalysis generally wastes time and money. When looking for professional help, remember what you need most: practical information, workable solutions, and coaching for both you and your teen in methods and techniques that help compensate for ADHD difficulties. As ADHD affects all family members, in addition to a cognitive-behavioral approach, the therapist should use a family-systems approach. With teens you will need someone who knows how to train families in problem solving, communication, conflict resolution, and other forms of behavior management such as contracting. These are discussed in subsequent chapters.

Once you make contact with a treatment professional, don't be afraid to ask directly about his or her training and expertise. Ask how they view your role. You are a part of the treatment team. ADHD cannot be managed with a top-down approach. I would also be wary of any clinician who seems to have all the answers at the first meeting. Therapy is a discovery process. A diagnosis is merely the first part. Treatment revolves around the business of sifting through the problem and trying solutions. There may even be homework involved!

Often by the time a family gets outside help for ADHD, they have an angry family mess going on. "My job," says clinician Richard Zakreski, "is to try to go where the family has been unable to go or has tried to go and been unable to successfully get there. I'm a neutral figure. I try to understand how everybody feels and what's beneath the anger." To do that with the teen, he generally finds he needs to spend some time alone with him or her. We parents may sometimes look to the therapist to be our ally. That's not a good idea. As Dr. Zakreski explains, "If I allow the therapy visit to become the mother and father and me getting on the kid's case, then the kid has no interest in coming back. I don't blame him or her," he adds. "I wouldn't, either."

Initially when you seek help, you will spend a lot of time with the clinician. This "burst of intervention," as Dr. Robin calls it, actually gets your situation stabilized. After this burst, you basically learn to use your bag of tricks. What's great about adolescents is they can learn to use the tricks, too. Your visits to the clinician eventually become tune-ups unless you hit some ruts. Then you will be doing that necessary intervention work.

ADHD generally is a lifelong problem. Aim to cope. Don't expect to cure. Some tools work better than others at given points in time and for various reasons. Sometimes you may not be emotionally available to deal with the problems. Then you have to wait a day or two and come back. When you've tried everything you can think of and no solution readily appears, you may have to wait it out. You have to draw from the assembled wisdom, avoid the cracks, take time, have patience, and learn to live with trial and error.

Transferring Responsibility to the Teen

A day will come when your teen will be able to manage the disorder him- or herself, as countless adults with ADHD now do. An essential part of ADHD treatment involves teaching and helping the teen to become his or her own advocate. The teen will learn how by being involved in decision-making processes and by seeking solutions for problems he or she identifies. Each teen needs to find his or her strengths and to get help to mini-mize difficulties. By the last of the high school years, the teen should be an equal member of the treatment team and be ready to move into the role of director—provided, of course, that he or she is ready. Readiness has arrived when the teen demonstrates the know-how and responsibility to be his or her primary advocate. As with so many things with ADHD, that growth happens a step at a time.

CHAPTER FIVE

Behind and Beyond
the Storm and Stress

ADHD and emotional overreactivity often go hand in hand. Recent research helps us understand that emotional control or the lack of it has a great deal to do with the areas of the brain affected by ADHD. This chapter looks at the neurological underpinnings of emotional control and how problems in this area may lead to the poor emotional affect so often seen in teens with the disorder.

"I'm not a very social person," 15-year-old Hallie Banks says. "I get upset easily. I'm one of those people who thinks everyone is out to get her. And I know I'm wrong. Yet I still believe these things."

How can Hallie think everyone is out to get her and at the same time know that's not true? Her rational side can size up situations. She can look at facts, figures, actions, and inaction. These give her a pretty good thought about what's actually going on in her world. But underneath this external cover of thought, Hallie has a different belief system—one that has been created by her emotions. Her world of thought and her world of feeling are a black hole apart. For reasons that are explained in this chapter, this gap seems to be a fairly common problem of ADHD. It often leads teens to misbehave, miss social cues, draw wrong conclusions, and be fearful, anxious, and defensive.

The neurological problems that cause the core ADHD symptoms have a huge impact on the social and emotional aspects of life. Surprisingly, as Dr. Thomas Brown points out, "There's not a damn thing in the

DSM-IV criteria that picks up on affect." Yet affect, the emotional side of self, causes people with ADHD great difficulty. They have a hard time managing their emotions. Others have a hard time dealing with their emotional natures. What you see isn't always how they feel, either. For example, Adrienne Milstein says her son "is not real honest about how poorly he thinks of himself." Instead, she says, "he gets angry." When he's having trouble in school and gets frustrated, he blames it on the teacher.

Teens with ADHD are "overly present" emotionally, particularly those who are hyper and impulsive. They bring a lot of gusto to life. They also bring fire and rain. When they've got it together, they bring incredibly uplifting, inspirational energy. But when they're "in a state," watch out. You may see temper the likes of which you've never imagined. You see frustration, a short fuse, and a lack of predictability. You may also see chronic worry and low-level anxiety. The less aggressive types may withdraw to the sidelines, as did Brian Ballard, the football player you met in the previous chapter. As Dr. Barkley says, "ADHD doesn't cause a mood disorder. What it creates is an inability to manage the moods you're going to have."

The hideous irony of ADHD is that many of these teens can be so aggressive and moody that they seem anything but anxious, worried, and thin-skinned to those around them, like "easily upset" Hallie. "I freak out on people when they are bothering me, " she tells me. In actuality, she just wants to be liked and accepted, like everyone else. She's a sweet young lady who is defensive as hell. As you will come to know shortly, Hallie's social misinterpretation, her difficulty holding back until she can think through a situation, and her hair-trigger responses have a lot to do with the balance between the brain's emotional, thought, and memory systems. As Dr. Brown notes, "Neuroscience and neuropsychology have only recently paid more attention to the biology behind emotion."

The Biology of Emotionality

We sometimes talk about our brains as though underneath our bony skulls are a bunch of separate parts that sometimes work together and other times do not. Actually, the billion neurons that comprise our brains operate through a series of systems and subsystems. Some of these are dedicated to specific functions. There is not really an emotional brain or a thinking brain. Instead emotion and thought are governed by separate brain systems that interact with each other.

At this present time in our species' evolution, connections from the emotional system to the cognitive (thought) system happen to be stronger than those from the cognitive system to the emotional system. That's a holdover from our primitive days. Our brains respond to sensory information. A stimulus that threatens our physical well-being gets our biggest response. Our brains had little thought and problem-solving function in earlier days because humans were mainly involved with the business of survival. Rapid response to threat is a brain mechanism that continues to serve us well.

As many thousands of years went by, the human brain developed a prefrontal cortex. With it came higher-order thinking skills, the so-called executive functions, which, as explained in Chapter 2, allow us to think, plan, organize, problem-solve, and so on. In other words, it allows us to be thoughtful and reflective. These cortical areas of our brains help us control our wild and wooly sides and prevent us from expressing them in inappropriate situations. Children, whose prefrontal areas are coming on line into adolescence, have less capacity to keep a lid on their emotional responses. Those with ADHD, who have inefficient executive function, often blow up at the slightest thing, as Hallie Banks does.

"I don't really get along with kids," Hallie says. "When I was in third grade, I hit a girl because she stole my place in line. It was during the first few minutes of school, and this was when being ahead in line was everything to a kid. I thought I had gotten there first and she thought she had gotten there first. We started arguing, and I hit her because I was really upset. I was never anywhere except last, and now I was actually in front of a person."

The Emotional Edge

Dr. Daniel Goleman writes that all emotions are "instant plans for handling life." When Hallie hit her classmate, she probably had what Dr. Goleman refers to as a "neural hijacking." In other words, she had a rapid-fire emotional reaction that led to an action. That action happened before the reflective system of her brain had the opportunity to think the situation through and plan a more socially appropriate response.

Why did Hallie have this emotional reaction? The answer may lie in the fear research done by Dr. Joseph LeDoux. When a threatening stimulus comes to us, it sends a signal throughout our brain. Most of the signal travels to the prefrontal cortex, the area associated with executive functions. This route allows us to think about what to do. However, a smaller signal travels to the amygdala, the brain's emotional center. This smaller signal helps us make an instant determination about whether or not the stimulus poses an immediate danger. If it does, we may act so instantaneously that the amount of time it takes to react is imperceptible.

In a neural hijacking, the balance between the size of the signal that travels the thoughtful route and the size that travels the emotional route is out of proportion. When too much signal juice goes the emotional route, overreaction results. In people with ADHD, the executive function difficulties mean that these neural hijackings occur with greater frequency.

Let's think about Hallie on the school line. Hallie may or may not have gotten to the line first, but she was so aroused by the opportunity to be first (a stimulus) that she made a beeline for the front without noticing anything or anyone else around her. Arousal is an important part of all of our brain's functions. We become aroused when any new stimulus comes our way. Already aroused, Hallie became further aroused when confronted with the very large stimulus of another person. She became tense and anxious as a result. A threat signal went off. Fearful that she would lose the coveted first place, her amygdala went into overdrive and she flew into action, fists flying before she could stop and think about anything—for instance, whether the other girl really did get there first, whether she would get in trouble for hitting, whether being first really mattered that much, whether she and the other girl could do some peaceable negotiation.

As explained by Dr. LeDoux, arousal locks you into whatever emotional state you are in when the arousal occurs—unless something else occurs that is significant enough and arousing enough to shift the focus of arousal. The other person's presence was large enough to remove Hallie from her happy state of thinking she was first on line and send her into feeling defensive and aggressive.

After most emotional reactions, most people have a sense of what came over them. That may not be the case where ADHD is concerned. Again, due to inefficient prefrontal circuitry, the person with this disorder may not fully register that anything came over him or her. In fact, quite the opposite might occur. A characteristic of youth with ADHD is to blame others. Neural hijacking may be the reason why. It is possible that the youth doesn't see the full picture.

That's especially true during the preteen and early adolescent years. Developmentally speaking, these are the years when the maturing brain brings more executive function into play. Consequently, as the middle adolescent years arrive, we expect better emotional control. Those with ADHD may not be able to do this until they are much older. Even then, they will probably be prone to neural hijackings more than others are. That's also true for people with a lot of stress. As circumstances become overwhelming, the brain seems to become trained to send most of the stimulus signal along the emotional route.

Though the neurobiology of ADHD is a setup for poor emotional response, it doesn't have to spell disaster. Medication can certainly relieve the core symptoms and reduce neural hijackings. As Dr. Barkley points out, "There are coping strategies for kids prone to mood dysregulation." Many of these work for their parents as well. Such strategies aim to defuse an overaroused state. They aren't necessarily complicated, either. A teen can count to ten, blow raspberries when appropriate, walk away, or move into an activity known to soothe and quiet the mind—perhaps running or listening to music.

 INFORMATION LINK

You might consider giving your teen a copy of the teen self-help book, by Lynn Clark, *SOS Help for Emotion: Managing Anxiety, Anger and Depression*, Parents Press, Bowling Green, KY, 1998.

☞ TRY THIS

Take a moment now to jot down some strategies your teen can use to avert a meltdown or pull out of one. If you can involve the teen in this process, that's even better.

Post the list someplace where it can serve as a ready reminder—perhaps the refrigerator or the teen's bedroom door. You can cue your teen with one of two words from the list so the teen knows he or she is coming close to a meltdown and needs to avert it. For instance, when Hallie's voice starts to get louder, a simple reminder would be: "Hallie—raspberries." She would then blow air through her pursed lips and defuse the scream and anger or frustration build-up.

With a suggestion like this one, understand that the object is to interrupt behavior. If the teen breaks the cycle without blowing raspberries, then the objective has been met. Sometimes the teen may be too far gone in the meltdown cycle, or the teen may be in a particularly angry period to abort a meltdown. That doesn't mean the strategy doesn't work. It just may not be the right time.

The Very Thought of It

Dr. LeDoux notes that we have both an emotional memory and a cognitive memory of a stimulus. Our emotional memories play out as gut reactions to something. Often we don't have the vaguest idea of why we feel or act the way we do.

Memories formed mainly via the emotional circuit may explain why people with untreated ADHD can eventually come to see their worlds as dark, forbidding, scary places. Poor ability to think things through leads to emotional overreaction. Couple this biological problem with the social experience of people constantly jumping down your throat and giving negative feedback. Chances are you may become defensive, angry, withdrawn, or aggressive. When faced with new challenges, especially adolescence and the rapid changes it brings, teens with untreated ADHD may be prone to a greater number of neural hijackings. I emphasize treated versus untreated, because medication helps the prefrontal cortex to respond more efficiently. In turn, the person with ADHD is guided more by thought than emotion. Thus, the hair-trigger responses decrease, resulting in better emotional control.

Dr. LeDoux makes an interesting speculation. People who respond to stimuli primarily via an emotional route, with little or no thought, may form emotional memories based on these events. That raises a problem because these perceptions may actually be based on bits and pieces of neural information instead of the complete picture. Such people, he thinks, would have very poor insight into their emotions. Furthermore, their memory of events would be skewed. Thus, in future situations, the inaccurate memory of events may guide the way they look at things. That could lead to expressing emotions that are inappropriate. It is also possible that a person picks up only bits and pieces of a situation due to poor attention. Missed information leads to misinterpretation and the makings of misunderstanding.

One of Hallie's problems with her classmates is that she jumps down their throats the minute someone sits next to her. The reason may have to do with her emotional memory. Because kids in the past have sat next to her to taunt her, she has an emotional response when someone approaches her. She's on guard, and she lashes out. After the fact, she can think about the exchange. That is when she realizes that everybody isn't out to get her. "I know I'm wrong," she says. So why doesn't she just stop doing that? What happens inside her head?

Dr. Goleman explains, "The emotional mind responds by triggering feelings that went with remembered events. It reacts to the present as though it were the past." This response served us very well in our earlier days. Most of us only touch a hot stove once as a toddler. A point Dr. Goleman makes is that if you make a fast automatic appraisal (jump to conclusions), you may not realize that things have changed. Maybe the kids were taunting Hallie in earlier years. Now they don't really have a chance to even get close to her to show that they may have changed. Her memories of past abuse may get in the way.

When our teens behave in an overreactive and sometimes emotionally outrageous manner, it's important to understand what is probably going on in their heads—a neural short circuit. That knowledge alone may help lessen negative feedback, especially anger.

INFORMATION LINK

Daniel Goleman, *Emotional Intelligence,* Bantam Books,
   New York, 1997.
Joseph LeDoux, *The Emotional Brain,* Touchstone Books,
   New York, 1996.

The Stress Factor

Reactive ADHD behavior certainly has a negative effect on interpersonal relationships. Teens who are aggressive and oppositional may spark neural hijackings in others. Those teens who tend to be anxious and chronic worriers may trigger a less volatile but nonetheless emotionally overreactive response in self and others, too. By the teenage years, ADHD, left untreated, often lives in conflict-laden families. Such conflict exists in friendships, too. Neural hijackings are crisis creators for most everyone. A neurally hijacked family is a family in crisis.

"Because of the frontal lobe aspects and the emotional overload, these adolescents are vulnerable to a lot of stresses," Dr. Freund observes. Sometimes that vulnerability gets hidden behind the external display of behavior. As Dr. Freund explains, "When you have an adolescent with opposition, anger, and frustration, the parents aren't thinking about how stressed and harangued the kid is, because they are dealing with the anger and opposition, not where it's stemming from." Since ADHD puts individuals and families under extraordinary stress, it seems important to understand the nature of stress, how it affects the body, and what to do about it.

Stress triggers the release of hormones and other chemicals. These help us cope physically, emotionally, and mentally. Once the stress passes, the stress chemicals return to their normal levels. Psychobiology researcher Dr. Bruce McEwen discovered that under periods of stress, repeated hits of stress, or extraordinary stress, the stress chemicals stay at elevated levels. Over time, our bodies adapt to the elevated levels of these stress chemicals. We may think we are doing great when we function at the coping level, but Dr. McEwen's research tells a different story. While these chemicals help us during a time of stress, if our levels can't or don't

TRY THIS

Identify things that create stress for you or your teen. Make a list. Brainstorm about how to get rid of the cause or reduce the effects of the stress. Try out an idea. If it doesn't work, try another one. Eventually, you'll find a way to ease the situation.

For example, suppose waking your teen for school creates stress because you have to get ready for work, and he or she rarely gets up the first or second time you call. Here you want to eliminate the cause of the stress, so you brainstorm to come up with ways to get the teen up. Perhaps use multiple alarm clocks, or set a radio alarm to a station the teen hates. The stress is reduced for the parent because you are not directly responsible for waking the teen. You can use the additional time you gain for some light yoga, relaxation breathing, working out, or watching a morning news program. Getting up may still be hard for the teen, but he or she doesn't have the added stress of being "bugged" by another person.

drop down to normal range, the body remains on heightened alert, and this can lead to health problems.

Most people know that chronic stress can cause heart problems and autoimmune diseases. It also kills neurons in the hippocampus, which is a brain area associated with memory and emotion. Lasting stress may lead to stress disorders, such as recurrent depressive illness and posttraumatic stress disorder.

When we're engaged in the daily business of coping with ADHD, it's hard to think about what effects that stress may have in the future. Yet if we don't, we may be dealing with health problems tomorrow. Efforts must be made to alleviate stress.

What can be done? Although Dr. McEwen doesn't work with ADHD populations, he is familiar with the disorder. He thinks these kids need to break bad habits, establish new ones, and gain a sense of mastery and control. That goes for parents, too. As you and your teen learn some of the ADHD management tools described in the remainder of this book, these suggestions from Dr. McEwen will be put into play. Meanwhile, practice stress relief.

Plenty of stress-reduction techniques exist. They include physical exercise; meditation, which quiets the mind and slows the body; laughter, which restores good feelings; and many others. There are hundreds of books and tapes on this topic and many ways to get instruction through community-based programs or private practitioners.

It's so easy to overlook good health practice while dealing with the more demanding aspects of ADHD. Even putting the benefits of future good health aside, stress management helps with daily living, too, by helping us to stay in emotional control. Decide to do something stress-reducing today. Then do it.

Emotional Intelligence

Whether we're talking about intimate relationships, getting along with friends, or getting along as a social being, emotional intelligence comes into play. Many ADHD social problems seem to come from poor emotional intelligence, a term coined by Dr. Goleman. He considers it critical for success in today's world. According to Dr. Goleman, emotional intelligence consists of these abilities:

- self-motivation
- persistence despite frustration
- impulse control
- delay of gratification
- mood regulation
- thoughtfulness under distress
- empathy
- hope

Dr. Goleman thinks of emotional intelligence as an aptitude. Childhood and adolescence are the years when that aptitude is mainly under construction. It takes but a quick glance at his list of abilities that go hand in hand with the development of emotional intelligence to see how ADHD can interfere. "Nature and nurture are partners in our emotional life," Dr. LeDoux says. Skills our teens don't come by naturally can be taught.

Youth have a wonderful opportunity to shape some of their personal characteristics. (Of course, adults do, too.) To do so, they need great guid-

---

TRY THIS

If you'd like to try to help your teen identify and shape some of the abilities needed for emotional intelligence, take another look at the list on page 103. Place a check mark next to those skills that your teen has to some degree or another. Think about your teen in all his or her social worlds: home, school, extracurricular activities, relatives, neighbors, friends, clubs, organizations, religious institutions. (As parents, we can take pressure off ourselves by remembering that our teens live in a larger world. Everyone in this larger world can in a sense become part of the treatment team.)

The check marks you make help to identify your teen's good stuff. Doing that helps us parents in two ways. First, we may be so embroiled in trying interactions with our teens that we lose sight of their natural goodness. Second, we can use this list to help our teens build emotional aptitude. How?

- *Let's say you checked empathy. You can look for instances during the day when your son or daughter behaved in an empathetic way. Point that behavior out to them. Label it as empathetic. Give praise and appreciation.*
- *Suppose you put persistence despite frustration on the list, even though that happens quite rarely. In addition to looking for instances to praise, you can also bolster this skill by presenting barely challenging situations that you know will be mildly frustrating yet within your teen's reach to complete—perhaps shooting hoops with him or her. Of course, regardless of what practice situation you set up, the minute your teen starts to get frustrated, create a distraction into a totally soothing activity.*

ance about the appropriateness of an emotion and the way it is expressed. Emotions in and of themselves are not bad or good. But what any of us do with them is another story.

Social Basics

You can also make a list of the things you did not check, the not-so-good stuff. Perhaps your adolescent doesn't delay gratification. When "gotta have it now" happens, don't get angry. Try to remember that it's only one part of your son or daughter's emotional intelligence and that it is under construction. After you build on the strengths, you can help them beef up the weak areas.

During their early years, many children with ADHD do not learn basic social competency skills, though not because we parents didn't try to teach them. Rather, under normal circumstances this skill development begins around age two. The developmental delay of ADHD makes this toddler a less than ready or eager pupil. What skills are we talking about? The stuff of ordinary good manners: Speak when spoken to. Speak in sentences—not grunts, groans, and one-word replies. Initiate social contact. Say please and thank you. Share your toys. Show appreciation and gratitude. Let others go first, too.

It's never too late to teach the basics. However, in the teen years, parents don't usually make the best strategy-building partners. Your teen wants to fly on his or her own. What you can do is model socially appropriate behavior. You might also give reminders—provided these don't turn into nags. For instance, if your teen walks out the door and forgets to say goodbye, go to the door and politely or even humorously give a reminder. Avoid anger, criticism, and harsh, reactive punishment.

Some teens may also benefit from formal social skills training programs. A therapist can help you locate such programs, or your teen's school may have a program as well. Such programs teach strategies. Keep in mind that these strategies do not prevent an emotional reaction. They help the teen get a grip once it has occurred. In order for social skills to improve, they have to be practiced in the natural setting.

As explained by Dr. Goleman in his book *Emotional Intelligence,* Yale psychologist Peter Salovey says there are five domains of emotional intel-ligence, which I have listed below in italics:

Knowing one's own emotions. People with ADHD tend to be unaware of how they are feeling. That might be because they have mini neural hijacks as well as major meltdowns. Will people with ADHD get self-awareness? "Yes," says Dr. Barkley, "but at a later age than others."

Managing emotions. While the ADHD hair-trigger response is a par-ticularly hard cycle to change, we can try. You may not get an immediate response, but today's lesson becomes tomorrow's skill. I have interviewed teens with the shortest of fuses. Some have even been in trouble with the law and been placed in residential treatment centers. With the right guid-ance, structure, and possibly medication when indicated, they do manage their emotions. You'll meet them in Chapter 9. You'll get some tools in Chapters 6, 7, and 8.

Motivating one's self. Goal-oriented behavior, self-control, and turn-ing away from impulse are the bane of their existence for most teens with ADHD. Often when they find their passions, the picture changes. If you have a son or daughter with ADHD and he or she finds a passion, shout "Hurray!" Encourage him or her in every way. It may just be through the passion that the other skills can be coached and improved.

Recognizing emotion in others. Teens with ADHD have a hard time bringing mindful observation to what they see. In fact, they often read other people as being angry. Clearly they need cool, calm, collected prac-tice in learning to judge what they see.

Handling relationships. Knowing how to participate in a relationship is the art of social competence and the fabric of our lives. One of the biggest problems reported by adults with ADHD is their lack of ability in this area. They have more broken marriages and more job changes than others. When the core problems of ADHD get arrested, usually with the aid of medication—then therapy, coaches, and self-help groups can assist in developing better relationship skills.

In addition to these elements of emotional intelligence, researchers generally recognize a core group of basic emotions as common to humans: surprise, happiness, anger, fear, disgust, sadness, interest, and anticipation. The core emotions have themes and variations. For instance, joy can mean happiness, relief, delight, pride, and so on. While such words are the spice of writers, I also think they help us home in on how we actually feel. Many teens with ADHD (and without) have poor emotional vocabularies. They may know the words *pissed, frustrated, awesome,* and *great.* But these words are so nonspecific. One thing we can do for teens with the disorder is to help them develop their emotional vocabularies. That in turn may help to improve self-awareness, awareness of emotional states in others, and the ability to use words to handle relationships.

Emotional Words

In *Emotional Intelligence,* Dr. Goleman comes up with a list of primary emotions and their themes and variations. I've adopted his idea to help you expand your teen's emotional vocabulary. Following is a list of core emotions and associated words. You might have a few of your own to add to the lists.

Angry words: *burn up, enrage, incense, infuriate, ire, madden, provoke, fury, outrage, resentment, wrath, exasperation, indignation, vexation, acrimony, animosity, annoyance, irritability, hostility, agitated, cranky, frustrated, impatient, upset*

Disgusting words: *contempt, disdain, scorn, abhor, aversion, distaste, revulsion, nauseating, repelling, revolt, sickening, filthy*

Fearful words: *anxiety, apprehension, nervousness, concern, consternation, misgiving, wary, qualm, edgy, dread, fright, terror, alarmed, horrified, panicked, trepidation, victimized*

Joyful words: *happiness, relief, contentment, bliss, delight, amusement, pride, thrill, rapture, gratification, satisfaction, euphoria, whimsy, ecstasy, glad, merry, exultant, jovial, amazed, cheerful, wonderful, up*

Loving words: *accepting, friendly, trust, kind, affinity, devoted, adoring, infatuated, affection*

Sad words: *grief, sorrow, cheerless, gloomy, melancholy, self-pity, lonely, depressed, dejected, down, despairing, dismal, joyless, let down*

Shameful words: *guilt, embarrassed, chagrin, remorse, humiliated, regretful, mortified, contrite, disgraceful, blatant, brassy, infamous*

Surprised words: *shock, astonish, amaze, wonder, startled, taken aback, stunned, rattled, disconcerted*

Interested/not interested words: *alert, ambivalent, bored, curious, energized, enthusiastic, excited, focused, jazzed, prepared, ready*

☞ TRY THIS

Without being obvious, model the use of emotional vocabulary.

You might talk with your teen about something that happened to you during the day that had an emotional kick. When describing the situation, avoid using common words such as angry, sad, afraid, fine, *and* love, *or the teen's common phrases* pissed off, scared shitless, *or* fucked up. *Substitute words closer to your actual feeling—for instance, "I felt relief when I avoided an accident after someone cut me off today."*

You can also do this modeling when watching television or movies with your teen, or when you are out in a place where you observe people in action. If your teen receives this type of modeling well, then you might even try a TV/movie game. Here, you watch a show together (maybe even with friends). While viewing, use the word list and identify emotions in characters. Figure out with your teen some system of determining a win and what the win will be worth. Of course, give penalties whenever the usual words are used: angry, sad, afraid, love, felt good.

This type of modeling game probably works best with early adolescents. However, teens at any age can get agitated when they think they are being manipulated. So don't make it an issue. You can still model words—as long as the teen doesn't think you are doing so as a teacher.

Some good rules of thumb for modeling: Be brief, be gone, and don't beat a dead horse.

Empathy

In his book *The Lost Boys,* Dr. James Garbarino, a leading expert in youth violence, says empathy is the foundation of all emotional intelligence. Most people have the capacity to understand how another feels. He notes that early adolescents, who are naturally melodramatic, impulsive, and self-centered, lack this skill. Because ADHD, with its hair-trigger responses, stifles empathy, it may need to be taught. This skill may take time to build. School-based peer-mediation programs and conflict-resolution techniques have been shown to be very helpful. Family communication patterns can cultivate empathy as well.

Often teens with ADHD are clueless about how their behavior affects others. One way to clue them in and to help them develop empathy is to call attention in a nonjudgmental way to the distress caused by their behavior. Dr. Peter Jensen underscored this point in a personal anecdote about his family, especially as it related to his son with ADHD, who is now a young adult. This young man struggled with aggression. He picked on his younger siblings a lot, especially his sister. During a peaceful time, Dr. Jensen sat down with his son and let his heart be known. He said to his boy, who was about 16, "You know, I'm really concerned about this. I don't know how to help you. It has an impact on me and your sister. I really feel bad. I don't want you to feel bad, but I don't want to feel bad, either. And I don't want to be riding you." Seven years later, while on a sports outing, this son told his father how deeply that conversation touched him.

What worked here? Dr. Jensen explains that he didn't come into the conversation with any sense of criticism. He just showed his son that he was in pain. Did it change the young man's behavior toward his sister? "I wouldn't say it was an overnight change, but his behavior got better over time." As Dr. Jensen says, "It's like steering a giant cruise ship. You jerk the rudder, but that ship may not turn for seven or eight miles." That's true for a lot of what happens in emotional development. It may not show up for years.

Just as teens with ADHD need to develop empathy, they also need to receive it. Youth who live in a harsh, forbidding, punitive world may not sustain the feelings of self-worth to make it in life by positive means. That's what was beginning to happen to a former student of mine. Every day he disrupted the class. He tried to be a wise guy and the class clown. I took his snickering and calling out in stride. His lack of work and his poor grades concerned me. However, his anger and his snarling at classmates and at me whenever I tried to get him back on track began to tick me off. When I found myself reacting, I knew I needed to do something else. One day I gave him detention. When he arrived, I looked him straight in the eye and said in a very pleasant tone of voice, "Tell me what you are working for. If I know what you want with this behavior, then maybe I can give it to you and we can skip the acting out."

His mouth dropped and he hedged a bit before replying, "I'm not good at anything." I tried to assure him that it's not unusual to feel powerless and ineffective during early adolescence, and I told him that if he was patient, his special talent would reveal itself. We began to explore his likes and things he might want to pursue. We didn't find that special something that day. In the days that followed I still had to call him to attention when he was off task or disruptive, but he never gave me attitude again. A month or so later, a most amazing thing happened. The boy wrote a phenomenal poem that I encouraged him to enter in a contest. It's published today. His poem was about not fitting in.

In a way, this student's acting out was a good sign. Some youth get so derailed, they barely operate at all. The term for this state is "learned helplessness." Youth with this problem are so sure they won't do well that they may not even try. They make statements like "So what?" "Why bother?" "It doesn't matter." "I don't care." In other words, they expect a poor outcome regardless of what they do.

As the anecdote shows, everyone needs some type of passion or confidence booster. What can be done for a turned-off teen with little to no self-esteem? Help them to do the following:

- develop a hobby that requires physical action
- perhaps try an intense confidence booster, such as a wilderness program
- develop a passion or a special interest

Don't be surprised if your teen resists efforts to steer him or her in any of these directions. He or she may truly believe, as my former student did, that "I'm not good at anything." The process of discovering a passion or an area of competence takes trial and error. Don't let your teen quit something too soon. Teens will often protest as a way to avoid the challenge they don't think they can meet. They need to stick it out—at least for a reasonable length of time. By all means, listen to your teen's protests. Investigate them. Try to alleviate problems. Talk and strategize with whoever is in charge of the activity. Involve your teen in discussions, too—which has the added benefit of developing self-advocacy skills.

An advantage that adolescence brings for the teen with ADHD is more opportunity and a greater variety of possible areas of interest to choose from. You may have to try a number of ideas out, but eventually something will turn up. "Individuals are a collection of aptitudes," writes Howard Gardner in *Multiple Intelligences,* the book about his theory. "Because of a particular combination or blend of skills," Gardner explains, "he or she may be able to fill some niche quite well." When people with ADHD find their niche, they tend to soar. Read what these teens and parents had to say about their special aptitudes. What they have to share may trigger some thoughts about special areas that your teen can further develop.

- *Need child care?* "I spoil all the kids I baby-sit. I have fun with them, and baby-sitting is when I get to be a kid again." Becky Needham, age 16, is the most sought-after sitter around. Her family calls her a "baby magnet." Becky is very thorough. She actually keeps a ledger sheet for each family in a three-ring binder. On it she records emergency numbers and special information about each child such as allergies, likes, dislikes, and birthday. Whenever she goes on a job, she takes that family's ledger page with her, so she always has what she needs at her fingertips. Becky loves kids, "especially those with disabilities," she tells me. Through baby-sitting Becky has found unconditional love from the kids. She plans to work in early childhood care or education.

- *Need a shrink?* "I like to know what's going on with all my friends. I try to figure them out. For someone like me, college is like having ten million people to analyze," says Ted Harris, age 20. Ted spent many years being helped by a psychologist for his ADHD-related problems. Now he puts what he's learned to work for others.

- *Need someone with camping skills?* The psychologist encouraged Ted to join the Boy Scouts. That's where his big turnaround began. "Scouting always gave me reality," he tells me. "Without the structure scouting gave me, I would be up in the clouds." Through Scouting-sponsored camping trips, Ted learned to problem-solve with a group. They learned to divvy up chores and to keep the campsite clean and safe. They learned how to plan for an event and an emergency. Eventually Ted achieved the rank of Eagle Scout.

- *Need a lift?* "I like flying planes," says Joel Milstein, age 13. Joel still needs some help with aerodynamics and wind currents. At present, though, he's working on charting, which he needs to get his pilot's license. "It's like eight hundred times more complicated than flying the plane itself," he tells me. I gather from Joel that private aircraft pilots have to know where the military zones and hang gliders are, and "other stuff like that." Joel's flying costs $99 per hour, so he works part time to support this passion.

- *Need some comic relief?* Hallie Banks, age 15, has found a new friend because they share a passion: Japanese *anime.* She loves to write. He can draw. So together they work on comic books, which they plan to market through a Web site they've created.

- *Need fast action?* In high school, George Winston's parents actively supported the creation of a school ice hockey league. "It seems to be a sport for boys with ADHD," his mom says, "because it's fast-moving, keeps attention, and is a good place to release stress and aggression."

- *Need to capture the moment?* Michelle Prior's son, Marty, age 12, likes photography. In fact, his interest developed out of something he couldn't do well, bike jumping. Because of his size, Marty has been unable to get the lift he needs. When he came home one day and asked for a camera so he could shoot the other kids in action, Michelle bought him a little throw-away one. Now, he's graduated to the family camera and hopes to go to vocational school to be a photographer.

- *Need one thing after another?* There's nothing like a good job to help a kid feel good. Cliff Haskell, now 18, has had a job since he was 10. He started his work career helping out on a boating dock. He learned to pump gas and do small-engine repair. He loves food preparation and eating, so he got a job at a local deli. He's not a great student and doesn't care to be. He once planned to join the service upon high school graduation, but now his plans are uncertain, as he has also become quite involved with the police explorers. He gets to ride around in patrol cars on weekend nights and hang out where the action is. He's thinking he'd like to become a police officer.

The possibilities are limitless. Some kids have great luck and know what they want from the get-go. Others stumble on their passions, as my son did. A friend asked him to try out for track, so he went to keep his friend company. He found out he could run really well, and he learned how to be part of a team. As a young adult, he's carried that sense of team play into his work world. He always shows up for the job and is on time. He also has a great sense of responsibility to his employer and coworkers and appreciates their reliance upon him to carry his share of the workload.

As Dr. Jensen says, "Everything is a social skill in one sense." While special programs target the development of specific skills, such as anger management or group dynamics, day-to-day living allows countless opportunities to identify and practice improving the social self. As a parent, you can help nuture these skills by taking interest, being supportive, and being available. The bonus is that your involvement sends the teen a powerful message about your commitment to him or her. There's no measure for the worth of that social message.

PART TWO

Within the Family

CHAPTER SIX

Family Matters

ADHD usually has an impact on the entire family system, and certainly it's been known to get in the way of a parent's best intentions. The next four chapters cover home-management issues. These chapters are organized in a progressive manner. This chapter starts with problems in the family system and offers suggestions and guidelines that help parents begin to reclaim their parenting role. Many of the strategies are basic parent-management tools that are good entry-level treatment approaches. The next chapter delves into parenting teens through the use of a conflict-resolution approach. Chapter 8 deals with teens whose behavior is a bit more problematic because it is more oppositional and defiant. Chapter 9 discusses the seriously defiant teen and what can be done. Many of you may not have problems as severe as those described in Chapters 8 and 9, although some of the information may be useful.

"I'm somewhat burned out from dealing with all this. Essentially, I've been a single parent, mother and father," Ann Eckhart says. Ann's kids and husband have ADHD. About a year ago, she found herself in a "borderline nervous breakdown." Much of Ann's stressed state stemmed from the role she's assumed in the family. She sees herself as "exoskeleton," meaning the framework that holds everybody together. When it comes to her needs, support is in short supply.

When life's troubles hit critical mass last year, Ann caved in from the pressure. She couldn't concentrate and could barely string words together to make sentences. She began to cry for no apparent reason. Every day she needed a glass of wine to soothe her nerves. She had to quit her job. At present she's being treated for a stress disorder.

"My kids and my husband are great people," she says. "It's just hard to take things as they come." Thanks to therapy, Ann is learning how to carve out a role that she can comfortably manage. In essence, she's learning to balance.

Families, too, strive for balance and harmony. What a tall order that can be! No two family members are the same. Families are dynamic, inter-active, transactive. When we look at families, we look at systems. When ADHD is present, we have to look at ADHD systems. These may be rela-tively easy to manage or difficult, depending on what the family is dealing with. Is it ADHD only? Is it severe? Does more than one family member have it? Are we talking anxiety, opposition, defiance, or other comorbidi-ties? Are there other psychosocial stressors?

Restoring order in an ADHD system is not just about fixing disorders. You have to untangle the transactional patterns that form in family sys-tems. By the time adolescence comes, there are usually a lot of knots. We may be troubled families.

Let's begin to untangle this subject of the troubled family by look-ing at how the ADHD core symptoms intrude into the family mix, as described by author and clinician Dr. Robin. Inattention makes it difficult to stay on task when resolving conflicts, to carry out agreements, to complete schoolwork and chores, and to fulfill other responsibili-ties. Impulsivity leads to "losing it" in conversation and negotiation. Hyperactivity creates a "stick-to-it" style when letting the matter drop would be more socially appropriate. Clearly, these characteristics have the potential to create extraordinary family difficulties, especially when more than one member of a family has the disorder, which is often the case.

Philip Banks finds himself constantly at odds with his daughter, Hal-lie. "It's probably because she's more or less my clone. A lot of my frustra-tion has to do with my seeing myself in her," he tells me. I have to chuckle, because without having heard the conversation between his daughter and me, he echoed her words. "He acts a lot like me," Hallie said. "He gets short-tempered and stuff like that. Did I forget to mention that we clash all the time? So much so, it's scary." Hallie's mom knows exactly what her husband and daughter mean. She says to me, "They are two faces on the same body. When they are going in the same direction, it's like Broadway lighting up." Most of the time, though, it's lightning that flashes in this family's sky.

Families are systems of reciprocal emotional relationships. Each person's behavior has an effect on the other and vice versa. A unique study done by SUNY Buffalo researcher Dr. William Pelham and colleagues underscores this point. Dr. Pelham wanted to look at the effects of ADHD on parent behavior, specifically alcohol consumption. He took parents who had never had an alcohol abuse or addiction problem. He trained their kids to act like they had ADHD. Dr. Pelham's research team kept careful record of the mothers' alcohol consumption during the period of the study. Lo and behold, the mothers of the "ADHD imposters" drank more. Other studies found that mothers reported less satisfactory relationships with their children who had ADHD. They used more negative commands and were frustrated a lot of the time. They said the disorder had a negative impact on the family, its financial resources, and their social lives.

Negative interactions between parent and child, regardless of age, can breed oppositionality. As Dr. Robin points out, "Negative parent-teen interactions lead to poor parental monitoring of what the teenager does." Of course, when we throw up our hands, the likelihood that our teens will get involved in risky behavior increases.

Given the types of problems that ADHD causes, it's easy to fall into the perception that ADHD is the root cause of what ails the family. It's not that simple. Each family member has personal characteristics and coping styles. Some of these "get along" better with ADHD than others. Stress of any sort can throw a family off-kilter. Perhaps marital troubles or financial concerns exist. Parents may be coping with the needs of their aging parents, or they may have health issues, such as cancer or migraine headaches, that can make it hard to manage a teen.

Forty percent of the parents of teens with ADHD have mental health issues of their own. A number of mothers and fathers have ADHD. Many mothers suffer from major depression or dysthymia, an overall feeling of glumness. Fathers don't tend to have major depression at the rate mothers do, but family histories reveal a higher incidence of substance abuse and antisocial personality disorder, though certainly some moms have these conditions, too.

There have been some dramatic findings regarding alcoholism and ADHD. Dr. Joseph Sergeant reports, "Children who show the greatest loss of executive function control came from the group of kids with ADHD born into families of multigenerational alcoholics." It's no secret that alcoholism runs in families. From a neurological standpoint, the disease is seen as a reward problem. Alcohol is known to stimulate the brain's pleasure centers. Some people are predisposed through multiple genes to seek the feel-good effects that result from alcohol's ability to activate the reward system, which in turn may lead to cravings and addictions. Youth with a double load, ADHD and a family history of alcoholism, "have a reward problem and also an inhibition problem," Dr. Sergeant explains. The combination of poor ability to turn off behavior and getting turned on by reward make this combination potentially disastrous.

While genetics predispose an individual to certain difficulties, the environment also comes into play. Youth with ADHD require parents with an even temperament and excellent parenting skills. The types of problems listed above drain valuable parent resources and create poor parent-adolescent relations. Teen behavior tends to worsen as the result of parental problems that interfere with the parent's ability to make rules, set clear guidelines, follow through on consequences, problem-solve, and communicate effectively. That's how families with troubles turn into troubled families.

Roles and Structure

"Cohesion, hierarchy, and the distribution of power in families are the molecules of family structure," writes Dr. Robin. In families, we hope for good glue to connect us to one another in positive ways. Conflict, of course, can disrupt these molecules. Out-of-whack molecules can create more conflict. Eventually the roles and structure fall into disarray.

Consider cohesion, the bond between family members. When certain disorders are present, these bonds lose a lot of their grip. Many developmental experts believe the initial attachment between parent and child sets the stage for life adjustment. While there is no literature that specifically looks at the bond of attachment between a parent and infant or toddler with ADHD, Dr. Robin surmises that when ADHD is present, "there might be an initial attachment, but the disorder might interfere with a continuing positive parent-child bond." In the teenage years, the warmth of nurture may be cooled off by the amount of time parents and teens spend in negative interactions.

What's important about this information is the understanding that the relationship today between you and your teen may be rooted in much earlier days. We parents may spend a lot of time focusing on the issues of the day when perhaps part of the solution for a twisted dynamic has to do with reattaching the earlier bonds.

A way to do that might be to follow the intent of the words writer Maya Angelou spoke to an *Oprah* audience. To paraphrase, when you see your child, your eyes should light up. That unspoken gesture reveals what's in your heart. Though a lot of upheaval may be going on, if each time your son or daughter sees you, he or she sees a quick flash of your unconditional love, then your teen knows that at the center of difficulties, there's a safe and loving home base.

Friendship between parents seems as important to marriage bonds as unconditional love is to the parent-child attachment. Fondness and admiration go a long way toward helping parents stay partners. As Dr. William Bumberry, a marriage and family therapist as St. John's Mercy Medical Center in St. Louis, explains, "People who stayed happily married for fifty years down the road remember what they really liked about each other and stay focused on that rather than allowing their minds to go to all the negative things."

Jill Gillingham and her husband, Bob, have three children. Two have

ADHD. The younger of these two used to have such severe meltdowns and rages that the family couldn't go out together. To this day, Kevin's needs continue to demand most of the family's resources. When asked how she and Bob kept their marriage together through all the turmoil, without pause Jill replies, "We just became like perfect dance partners. When one had had it, the other moved in. As a result of some miracle, we never fried together in a crisis or in need." The Gillinghams sought help early on. They also use their own common sense. They discuss Kevin's problems. They do not take ownership of them. They use many of the positive parenting practices mentioned throughout this book. They also maintain a friendship with each other.

Destructive Imbalances

Often when disorders exist in families, aside from attachment issues, you see either what psychologists call enmeshment/overinvolvement or disengagement/cutting loose. When teens feel smothered (enmeshment), they don't develop independence and identity easily. When one or both parents disengage, the isolation erodes self-confidence. Parents of teens with ADHD have to hang in there, but in a deliberate, systematic way. Generally, this is accomplished through effective parenting techniques and perhaps the use of behavior-management tools, as described in the last section of this chapter.

Families are supposed to have a hierarchy. Parents are the guides who lead the way and set the course. Children follow the lead. They may have input into decisions, but the decision-making power does not lie with them. That should be up to the parent. In conflicted families, that order generally goes out the door.

"One of the basic foundation issues of family therapy is determining if the parents are actually parents and if they work as a team," says Dr. Bumberry. Two common hierarchy problems found in troubled families are coalitions and triangles. These make for ineffective family management, because in each case the parents are not on the same page.

In coalitions, two parties join against a third to get what they want. You know this scene. One parent says no. The other parent says yes. "Kids are not stupid," says Dr. Zakreski. "If they want to go to a concert, they figure out that it's better to ask Dad, because he's more likely to say yes." Similarly, he's had many teen clients who basically tell him, "I can always get my mom to side with me against my dad," or vice versa. The problem with that, he explains, is that it renders the parent ineffective. Teens will manipulate situations to their advantage. While they get what they want, they don't get what they need—consistency and dependable discipline.

Triangles involve a victim, a rescuer, and a villain. "People in a family can occupy different angles in that triangle," says Dr. Zakreski. He observes that very often the teen sees him- or herself as the victim. The parents might flip roles between villain and rescuer. Dr. Zakreski offers the example of the teen who comes home drunk. If there's a triangle going on in the family, generally one parent will attempt to punish the teen while the other comes to the teen's rescue. So even if the bad cop gives a consequence, it becomes ineffective because the good cop invalidates the consequence and lets the teen "off the hook." The alliance of one parent and teen comes at great cost to the marriage and to the relationship between the other parent and teen. The teen becomes way too powerful in the family system while the parents are rendered impotent and unable to control him or her.

What a mess that makes. When roles and structure go awry, the distortions send families into deep trouble. Destructive imbalances often lead the teen down an oppositional and defiant path. One of the worst things that can happen in a home and to a teen is to have two parents who publicly disagree over rules and consequences and who can't settle their differences and come to agreement.

Often a therapist can help parents negotiate a few rules and consequences they can agree on. Sometimes there may not be any way to get parents on the same page—even with the help of the most skilled therapist. That may happen in cases of an embattled marriage or a divorce situation, or should one of the parents have a mental health problem, perhaps an addiction or a thought disorder. Whatever the cause, it can be a tragic shame.

Siblings

In addition to the victim, rescuer, and villain roles, two other roles are commonly seen in families. The children are usually the ones to star in these. Generally with ADHD and related disorders in the picture, you will see the black sheep and the white knight. The black sheep, as you know, is viewed as the cause of what ails the family and its individual members. Dr. Bumberry points out that clinicians easily identify the black sheep, or family scapegoat. "The thing we often miss as clinicians," he explains, "is the counterpoint to that role: the white knight, the hero, the golden child." Of course, families do not deliberately assign these roles. They tend to unconsciously fall into them as a way of dealing with distress.

Eleven-year-old Jenny Prior finds it hard to be the sister of her brother, Marty. He has severe ADHD and oppositional defiant disorder. Although Jenny loves her brother, she also fears him at times, especially when he's in a bad mood. Sometimes she tells him to be quiet, such as when he screamed at his mother and told her he wanted a new family. Sometimes she withdraws to her room "because I'm kind of scared he might hit me or call me names," she says.

Marty has not hit his sister, but because he can be so explosive, Jenny cuts him a lot of slack. For instance, she'll do his chores to stop his complaining, "because if I don't, there will be a problem, and I want to have peace." Jenny's learned from experience that her brother's complaining picks up momentum and turns into shouting and slamming things.

Once when she was much younger, Jenny took one of her brother's GI Joe toys. He got really mad, so she never did that again. Of course, that's fairly normal. However, there is not an equal distribution of power in the family. Marty takes Jenny's things all the time. She allows it and says it doesn't bug her. Jenny's mom describes her daughter as "good-natured, easygoing, nothing at all like Marty."

We might be fooled into thinking that the golden child has an easy go of it. But, as Dr. Bumberry points out, "They have an equally narrow way of operating. They have to please. They can't disappoint."

Dr. Bumberry says, "Those types of dualities need to be integrated.

Nobody is all good or all bad." Take a look at your family. Do you see these roles? If you do, you may want to get some help to put your house in order.

The Minnesota Parent Advocacy Center for Educational Rights published an article by Patricia Bill about siblings of children with disabilities. She writes about the opportunities and challenges a brother or sister with a disability brings to a sibling. While the article is not ADHD-specific, I think many of the observations about sibling effects apply.

Opportunities:
- insights and empathy—to recognize strengths in others and value individuality
- maturity from successfully coping with sibling's special needs
- pride in brother or sister's hard-earned accomplishments
- loyalty to sibling and family
- appreciation for their own good health

Challenges:
- feeling embarrassed by sibling's behavior
- feeling responsible for the care and well-being of the sibling
- feeling isolated and left out of the family information loop
- feeling resentful
- perceiving pressure to excel in sports, academics, or behavior
- feeling guilty for being spared the condition
- feeling they will catch the disability

The last on the list, feeling they will catch the disability, may not be too far off base. As Dr. Barkley explained, some siblings may develop oppositional defiant disorder or conduct disorder due to being raised in a chaotic home where rules are seldom enforced or where there is little to no consequence for misbehavior. Often under these conditions, family patterns become enmeshed in negative and hostile interactions. These, too, may breed oppositionality. So while siblings don't catch ADHD, they can catch hell. They may also become fearful of the sibling, anxious, worried, or depressed, as happened in Jenny's case.

What can you do for siblings without ADHD?

> ☞ *TRY THIS*
>
> *Read over the list of challenges. Check off those that apply to your children who do not have ADHD. Brainstorm to find ideas that compensate for the negative side effects experienced by your son or daughter and make a conscious effort to use them consistently—perhaps work on one at a time.*
>
> *For example, if feeling resentful is a problem, your brainstorming might generate the following remedies:*
>
> *create time alone with you*
> *spend less time in family activities*
> *carefully structure the activities you do together*
> *assign separate chores*
> *don't ask the sibling to pick up the slack*
> *don't complain to the sibling about their brother's or*
>   *sister's behavior*
> *try to behave peacefully*
> *don't make the sibling your ally*

When Parents Are Split

The subject of divorce and alternative family structures goes way beyond the scope of this book. Still, some points must be noted. First of all, since ADHD can add to ordinary troubles, you may expect extraordinary swings during the entire divorce process, which includes the time leading up to the divorce as well as during and the aftermath. Most studies find that two years after a divorce, the trouble it caused subsides for most adolescents.

"The real negative impact on kids is the acrimony between parents," whether they are divorced or not, notes Dr. Bumberry. In fact, most studies find that teens whose parents stay together in an angry marriage are more likely to be disturbed. "Stay out of the battle," advises Dr. Bumberry. If a spouse or ex-spouse wants to keep a war going, there are ways to cut the losses. Dr. Bumberry advises parents to develop a personal relationship with the teen and to avoid vengeance or bitterness against the other parent. Be careful about "innocent" comments that are disguised critiques. Don't criticize the other parent in any way. Needless to say, the best scenario is when both parents are on the same page and remain involved in the teen's life and upbringing.

Single Mothers

A major pitfall single mothers of kids with ADHD face has to do with their parenting style. According to Dr. Barkley, "Researcher Pat Cohen has found in her work on divorced women that they need to adopt a mixed strategy of parenting. The mother can no longer fall back on the typical feminine parenting style." Mothers tend to talk and reason more and to be naturally nurturing and loving. Dr. Barkley says, "They are inclined to use affection as a social tool to influence an adolescent, particularly a male adolescent." Single moms have to shift and become more like a father would be. "That means," says Dr. Barkley, "you make rules and you do not flinch on them. You are going to be very outspoken and back up your word with your deed."

Mothers, you should know this information about your sons. "Adolescent males test people's resolve, particularly their mother's resolve on the household rules," Dr. Barkley explains. The reason has to do with hierarchy. "Males want to find out who means business in this social hierarchy," he adds.

Dr. Barkley advises single moms to move to a mixed parenting strategy. Set firm limits. Deliver consequences. And, he adds, "you are not going to discuss it. No amount of talk, no amount of reasoning, and no amount of bull that a teenager is going to try to run by you is going to get you to change those rules you have." With a laugh, he adds, "Even if that means taking testosterone injections."

Single moms need a lot of support to follow through on Dr. Barkley's advice. You may be socially isolated, scared, and overwhelmed. If your child is aggressive and defiant, your hands may be overly full. What can you do? Find another adult who is stable, responsible, and even-tempered to be a support system for you. This person might be a member of the clergy, a friend, a relative, or someone from the Big Brothers or Big Sisters organization. If possible, it would be great to have your buddy trained in the management techniques that work well for teens with ADHD. The goal here is to help the single mom.

Remarriage

Stepfamilies need to strike an interesting balance. If at all possible, both homes should shoot to have the same expectations, to ease transitions, and to share in decision making. When ADHD is present, it's wise to have a trained counselor to provide anticipatory guidance to avoid the many glitches that can arise.

Before anything else, the stepparent has to establish emotional rapport with the stepchild. That usually doesn't happen if he or she steps immediately into a disciplinary or supervisory role. As Dr. Zakreski says, "You want to avoid getting into the place where the kid delivers that old phrase 'You are not my mother/father.'" He advises stepparents to try to take on more of an advisory role rather than a front-and-center approach. "It's the responsibility of the biological parent to make the rules and enforce them. The stepparent should assume a role supportive of the biological parent," Dr. Zakreski adds.

Even when mutual love and respect exist between the stepparent and child, potentially loaded situations also need to be avoided. The Primaveras could have used a little anticipatory guidance on this front. Dan Primavera enlisted the support of his wife, Annette, to help his younger son organize his belongings and supervise homework. What seemed innocent to him had the makings of disaster. Dan recalls, "Annette's sitting down trying to do homework with him and he's getting pissed off. Now she thinks it's an attitude problem—that Tom is getting pissed off because she's making him do his homework. She and I are really banging our heads because now the relationship between the two of them is horrendous. It went from good to bad that fast."

Stepparents also need to be aware that when they come into this role during the adolescent years, the teen is highly unlikely to accept this new person as an authority figure. At this stage, Dr. Zakreski explains, "the teen's looking for self-control, not more parental control."

Distorted Beliefs

Before Dan Primavera knew his oldest son had ADHD, he came up with a number of explanations for Louie's troublesome behavior. He assumed some of the problems stemmed from "teenage-itis." Others he saw as the result of family dysfunction. Although he hadn't had a drink since Louie was quite young, he blamed alcoholism, the divorce, and his former wife's dysfunction for many of Louie's problems.

Dan found his son to be lazy, unmotivated, and rebellious. He felt Louie could do better. "Given all the time and work I put into the relationship, I felt like he was throwing stuff in my face," says Dan, shaking his head. Dan took his son's lack of effort in every area of his life as a personal affront to the work ethic he had tried so hard to instill.

Before the diagnosis, Dan drew the erroneous conclusion that his son deliberately chose to screw up. In response, he did what he thought he had to do—he took away things. "Louie started to play hockey and his grades went down, so I made him quit the team," says Dan, who recalls the tremendous upheaval it caused. "He was crying, but his teachers thought I was great—tough dad." So tough that Dan still cringes at some of the stuff he did to get Louie in check. "I even withheld Christmas gifts one year. I gave him the gifts but said he couldn't use them for a month. I did horrible, stupid things." Louie's diagnosis helped Dan to see his son differently. "I'm noticing for the first time how really tormented he is."

Clearly, Dan's reactive parenting style needed some redesign. Instead of responding to the problems in a planned and thoughtful way, Dan got angry and upset, behaved inconsistently, constantly derided his son, made threats, punished a lot, and seldom praised. Dan's reactions seem to have been fueled by extreme thinking. As Dr. Robin explains, parents and teens each develop a set of unreasonable beliefs that commonly disturb their relationships. Of course, some of Dan's beliefs came out of his own upbringing. Despite how much we tell ourselves, "I will never be like my mother/father," rare is the individual whose past does not inform present action.

Teens with ADHD and their parents don't hold the patent on unreasonable beliefs, either. All parents and teenagers have them to some degree. The problem as seen by Dr. Robin has to do with the extent to which these beliefs are held on to. These beliefs prevent good problem solving and conflict resolution.

Following is a list of types of unreasonable beliefs that parents may have about their teens, which I've adapted and modified from Dr. Robin's book. You may recognize some of these types of beliefs as ones that you have. You will probably recognize the examples, too. They are the beliefs that Dan Primavera had about his son Louie.

Parent's Beliefs
- *Ruination.* He's got no work ethic. He'll be a total failure.
- *Obedience.* He should study and work hard like I told him to do—no ifs, ands, or buts.
- *Perfectionism.* He's deliberately choosing to screw up. He can do much better.
- *Malicious intent.* I felt like he was throwing stuff in my face.
- *Self-blame.* I blamed the divorce. I figured he needed a strong father figure.
- *Love/appreciation.* If he loved me, he'd respect my work ethic.

Of course, adolescents also have unreasonable beliefs about their parents' reasons for acting the way they do. I've never spoken with Louie, so I can't tell you what he actually believed about the interchanges with his father. However, I bet he had the typical types of adolescent unreasonable beliefs.

Adolescent's Beliefs
- *Ruination.* He's making me quit hockey! He's trying to wreck my life.
- *Unfairness.* Nobody else's parents are pulling them off the team. I tried to do my best. He's not being fair.
- *Autonomy.* I don't need him to run my life.
- *Love/appreciation.* How can he say he loves me and then take away the one thing that makes my life worth a damn?

As we saw with Dan Primavera, the ADHD diagnosis is often a first step in changing some distorted belief systems. Still, even parents of kids who have been diagnosed from their earliest days will fall into this type of thinking and seeing from time to time. The way to get out from under distorted belief systems is to make a conscious effort to recognize them in all our daily interactions.

☞ *TRY THIS*

Think of a recent situation in which you had a run-in with your teen. Do you recognize any unreasonable beliefs at work? What was going on in your head at the time? Perhaps your teen asked to stay out later than usual, or to borrow the car. Write down what happened and what you may have said to each other. If you feel especially motivated, jot down exactly what unreasonable beliefs you were thinking. Next to it put a more reasonable belief. Try to catch unreasonable beliefs and change them before you respond to the teen. Of course, your teen can also benefit from self-monitoring, although ADHD may make it hard for the teen to do so without a prompt from the outside. In either case, the object is to correct distortions.

Parenting by Drowning

I have never met a parent who sets out to have a negative, hostile relationship with his or her child. For the most part, I think parents have the best of intentions. So how do things get twisted? No one has the definitive answer to that. Each family, each interaction within the family, each family history, the society, the culture, and the state of health and well-being are some of the factors that come into play.

Part of the challenge of ADHD comes from what I call the "last-minute lifestyle." It seems there's always a rush, always a crisis, and little time to think things through. The floodgates open. The dam bursts. Our kids may train us to react through temper outbursts and rash actions, or by putting things off until the last minute has come and gone. Woeful is the parent with other life issues and stresses. ADHD requires vigilance, parents who can navigate in any waters, and a parent team that understands how to sail a boat together.

Dr. Barkley and his research team have studied ADHD and parent-child relationships for many years. Dr. Barkley has identified four patterns, or management strategies, that parents fall into that fuel disorder and conduct problems.

- *All talk/no action.* "To these parents, yelling, screaming, arguing, threatening, and voice escalation are discipline," Dr. Barkley says. "These are the families you hear screaming at each other from down the street." Beyond verbal abuse, nothing happens that resembles discipline. What is discipline? According to one dictionary, to discipline means to train by instruction and control; to teach to obey rules or accept authority. Yelling and the like are not action. They're reaction. They blow smoke over the issue.

- *Tit for tat.* In other words, you get what you give. Dr. Barkley calls this reactive pattern "a very immature style of parenting." So much so that when the voices of the parents and teens on the research audiotapes were disguised, researchers could not tell the parent from the teen. As Dr. Barkley explains, tit for tat means "My behavior as a parent is determined by how my teen treats me." If the teen threatens, the parent threatens. If the teen pushes, the parent pushes. "Nothing governs this interaction other than what the person just did to you," he notes. Of course, we want rules to govern behavior, not reaction.

- *Be nice/forget.* This strategy appears to progress from tit for tat. Tired of getting into it, parents disengage. It's the "Oh well," "Whatever you want," "That was yesterday. This is today" attitude that ignores issues and conflict. It's like being a buoy in the water, bobbing with the waves and the tide. The problem is the teen has no consequences, no responsibilities, and no standard to live by. We may think being nice helps the teen feel okay, but don't mistake giving up with a polite smile as being warm and caring.

- *Russian roulette.* Unpredictability and harshness is the name of this game. Dr. Barkley finds that ineffective parents are inconsistent: "They drift over time toward an even greater use of harsh punishment, or extreme discipline, but inconsistently." The parent makes a threat. Regardless, the teen does not comply with the rule. Nothing happens until the next time, or the time after that. Then, kaboom!

Why do parents sink into these patterns, which don't get any of the desired results and may actually do harm? Dr. Barkley's research group identified a large contributory factor. Parents, it seems, may be drowning in their own emotion. According to Dr. Barkley, "These parents seem to decide how to act on the basis of the feelings they feel at the time. Perhaps they are depressed at the time, or they are angry at the stars, or they just had a marital dispute. It was truly their emotional status at the moment that mainly determined how that parent would come across."

While mothers don't use these reactive parenting strategies any more than fathers, they do have more conflicts with their teens than fathers. "That's because the mothers tend to assume more of the custodial scut-work," Dr. Barkley acknowledges. More time on the job means more opportunity to clash.

Dr. Barkley emphasizes that the teen's behavior should never determine the parent's actions or inaction. This principle holds true whether the teen threatens, acts out, or says, "I hate you." Parents need to have a predetermined set of guiding principles for what they are supposed to provide and what the teen is expected to do.

Dr. Barkley's research team has observed that effective parents have what he calls a "stay-the-course" strategy. A parent who "stays the course" treats the teen based on what the teen does or does not do. And the parent has a goal. As Dr. Barkley explains, the goal is to see the teen through adolescence. Nothing deters the parent from keeping that goal in mind.

A "stay-the-course" parent does not take any of the teen's bait. "You can swear at me," says Dr. Barkley, speaking as if he were a parent talking to his teen, "and you can insult me. You can try to get me angry. You can use every little coercive strategy you want. But my goal is to see you through your adolescence, to see that you uphold your responsibilities around the home. It's also to see that you know I love you. I respect you. I'll show you that by holding you accountable to certain standards."

Strategies to Stay the Course

Maybe you've been floundering for a while. Perhaps you didn't know your teen had ADHD. Or maybe you did know, but you got caught up in life and went a little off course. Or maybe your teen's problems escalated due to other circumstances. Perhaps you got burned out and needed to take a hiatus. Whatever the case, you might be in need of some outside help to get back on course. As Dr. Zakreski says, "Parents come for help when their child's behavior has become the parents' problem."

When parents seek help, they know it's time to make a change because standard operating procedure is not working. Most adolescents don't tend to see things the same way. They may agree that something has to change. Usually they think it's the parents and their rules and demands.

Don't be surprised if they balk at outside help. In general, early adolescents tend to be more resistant than older teens. Whether we are talking about resistance to medications or the support systems that need to be put in place, treatment-resistant teens often need education about ADHD before they become even slightly willing to consider a change. In some cases the teen has been educated about the disorder and resistance has to do with "normal adolescent stubbornness," as Dr. Barkley puts it. At that point, he says, "parents need to realize they control a variety of resources." These can be withheld as needed.

In some families, many of these resources are seen as entitlements. From Dr. Barkley's point of view, they are privileges. Dr. Barkley says parents need to take stock of the variety of resources they already provide the teen in their home. For instance, does the teen have a computer, a television, a phone, a stereo system? Does he or she have or borrow a car? Who pays for insurance? Then parents need to assess what they do with these resources. Does the teen earn this good stuff or get it just for breathing? Is the good stuff taken away when they misbehave? "Empower yourself," writes Dr. Barkley. That means you take control of the stuff you give freely. Have the teen earn it. The best way to do that is by setting up a behavior-management system like the types explained at the end of this chapter.

Parenting a teen with behavioral difficulties is like using a compass to navigate. There are basically four directions you have to follow depending on where you are in your journey.

- *Create a scaffolding.* Provide structure, routines, assistive devices, external supports, and guides for organization.

- *Develop behavior-management strategies:* Provide positive attention, rules and consequences, and formal systems when needed.
- *Use problem solving:* Develop skills in the art of negotiation, learning to give and take, and resolving conflict through peaceable means.
- *Polish communication skills:* Learn to say what you mean in a firm, loving manner, to practice listening without judgment, and to discuss without attack.

These compass points do not specifically cure the core ADHD problems. Scaffolding helps an individual with a disability manage his or her way around tough environments. Behavior-management strategies, problem solving, and communication skills help with the side effects. They may reduce conflict. Less conflict means less negativity, aggression, and hostility. The techniques also help parents get on the same course and feel as if they've got a grip—even if the conflict continues. They help the parents avoid getting sucked into the whirlpool of parenting by emotion. Effective parents learn how to get into the eye of the storm, that place of calm.

Behavior-Management Principles

Behavior management is actually a style of responding to your son or daughter. "Stay-the-course" parents follow these general principles:

- They give a lot more positive than negative attention.
- They are consistent about rules and consequences.
- They use specific consequences.
- They give feedback immediately, or as soon as possible.
- They give more rewards than punishment.

If these principles don't guide your current parenting practice, you'll probably want to make some changes. The first thing you want to do is *catch your teen being good!*

If you have trouble finding things to praise, Dr. Barkley suggests that parents make minor requests the teen is likely to obey spontaneously, for instance, "Please pass me the salt," or "Would you hand me the newspaper?" In other words, you *rig the gig.* Once the teen complies, give praise. A simple "I appreciate it" will do. Don't lavish praise, as the teen will hear it as hollow or phony.

You also need to *pay positive attention.* Do something special with your teen. Make it an activity where you are not the supervisor, judge, and jury. You might involve yourself in an activity the teen is already doing, for instance, playing a computer game or shooting hoops. Teens' and adults' lives can be really hectic, but if you can find fifteen minutes at least three or four times a week to do something positive and rewarding with your teen, that would be great. Also, bear in mind Dr. Barkley's admonition: *One-on-one time is not a reward!*

Finally, you may also need to change the way you ask your teen to do things. *Be clear and specific.* Try not to ask your teen to do something while he or she is in the middle of a highly pleasurable activity. In addition, Dr. Sergeant reminds us that "you should not ask a kid with ADHD or ODD to stop something when they are actually in the process of doing it, because they've gone past the point of no return."

Behavior-Management Guidelines

Having a problem with rules, consequences, setting limits, being consistent? Maybe you need to use some type of formal behavior-management approach for a while. If you're not good at managing behavior, you might want to start with what Dr. Barkley calls an "artificial consequence system." To understand how these systems work, you need to know the behavior ABC's.

- *Antecedent* is what comes before a behavior. The time to interrupt a behavior is before it begins. That means you may have to study a behavioral problem to see what sets it up. For instance, suppose your teen is prone to forgetting to bring things needed for school. Is there a routine missing?
- *Behavior* is an action. It can be good or bad, important or not. Taking out the trash is a behavior. So is spitting.
- *Consequence* means that which follows an act. Consequences and punishment are not synonymous. Consequences can be positive or negative, artificial or natural. Grounding a teen for

being late is a logical and artificial consequence. Smiling
when the teen comes home on time is a natural and positive
consequence. Consequences are feedback. They tell the teen
how he or she is doing.

Behavior-management systems basically work on the principle that
behavior is a choice and that you can influence behavior by changing
antecedents and providing consequences. A good choice gets a reward
and a poor choice leads to a penalty.

Behavior-management systems come in two basic styles: point systems (generally for teens under 14) and behavioral contracts (for teens 14
or over). Both operate under the principle that privileges are earned by
behaving appropriately. That means the teen follows rules, meets responsibilities such as chores and schoolwork, and behaves in a socially appropriate way.

In a point system, the parent comes up with a list of rules the teen
should obey or desirable behaviors the teen should use. Each item on the
list gets assigned a point value. By doing what is expected, the teen earns
points. These are exchanged for privileges. Of course, each privilege has a
net value. Parents and teens determine each privilege's worth before the
system begins. Dr. Barkley advises against extending credit. In other
words, no privilege is granted until it is earned.

Contracting is exactly as its name implies. In a formal written statement, the teen agrees to certain terms in exchange for privileges. For
instance, you and the teen may sign a contract in which the teen agrees to
do the dishes after dinner and you allow the teen to use the phone in the
evening in return. Contracts need to be carefully worded to eliminate
areas of confusion.

Both contracting and point systems can also work on a response-cost
basis. That means the teen starts off with privileges but loses them for not
meeting behavioral expectations. What privileges will be lost and under
what circumstances is determined ahead of time.

While these systems seem to be an easy do-it-yourself method, they
usually require the help of a trained professional to get started. That's
because the parents need training in how to set up the systems and how to
keep them in place against a resistant or clever teen.

Some parents have been known to resist these systems, too. They may see the systems as extreme or as catering to a teen who should be behaving. However, when ADHD is viewed from a disability perspective, it's apparent that these types of efforts are periodically required to help parents and teens interact better.

Parent Basics

There are a number of basic techniques that are not ADHD-specific but that can improve your life and your teen's life considerably. I've given them catchy names, but don't be fooled. The approaches listed below are basic, time-honored methods—nothing fancy, just effective.

- *Believe none of what you hear and half of what you see.* Adolescents do care what parents think despite what they may say. And they listen, even though they may ignore you or disagree. The data goes in. It may not register for a long time, but it does go in. So continue to give input even when it appears you are up against a brick wall.

  Adolescents want you in their lives, even though they may say otherwise. They want their freedom, but they also want parents who show they care.

  Adolescents want limits. Boundary lines give them security and less to master at one time.

- *Roving eye.* Early and middle adolescents need to be monitored. Insist on knowing what they are doing, with whom, where, when, why, and how. Ignore the "Don't you trust me?" question. Or answer it with "I'm just doing my job." Expect flak. Don't take it to heart. If you suspect something is up, don't be afraid to call the place where your teen says he or she will be. Beepers and cell phones help you stay in touch. Still, there's nothing like a good old-fashioned phone call to talk with another parent about the plans. If your teen wants to do something that can't be monitored, you probably want to just say no.

- *Network.* If you want to know what's going on in your teen's world, step into it. Go to sporting events, school plays—even if your kid isn't participating. Join the school parent organization.

There's a lot of "who's doing what" chatter that can be very helpful. And you also find out about the notices the school sends home that never get to your hands, such as those about college planning meetings or SAT dates. Most important, you also show the teen you care to be involved in his or her world.

- *Plan ahead.* Figure out what rules you need to make before a situation arises where you might need a rule. Know your bottom-line rules. Know your position on those things that your teen will suddenly remember that require you to drop everything and run. Review your situation. Do you occasionally bail your teen out, or has your teen's lack of planning become *your* last-minute lifestyle? If so, it's time to add more structure and consequence.

- *Elastic contract.* Know what rules are negotiable. For instance, if you set a curfew, are you willing to alter it for special circumstances? Be sure your decisions to modify rules are based on discussion and input ahead of time, and that your teen realizes that you are making an exception for special circumstances—not revising the rules.

- *Mean what you say.* Adolescents like consistency. They understand accountability. Mean what you say. You can agree to revisit issues and rules later, but until you do, stay the course, despite how hard that is on you.

- *Don't beat a dead horse.* If your teen has already paid handsomely by a natural consequence or at the hands of someone else, like a police officer or a coach, you may not need to give another consequence. Ask yourself, "Do I have anything to add to this situation, or am I just ticked off and looking for a little vengeance?"

- *If-then.* Understand how to use contingencies. "If you want to _____, then you must _____." Or "If you do _____, then I will _____." As Dr. Curry points out, parents have more contingencies when kids are younger, but the ones we have with teens may be stronger—for instance, the car and the curfew. You might say something to this effect: "If you can't tell me who you are going out with, where you are going, and when you will be home, then no keys." Or "If you are late, then the next time you go out, you have to come home that much earlier." Just be sure that you don't get yourself into a mess with the if-then stuff. There's a potential here to make a rash decision. You want to be sure that the contingencies are harder on your teen than on you. Of course, that holds true for any negative consequence you give.

- *"I'll think about it."* No amount of planning will ever take into account all the little situations that can arise. Also, if you are living with a reactive teen, or one who's constantly trying to modify the rules "just a bit," the best words you may ever learn are "I'll think about it." Buy yourself time to know what your position is and to take careful action. The same principle holds true for consequences. While consequences should happen very near in time to the behavior, if you're not sure what to do, let the teen know one is coming.

- *Be brief.* Say what you need in as few words as possible. "Tom, your laundry." "Alice, homework." Most commands and requests require little or no explanation, especially if you've already sat down and made rules with your teen, along with a list of who will do what around the house. Lecturing doesn't work. It takes too long. It's boring. Nagging backfires.

- *Write it down.* Keeping track of who said who would do what, when, why, and for what is too much for most brains. Most of us have lots going on in our lives. Whatever agreement or rule you reach with your teen needs to be written down.

- *Grounding.* If you ground your teen, make sure it's a decision and not a reaction or retaliation. The purpose of this method is to punish by withholding all forms of positive activities, whether these are outside or inside the home. Effective grounding needs to be well thought out. Also, it probably should not be used for those teens age 16 or above. For any age, consider substituting a work detail for grounding. It may be more productive. If you do decide to ground, avoid these common holes Dr. Barkley finds many parents get into.

1. Misuse or overuse. (Perhaps you ground the teen and remember something she or he had to do, so you have to retract. Or you ground so much that the teen is used to it and the penalty loses any effect.)
2. Not really grounded. (The teen may be under house arrest but still has access to everything: phone, e-mail, the stereo, TV.)
3. Goes on too long. (The point of grounding is to make point. If you ground for too long, it doesn't really change the misbehavior. Short and to the point works best.)
4. No monitoring. (If you can't be there to enforce the grounding, it usually won't work. If anything, you may make your teen into a clever "criminal" who figures out how to slip in and out or go around your grounding rules so you don't even know.)

• *Eyes wide shut.* If you get on your teen for every little thing, you may turn your home into a combat zone. Prioritize. Pick your battles wisely. Learn to ignore minor misbehaviors. If your teen comes in slamming doors and stomping feet, hold back for a calmer moment. You want to have open communication and know the reason behind the frustration or anger. You can work on fine-tuning the self-expression later.

Finally, *keep a sense of humor.* In the spirit of this suggestion, I pass along an e-mail I got recently: If you find yourself in a hole, the first thing to do is stop digging!

☞   TRY THIS

Review the list of parent basics. Are there any you don't use that you think might work? Circle them and select one a week to practice and implement.

CHAPTER SEVEN

Home Rule

"Home rule" refers to the style of parenting we use to rule our homes. Teens require more input into the issues of their lives. That means families need to use a wide variety of management tools. Conflict-resolution skills come in handy during these years. Such skills are not specific to ADHD. However, when used for ADHD in combination with the behavior-management techniques mentioned in the last chapter, the home can be a more peaceful place. This chapter explains how to use conflict-resolution tools. It also delves into some issues that are not ADHD-specific but that need to be seen in an ADHD light.

"Sometimes you wish you could push them back in the womb," David Milstein tells me over a cup of coffee at the kitchen table.

"Yeah, that's because it's my womb," his wife, Adrienne, says with a big laugh. Though the couple is laughing, David's quite serious. When it comes to dealing with their son, everything, it seems, is an issue these days. David and Adrienne are used to being quite involved in the details of Joel's life. They've been intensively supervising him and running interference for years, which is what parents of children with ADHD have to do. But Joel's in his early adolescent years and becoming increasingly independent. He questions their authority and resists his parents' level of involvement. Yet he's far from ready to stand without a scaffold.

Think about what a scaffold does. It's not meant to be restrictive like a fence, although it can be. A scaffold serves as support until a structure can stand on its own. Most teens with ADHD need a flexible scaffold. It's best to use a mastery approach: As the teen demonstrates the ability to handle a certain level of independence or "mastery" with only minor difficulty, allow more freedom and personal responsibility. If the teen starts to flounder, tighten the support. There's no way to know for sure how much or how little supervision is necessary. It will be different for each teen and each circumstance.

It may be helpful to keep in mind what someone once said: "Good judgment comes from experience, and a lot of that comes from bad judgment." Mistakes happen. We want to minimize their impact, but not deprive the teen of the learning. Some parents are reluctant to try again when they've given the teen a certain degree of latitude and the teen has not handled it well. That's understandable. Nonetheless, it may be helpful to look at age as an acronym for "another growth experience," and mistakes as part of coming of age.

Parents have to shift into a new mode. As Dr. Zakreski points out, "Compromise and negotiation have a place in raising a healthy adolescent."

Conflict Resolution

While battles in families may be *over* disagreements or failure to follow rules, I believe they are *about* the lack of respect and recognition each involved person feels.

Mike Farnsworth feels the way he and his wife recognized their son's ADHD may have driven Neil to leave home his senior year in high school. When Neil did that, he also walked away from a college acceptance. As Mike explains, "Neil did not have much space for himself. He had a hard time being who he is. No one would let him be the kid with ADHD. We really didn't understand it, and quite frankly, I don't think in a real sense we would even accept it."

In a sense, the Farnsworths tried to parent ADHD out of Neil. Instead of supplying a scaffold, they were doing a makeover. In retrospect, Mike believes "he's had too much supervision from his parents in a real negative way." As many parents do, the Farnsworths had always expected Neil to excel in school and to go to a good college. In their circle, "being a good student is what being a good kid is about," says Mike. When Neil's academic life began to fall apart due to his ADHD, they made huge efforts, but the focus seems to have been more on keeping the college expectation in play. Managing ADHD was a way to do that. That's a very subtle distinction. Parents may recognize ADHD but lose sight of the teen.

The alienation between Neil and his parents has sparked Jane and Mike into taking a good hard look at the way they handled the ADHD problem. As Jane sees it, "I think most mothers probably kick themselves for certain things they said or did. I think of the things I said to Neil that I'd wished I'd apologized for at some point. They still do haunt me a bit." Jane says Neil would describe her as "an incredible nag." She had no idea that she'd been nagging. She saw her constant reminders and lists as an effort to help him learn. What Neil learned was to associate his mom's voice with judgment and criticism. The minute she spoke, he'd pop off with verbal abuse. Mike tried to step in, but, he says, "the conflict was too intense. I'd usually start by mediating and then discover that it was pointless, so then I withdrew. Jane got angry with me because my withdrawal indicated to her that I didn't care and don't take responsibility."

Conflict is natural and nothing more than a disagreement or problem that needs to be solved. It's not the problem that's the problem. It's how people deal with the problem. Conflict gets its reputation to do harm because families get caught in power struggles over control. These rob each family member of respect and recognition.

Dr. Katherine Kennedy, a northern Ireland conflict-resolution specialist, explains that the way to deal with conflict is "to empower people with the confidence that they can handle their conflicts." That empowerment happens through cooperation, good communication skills, and the use of problem-solving approaches that create win-win solutions. These conflict-resolution skills help a parent wade through issues with their teen like a well-skilled arbitrator.

Know Thyself

When problems and issues arise, most of us step into our typical patterns of managing conflict. These can be adaptive and helpful or maladaptive and somewhat harmful. Different issues require different approaches.

Issues of safety call for a direct and controlling stance, such as "Don't drink and drive." Issues that are negotiable require a cooperative or compromising style. Some issues call for accommodation, especially when the relationship is more important than the issue, or when flexibility is needed, like not getting hung up on your teen's clothing or setting curfews in stone. Sometimes it's helpful to avoid issues altogether, especially if the problem will work itself out or if the battle is not worth fighting.

If you find yourself locked into any one of these approaches as a knee-jerk reaction, you need to be mindful the next time an issue or problem arises. Assess what type of management would be best. Do you need to be controlling, or would collaboration work better? Do you need to be a little accommodating, or give in, or close your eyes?

Parents need to study the way they handle conflict so they can make necessary changes to become more effective. Though the tools that follow are not ADHD-specific, they will help with the broader and common conflict issues that each family, regardless of ADHD, has to face.

Communication

Certain ways of communicating bring us closer, and others serve as roadblocks and land mines. ADHD increases the potential for negative communication patterns. Consider how ADHD affects speaking and listening. Difficulties with working memory make it hard to follow words for very long. Impulsivity and hyperactivity make it hard to wait until the other person is finished speaking without interrupting or tuning out. Tuning out or not responding leads to more words from the other person. More words usually aggravate teens with ADHD. Having a motor in overdrive makes for motor mouth and loud speech. Poor self-control allows for inappropriate words and gestures at inappropriate times.

When these problems are coupled with the entire repertoire of ADHD behaviors, it's easy to see why some families find themselves entrenched in a negatively charged communication style. Parents may see the way the teen communicates as deliberately meaning to be hurtful or provocative. That misperception can lead parents, and siblings, too, into some bad habits as a reaction. Pretty soon the entire family may be using put-downs, name-calling, sarcasm, orders, threats, lectures, judgments, and dismissals. These habits might easily be called "fighting words." Of course, ADHD is not the only factor that contributes to this negative communication style. These patterns may be passed down in some families.

Very often people are unaware that the statements they make have great potential to provoke one another. Try to hear what you say to your teen. The way to break a bad habit is to be consciously aware of it and then to make an effort to replace it. A change in the parent's pattern often leads the teen to use these negatively charged words less, especially when parents label the true nature of comments that are made. For example, if you or your teen uses a put-down, you might say, "That was a put-down. I'd like to hear your point better, so please tell me again without the put-down."

The substitute sentence just given could be either a peacemaker or a peace breaker. It depends on two other important factors: tone of voice and body language. Suppose that sentence is said with a voice that has an edge or with a tight jaw and raised eyebrows. How we say what we say and how we look when we say it can often be more inciting than the words themselves. Screaming, yelling, speaking through clenched teeth, stamping feet, throwing things, sneering, finger pointing, holding someone's face, and making threats are violent forms of communication. They breed hostility.

Humans get ticked off. That's a fact of life. If you or your teen starts to lose control in a conversation, dismiss yourself. For instance, call a five-minute break and go to another room. The idea here is to avert an escalation of conflict.

Active Listening

Good communication takes motivation, effort, and skill. While what and how we say something are important, how we listen is equally important. Poor listening skills can ignite an emotionally charged or potentially volatile situation.

"She'd never really listen that well," 16-year-old Jeff Kain tells me about his mom. "She'd say she'd listen, but it didn't seem like she was listening." To Jeff, it seemed as though his mom would listen until he began to speak, and then she'd start talking. He would say, "You're not listening." Then his mom would say something else.

Basically, Jeff felt his words went unheard. Listening, while it sounds easy and natural, actually requires a certain style to be done well. There are generally accepted techniques that improve listening. They're described below. As with many of these techniques, they require practice until they become habit. Meanwhile, mindfulness—the fine art of being aware—helps us catch ourselves so that our teens don't experience us the way Jeff views his discussions with his mom. Also, parents sometimes need to listen between the lines. Teens often speak in code. Using active listening techniques can help you figure out what's not being said, which may actually be the point the teen wants to make.

Active Listening Techniques
- *Encourage* discussion by asking neutral questions.
- *Clarify* what is being said by asking more questions.
- *Restate* basic ideas and facts to check your meaning and interpretation.
- *Reflect* by making an observation of your teen's feelings to show you understand and are listening.
- *Summarize* major ideas, including feelings, to pull the conversation together and hear where the discussion needs to go.
- *Validate* to show appreciation for your teen's efforts and actions and to acknowledge his or her values and feelings. For example, "I appreciate that you took the time to help me understand the problems you are having in math class."

To develop a high level of listening skill, you might need to practice each of these techniques one at a time until you are comfortable with them.

Tips for Improved Communication
- Let the speaker finish sentences.
- Concentrate on what is being said.
- Show your interest with eye contact, facial expression, and body language (when culturally appropriate).
- Avoid provocative statements such as put-downs and judgments.
- Say when you agree and praise when you can.

Feedback

Normally, feedback is given as close in time as possible to when a behavior occurs. However, in good communication, there's a time and place for everything. "When you give feedback to a teenager, it's best not to do it when the heat is on," cautions Dr. Jensen. Wait until he or she has calmed down. Otherwise the potential for even more anger increases.

One way to deliver feedback is through the use of "I" statements. This type of statement basically follows a formula:

- I feel _____ (state your emotion)
- when you _____(state the behavior nonjudgmentally)
- because _____(state the principle).
- Then, make a request or share a need: I want or I need you to _____.

Do "I" statements change behavior? No. There's even some controversy about how important they are for ADHD. Generally, with ADHD, the fewer the words used, the better. Still, I think "I" messages might have a benefit. They give parents yet another tool to stay in control. Perhaps an added benefit could be improved emotional vocabulary if the "I feel" part uses a variety of emotional words rather than the gang of five: *angry, mad, happy, sad, glad,* or their equivalent slang terms. As with any tool you try, if "I" statements grate on your teen, after you've given them a fair trial, you may need to modify them.

Food for Thought

With or without ADHD, teens get frustrated when they need to talk to a parent and the parent is unavailable. Obviously, parents can't always drop everything to listen *at the precise moment* when the teen needs to speak, although I do think we can drop more things than we realize. A partial way around this availability problem is to have regularly scheduled family meeting times. I know that the teen years don't make this easy. Yet where there's a will, last-minute scheduling and even the family dinner can work.

Research studies show a correlation between behavior problems in youth and families that don't eat together. Dr. Curry believes that "it's important to keep communication during these teen years, and one way to do that is to eat together." In some families, dinnertime can be like the bell that calls the boxer to the next round. When this happens, it's easy to just stop eating together, but breaking bread is a tradition. An invitation to the table signals a peace effort. I would say if your dinner table has become a combat zone, don't stop eating together. Instead, structure the situation so that you can get to eat in peace instead of in pieces. Have ground rules. Limit the amount of time at the table. Do some family problem solving to deal with the table-time issues.

The Art of Problem Solving

Some families fall into a "confront and control" style. Problems and issues become a contest of will and power. As Dr. Bumberry notes, "Rules become easier to enforce when parents and teens basically get along." The parent-teen relationship needs to be about "getting to yes."

Negotiation and problem solving are the keys to good relations between parents and teens. When these tools are used, each family member is part of the decision-making process and thus each member receives recognition and respect.

A structured problem-solving approach probably will not stop the initial burst of reactive energy that many teens with ADHD release whenever they want to get something or get out of something and, in the process, meet resistance. Many seem to have an intense request style influenced by waiting until the last minute, missing deadlines, putting the pressure on, and tuning out before an issue or problem is resolved. That style puts the pressure on parents to be calm, clear about their positions, and committed to solving issues and disputes with a systematic problem-solving approach.

Consider the idea of being clear about your positions. Effective parents know ahead of time how they stand on certain issues. There are basically three types of positions and issues:

1. *Issues you will not negotiate*, which are usually issues of safety, health, or family values, such as no lying. Even though you have

non-negotiable issues, teens sometimes want to put them into play. When a closed issue is reopened, either the parent or the teen can assume that means it's up for renegotiation. Teens need to know up front when parents are listening out of respect or to reconsider a position.

2. *Issues that you will ignore* because you realize they are not that important. We parents of kids with ADHD may get trained to micromanage because we have to be so involved. By dumping certain small things, such as what the teen wears or how clean the room is, we lessen the negative feedback the teen receives. That, in turn, removes a bit of oppression out of the air, which allows energies to be devoted to more important matters. Pick battles wisely.

3. *Issues you will negotiate.* These types of issues range from mild to very serious. Some parents are naturally inclined to tackle the toughest issues first. That's probably not a good idea when a family is just learning how to use a structured problem-solving method. If you're using an approach like the one described below, it's best to begin with issues that are important but not so highly charged that they run the risk of causing a fight instead of solving the problem. For instance, curfew or doing chores.

If you know which issues fall into what category, then as they arise you don't spend energy floundering about what to do or where you stand. It's a good idea to communicate with your teen ahead of time to go over which issues fall into what category. When we parent without surprise, we stand a better chance of being effective.

☞   *TRY THIS*

Make a list of the issues you and your teen have. Sort them into the three categories. Then rate them by level of intensity, meaning how likely they are to cause a blowup. Use appropriate conflict-management styles to deal with them, such as negotiation, collaboration, and accommodation.

Problem-Solving Basics

Most problem-solving methods follow these simple steps. When using a problem-solving approach with your teen, it's a good idea to write down each step and what you agreed to, including all the details.

1. Define the problem without judgment—just the facts.
2. Brainstorm to come up with possible solutions or compromises. (Write down every idea that comes to mind—no matter how stupid or far out the idea seems.)
3. Evaluate the ideas.
4. Pick the idea that seems most likely to work.
5. Try it and evaluate its effectiveness.
6. If it fails, try another.

There are two important ideas to keep in mind when problem solving. The first is to *be clear about what the problem is.* Issues can be cloudy or entirely hidden. It's not uncommon to spend a lot of energy spinning over a side issue that's not really the problem. Tina Lyons, for example, thinks she has a big issue with her son over his clothes. "I spent a lot of money buying stuff that he picked out. It was nice, expensive stuff. Six months later, he adamantly refused to wear it. He wouldn't wear anything but these five white T-shirts, which made me embarrassed because the school probably looks at this kid and thinks he has the same shirt on every day." Every morning she got into a battle with him.

What's the problem here? Is it that Tina, a single parent on a tight income, would have preferred not to waste money? Or is she mainly bugged by the thought that the teachers would judge her commitment to her son by the clothes he wore (which is not an uncommon issue for parents)? While Tina thinks her son's behavior is the problem, it may just be that her issue is with herself, or that the issue she has with him is not that important.

Second, when problem-solving, it's a good idea to follow this advice: *Leave the past behind.* Parent and coach Charley Holman says that's what sports taught him. "I tend to look at things this way: There's nothing I can do about what went on before. I can only change the present or something in the future."

Problem Solving in Action

Dr. Robin has refined this problem-solution approach for matters of parent-adolescent conflict. In actuality, his method takes the problem-solving approach through the process to an ultimate end: a contract agreed upon and followed by all parties involved.

That contract consists of six basic areas. Dr. Robin advises parents and teens to discuss the problem, devise a plan, and then write down the following:

1. *Who does what, where, when, and how.* For example, the family might agree that the teen will take out the trash the night before garbage pick-up.
2. *Who makes sure the plan is being carried out and what method will be used.* Will Mom or Dad monitor? Will the teen be solely responsible?
3. *Decide the consequences for compliance.* That includes positive consequences for upholding the terms and conditions of the contract and negative consequences for not following through on the contract.
4. *Will performance reminders be given? If so, by whom?* Here you might want to resist the temptation to make Mom the enforcer. A performance reminder could be a note on the door or on the breakfast/dinner table.
5. *Be specific about what constitutes compliance.* If the trash is supposed to be out the night before and the cans brought in the following evening, then you have to decide if it's okay if the teen

---

INFORMATION LINK

Dr. Robin has created some great user-friendly forms for therapists to use when training parents in this approach. The "Family Outline of Problem Solving" and the "Problem Solving Worksheet" appear on pages 328–329 of his book, *ADHD in Adolescents: Diagnosis and Treatment,* Guilford Publications, 1998.

delays, for example, if he waits until before school to put the trash out. A lot of agreements fall apart because they're not specific enough. It may be okay for the trash to go out in the morning. If so, then your agreement would say so.

6. *Anticipate any difficulties that could upset the plan.* For instance, the teen might be hurried in the morning, so putting the trash out the night before would be the better method. Or the family may generate so much trash that missing a pick-up creates a real mess. In this case, it might be better not to leave this chore up to the teen. Weighing the pros and cons is also a part of problem solving.

Note: If your teen is very oppositional or aggressive, don't try to engage in problem-solving and contracting without first consulting a professional. Doing so may create a blowup that will only make matters worse.

Should you want to try a problem-solving/contract approach, follow these four rules of thumb:

1. Only work on one issue at a time.
2. Begin with an issue of mild to moderate intensity.
3. Select the solution that has the most pluses.
4. Use good communication habits (no blamers, shoulds, put-downs, etc.)

Significant Issues

Following are brief discussions about certain common issues that often cause a lot of concern.

Car and Driver

"The most horrible phone call you can get is from the police officer telling you that your son's been in an accident," says Maggie Prescott, who's been on the receiving end of that call. She and her son, Mark, live in a rural area about a half hour away from Mark's dad. Though Mark has ADHD, both parents encouraged him to get his license as soon as he could. In preparation, Maggie and Mark's father both spent a lot of time behind the wheel with Mark. They trained him under all sorts of conditions: snow, hills, icy curves, and dirt roads. His parents felt confident that when he got his driver's license he would be as prepared as he could possibly be. Maggie even had her son take a test that measured reaction time. Mark did superbly. Still, his attention span and focus leave a lot to be desired. Though he breezed through the road test, Mark took his written test three times before he passed.

Four days after getting his license, Mark was driving from his dad's house to his mom's house. He had the cruise control on, but at one point, he accelerated beyond where he had it set. His mom says that "when he came to a corner that had gravel on it, he let up the accelerator but forgot he had the cruise control on. He had no choice but to take the corner at a fast speed. The car fishtailed like crazy. With his wonderfully good reflexes, he chose to hit a tree rather than go off the cliff." Though he totaled the car, miraculously Mark was not hurt.

Dr. Barkley has done the largest study ever on teens with ADHD and driving. Based on the findings, he strongly believes that with ADHD in the picture, the driver's license should be delayed. "Adolescents are among the highest-risk drivers. Now magnify that fourfold by the presence of the disorder," Dr. Barkley warns. His studies reveal these risks:

- Teens with ADHD have a fourfold increase in the number of auto accidents.
- Accidents are two and a half times more serious in terms of injuries and damage.
- Teens with ADHD get three and a half times the speeding tickets.
- ADHD teens have a high probability for suspensions and revocations.
- They have a high probability (even with suspension or revocation) of driving without a license.

It's not just inattentiveness or impulsivity that causes the driving problems. "They brake when they shouldn't, and don't brake when they ought to. They don't pay attention to things that are important," Dr.

Barkley explains. Problems exist even down to the level of motor coordination: "They are not as coordinated in terms of steering, and in a sense of boundaries or space from other vehicles."

What can a parent do? First, Dr. Barkley recommends a graduated license system that you, the parents, create regardless of your state's law. He acknowledges that your imposition of this system will cause fights, but as he points out, "Your child's life is at stake. What's more important?"

Dr. Barkley's Graduated License System

- Start with a long learner's permit period—about one year driving with a parent or another adult in the car.
- Move to licensed driving only in the daytime.
- Don't allow other adolescents in the car for at least six months. (This rule avoids problems resulting from the social side of adolescent driving, which includes conversation, loud music, and joyriding.)
- If six months pass without significant incident, allow evening driving privileges, and allow other adolescents in the car— during daytime hours only.
- If six more months pass without significant incident—no citations, no accidents, no coming home with alcohol on the breath—then allow evening driving with other teens.

Under this graduated licensing system, it may take two to three years before the teen has total driving independence. Dr. Barkley acknowledges that this method is not foolproof. It doesn't guarantee a safer youngster, but it does limit the risk.

Stimulant medication has been shown to have a positive effect on driving practices. Thus, Dr. Barkley also recommends that when medication has been prescribed, parents adopt a hard line of no medication, no driving. He acknowledges that in the short run, many teens don't see medication as a help. However, as a matter of practicality, Dr. Barkley points out that they will negotiate. "You are going to have to pony up something to make it a win-win situation," he adds. Medication may also lessen road rage. The emotional overreactivity and vulnerability to stress frequently seen in ADHD can turn a car into a lethal weapon.

About Insurance

Insurance can be another area of concern. Aside from the issue of who will pay, which is a matter of negotiation, you will want to know your state's insurance regulations. My state, for instance, automatically charges parents with premiums for any child who is a licensed driver and living under their roof, regardless of that child's age—unless that child has his or her own policy. So even if you don't want to pay for your teen, you may have no choice. Personally, I believe it's better to be sure your teen is covered. We want to help them avoid lifelong consequences if at all possible. Of course, you shouldn't cover the teen forever. If he or she refuses to behave responsibly and you've tried everything to help him or her, you may have to withdraw support and let the teen deal with the effects.

Before your teen gets his or her license, you'll want to clarify your position—for instance, "Do I want to have my teen on my policy? What are the risks to me? If I decide that he or she will be solely responsible for carrying his or her insurance, how will I keep track and make sure payments are made so coverage doesn't lapse? If my teen lets his or her coverage lapse, does that make me liable should an accident occur? Would I be better off just paying the price for the security of knowing that should something go wrong with my high-risk driver, it won't result in financial ruin?" There's a lot to be said for being the gatekeeper as long as you can.

The Social Scene

"I still have trouble socially," says 16-year-old Kevin Gillingham. "Making and keeping friends in general is a problem for me. I was really hyper and kind of weird. I still am kind of weird. It's part of the baggage and the frustration. It's hard. It's not so much that I'm weird. That's probably the wrong word. Everybody has their own character. Some people fit right into the molds and some don't. You know the ones who do because they have an easier time fitting in. They are standardized sort of people."

Peers

During the teen years, when friends become everything, kids with ADHD are not different from other kids. "As teens attempt to leave their families and the influence of their parents, they find a group of kids that serves a similar function," explains Dr. Zakreski. "Young teens hunger for peer acceptance, so they diligently work to avoid rejection and gain approval." As Dr. Zakreski notes, "It's the kids who are truly isolated that we worry about." Why? These kids don't have a support network to help them make the transition into an identity-achieved adult. Social isolation also breeds poor self-esteem, which may lead to other problems, such as depression.

There are other concerns. "I'm fearful of Joel's friends," says his mother, Adrian Milstein. Joel has not had a good track record with keeping friends, which is the social hallmark of this disorder. Generally, with ADHD, making friends is not a problem. Acting in ways that sustain a relationship is. Joel has never had great social competence. So the fear his mom feels has to do with what types of friends he'll choose. "He tends to pick kids who also have ADHD. They set each other off," she says.

"Kids find other kids who share the same point of view," Dr. Zakreski observes. The kid with ADHD who has been unsuccessful in school or defiant might wind up with peers who are rebellious, who put down authority, and who are likely to experiment with alcohol and drugs at an early age. "They group together almost as a way to celebrate their shared failures," explains Dr. Zakreski. In fact, kids with low self-esteem can develop high self-esteem by being with the wrong peer group. They learn to take pride in being bad or in rejecting the social conventions within which they've never been successful.

All peer groups, friendships, and the like initially form around common interests and ideas. Then issues of friendship and intimacy come into play. "Can I trust you? Do we understand one another? Will you be loyal? Do I like your personality?" Dylan Holman, now 25, has been very fortunate. His father, Charley, explains, "He's never had any social difficulties whatsoever. As a matter of fact, he got along with everyone in school." Dylan adapts well to every social environment. Charley believes that has to do with the coaching he and Dylan's mother gave their son. "We always told him, 'Be yourself. Don't put on airs. Don't put on any fronts.'"

It's important for parents to pay attention to who their teen's friends are and what they do. The general recommendation is to be involved but not interfere unnecessarily. The closer the relationship between parents and teen, the better the chance that the teen will choose friends the parents like, and the more likely the teen is to resist negative peer pressure. By guiding the teen into certain types of activities, perhaps community volunteerism, youth fellowships, or sports, the parent may be able to influence the teen's selection of friends indirectly.

Parents ought to be concerned if the teen is secretive about friends, as that may mean there's something to hide. If your teen winds up in a less-than-positive peer situation, what can you do? Walk softly. "The selection of a friend is about the most personal thing a kid gets to do. They're not likely to willingly give up the control they feel they have in this situation," Dr. Zakreski points out. Attempting to solve the problem of friends who are poor influences with a head-on attack most likely won't work. In fact, it may even encourage more rebellion. Instead, Dr. Zakreski advises parents to be open and to ask good questions. As an example, he says a parent might say, "Do you think Joe is the right kind of person for you to hang around with? I understand he's a pot smoker, and are you aware of the consequences of that?" Your aim here is to share your concerns, but stop short of saying, "You can't hang around with Joe." He also counsels parents to provide alternative situations where other healthier relationships might be formed. In extreme cases such as defiant teens, Dr. Barkley strongly encourages parents to move the family to another community when their teens get involved with the wrong crowd.

Romance

Romance can be another area of concern for parents and teens. Where childhood friendships form around activities, the closeness that teens feel in their friendships is based on emotional bonds. Along with this change comes the natural development of sexual drive. Emerging sexuality leads to sexual relationships. The challenge, according to Dr. Feerick, is to integrate the need for intimacy with the need for sexuality in an appropriate way.

Girls generally begin dating around 12 or 13, boys between the ages of 12 and 14. "Early intensive dating may stunt interpersonal growth," notes Dr. Feerick. When teens wrap themselves in relationships, they don't experiment to discover who they are. Instead, they may adopt someone else's identity as a way to gain comfort and approval. That's true regardless of ADHD.

However, when ADHD is present, as you might expect, the picture becomes more complicated. First of all, according to Dr. Robin, there isn't much research on the dating process and this population. However, he notes that boys with the disorder tend to start the dating process later—around age 15 or so. Furthermore, he adds, "Boys with ADHD are immature and so they tend to do silly, goofy things. Girls their age may find them totally out of it and not be interested." He finds that the boys become more interested in dating as juniors and seniors.

Whether male or female, teen or adult, in many cases "People with ADHD have a lot of problems in intimate relationships," notes Dr. Robin. Many problems stem from an all-or-nothing style of interaction characteristic of ADHD. For instance, 21-year-old Louie Primavera fell in love when he went away to college. Though newly diagnosed with ADHD, he really didn't want to know much about what to do to help himself, despite his father pushing him to read about the disorder and take his medication. One night Dan received a frantic phone call from Louie because his girlfriend was pushing him away. Louie told his dad, "I'm all obsessed, and I don't know what to do. She doesn't want to see me, doesn't want to talk to me."

After the girl dumped him, a desperate Louie sought answers. He read a book about ADHD his father had sent months earlier. Louie zeroed in on the part about relationships. It seemed that his smothering demands cost him the girl. In ADHD romantic relationships, being dumped isn't the only problem. As Dr. Robin notes, "I have seen teens with ADHD who go through boyfriends and girlfriends very easily." Why? Aside from wearing out their welcome, he says, "They get bored very easily."

Girls with the disorder may have a different load to bear than the boys. Dr. Hinshaw's research on younger preadolescent girls in a summer camp program yielded this information. Though the girls made close friends and their friendships had a lot of positive characteristics, the girls were rejected more by peer groups and had more conflict. "It may be that one close friendship can outweigh a lot of peer rejection," Dr. Hinshaw says.

While that can be redeeming, such a search for the one close friendship could lead to trouble in matters of romantic relationships. The social rejection girls feel, coupled with feelings of poor self-worth, may lead them to mistake sex for intimacy, a ticket to a newfound friend, or a means of gaining popularity.

The Facts of Life

You may have some influence in the early adolescent years over your teen's social life, especially through careful monitoring of comings and goings. Once dating begins, your greatest influence may come in the form of education and not fighting the facts of teen life. Of course, you can set some practical guidelines. For instance, Steinberg and Levin suggest that you do the following:

- Personally meet anyone your teen dates.
- Know where the teen is going and what he or she plans to do.
- Limit the number of dates per week.
- Except in cases of mistreatment or regular curfew violations, tread cautiously if you dislike the person your teen is dating.

Regardless of whether a serious relationship develops, sexual curiosity, desire, and experimentation happen, and happen to be natural. Most of today's teens no longer view sex as a step toward marriage. This book is no place to hold a dialogue about what makes for moral or amoral sexual behavior. It is a place to report some ADHD statistics.

Dr. Barkley's follow-up studies reveal this troubling information. Forty percent of teens with ADHD are involved in a teen pregnancy before they are 19 or 20 years old. That means that almost one out of every two teens with the disorder may wind up being a biological mother or father, or having an abortion. They also begin having intercourse about a year ahead of the average teenage population. They have more partners and are less inclined to use contraceptives. They are also at a greater risk for sexually transmitted diseases.

"You've got an individual whose body yearns for sexual experimentation and maybe even full-fledged relations. Housed in that body is a mind whose self-control and sense of responsibility, forethought, and planning are not on the radar screen," cautions Dr. Barkley. "I think parents of teens with ADHD have got to be discussing birth control," he adds. "This is not optional, unless you want a teen who is a parent at the ripe old age of 16." Also know that 54 percent of teens with ADHD who became parents did not have custody of their children, and unwed teenage fathers who may be interested in having involvement with their children are often discouraged from doing so.

Money Management

"Credit cards are to be cut up and thrown away, no matter how many come in the mail," says Dr. Barkley. He's found that teens with ADHD can be like junkies with these cards. "They get sucked so deeply into debt, they can't get out," he adds. People with ADHD don't corner the market on credit card misuse! As reported in *USA Today,* a 1999 survey found that 55 percent of all college students and 7 percent of all high school students have a major credit card. One-third of these cardholders do not pay their bill in full each month. Prepaid debit cards may be a better alternative for all irresponsible spenders—not just adolescents or those with ADHD.

These youth also need help with the accountability, budgeting, and record-keeping aspects of money management. The earliest training usually begins with an allowance. Whether earned or given freely, allowances help kids learn to budget their money. For that reason, frequently making advances on allowance is not a good idea. Dr. Barkley advises parents to insist upon an imposed savings plan from part-time and summer jobs. Kids also need to be taught how to balance checking accounts—the earlier the better.

INFORMATION LINK

A good place to read about teaching kids sound money-management practice is Neale S. Godfrey and Carolina Edwards, *Money Doesn't Grow on Trees: A Parents' Guide to Raising Financially Responsible Children,* Simon and Schuster, New York, 1994.

Also, Teenvestor.com provides teens ages 13 to 19 with information, advice, and work assignments to help them understand the principles of investing in stocks and mutual funds. You might want to check out this site.

The Room

"What's your room like?" I ask 13-year-old Joel Milstein.

"What's hell like?" he replies.

While the number-one complaint of parents of teens with this disorder usually has something to do with school, "the room" came up as a sore spot in practically every interview I did. One mother actually showed me her son's bedroom. Frankly, having a son with ADHD, I was unimpressed by her son's mess. So what is it about the bedroom that gets us mothers going? I remember when my son was an out-of-control toddler and little that I did helped. My way of dealing with the chaos was to have a neat, orderly house. It created an illusion that all was well. Maybe "the room" continues to be a sign that all is not well.

Some parents let this issue drop entirely. Jill Gillingham and her husband came up with the "once a week your room has to be cleanable" rule. Notice the difference between *clean* and *cleanable*. In other words, the room has to be picked up to the point that Jill can dust and vacuum. By the way, many teens want to ban their parents from "their" bedrooms. Dusting, vacuuming, and bringing in clean laundry is a natural way to maintain access. This access is essential to keeping necessary tabs on kids. Of course, teens desire their privacy, and many will object to parents being in their rooms. There should be limits to a teen's privacy, however. While the parent and teen may decide what most of those limits will be, certainly the parent has to do what is necessary if safety or health issues become a concern.

Though they may appear to be lazy, teens with ADHD may have messy rooms for a couple of reasons. As Kevin Gillingham explains, "I might forget to take the time to throw my dirty sweater in the basket or whatever. Part of it is just me being too lazy to put my clothes in the basket. I just toss them on the floor. Part of it is I'm in a rush, and all sorts of things contribute to that."

Rushing, of course, is an executive function problem, as are organization and memory. Some teens with ADHD have trouble finding or putting things in dressers, files, cabinets, and the like, so they keep everything out in the open. Of course, that's an absurd way to do things. A master system can be put in place to help the teen keep things neat and organized. Use simple filing systems, such as drawers with labels, color-coding for categories of clothes, special places for collections and CDs and school stuff, and so on. If you can afford to do so, you might hire a clutter consultant to help your son or daughter come up with a workable system. Once the master system is in place, use a contract to have the room cleaned once or twice a week.

A Room of One's Own

Although times have changed and older kids are living at home longer, living independently continues to be viewed as a sign that the adolescent period is drawing to a close. Some teens want to move out before they're of legal age to do so, or before they are ready. Mark Prescott, 17, has older friends who have headed to the big city for college. When he told his mother and father that he wanted to move, his parents adamantly refused. "He can make that choice when he's 18," his mom tells me. "He may choose to leave before that, but if he does, he knows he can't take anything with him."

Is there a magic move-out age? Will turning 18 help this young man with ADHD stand on his own two feet? His mother knows the answer to that last question is probably no. Legally, once he is 18, she doesn't have a choice about making him live at home. If he decides to head out on his own, she can only decide how she will respond to him. For instance, will she help him set up his place or allow him to come home to do laundry and eat? She might also think about her position if things don't work out and he decides he wants to move back home.

We hope our teens will include us and allow us to guide them in this decision to live independently. When we do have a say, Dr. Curry thinks that, in general, "You should let them stand on their own two feet when you think they have a pretty good shot of being able to do it." For instance, does the teen have a financial plan? Can he or she pay for food, rent, and utilities?

Just as teens need to map out their financial plan, parents need to be clear ahead of time about their position regarding moves toward independent living arrangements. You will want to have your answers to these questions: Does your son or daughter have enough money to be self-supporting? If not, are you willing to subsidize him or her? If so, how much and for how long? If your teen leaves either against your better judgment or with your blessing, are you going to bail him or her out if it doesn't work? As with many issues, this one is not ADHD-specific. It's just that ADHD is an additional factor that can set the stage for a poor outcome. Parents have to be like an advance team that is sent in to secure the area before the persons in need of security arrive.

If the teen or young adult does decide to move back home after a trial of independence, before you open the door you'll want to set some ground rules. Decide first what is expected financially. Does the teen have a job? What expenses in addition to rent do you want paid? Also, decide if you want to set a deadline for when the young adult needs to become self-sufficient. Similarly, parents of teens coming home for college breaks will want to be clear about house rules.

When All Is Said and Done

No matter what the issue, conflict-management tools are necessary for effective home rule. These techniques enable parents to be guides instead of guards. They train teens in the valuable people-skills of respecting self and others. Though ADHD presents a higher-than-average potential for negative interactions, families can live chaos free and in a good deal of peace.

When all is said and done, remember that you may not see the fruits of your efforts until some later point in time, or perhaps not until the adult years. Trust that your care, concerns, and hard work will have a positive effect. Don't be surprised if you even get some appreciation along the way.

CHAPTER EIGHT

Power Surges

When defiance and anger get their claws into a family, power struggles feel more like power surges. These have the potential to shut the family and the teen out of any positive interaction and send them into a combat zone. This chapter delves into the main conductors of power struggles, whether the seizing of power happens within the family or between teens.

"When they don't let me do something, I just argue with them and make it so I can," 16-year-old Jeff Kain tells me. Unfortunately, Jeff doesn't stop at arguing. When his parents say no, he says, "Oh yeah?" For instance, whenever his parents told him he couldn't go out, "I'd go out at night when they went to sleep," Jeff says with a bit of remorse. When I ask him what happened, he answers, "I got caught a couple of times, but I never stole from them." Bringing up stealing is his way of letting on that he's not that bad.

Jeff says he's never been physical with his parents except once. "I pushed my dad because he hit me because I got arrested for graffiti. We were in the police station. That was the first time I got arrested." By "first," Jeff means the only time.

Jeff has a sweet face and an unassuming, soft-spoken manner. Yet that's not how he thinks people would describe him. He believes his teachers would say that he's "uncontrollable, disrespectful, don't listen, and probably that I am a bad kid." He's not too sure about his friends.

"They trust me and they respect me. I get in a lot of trouble, but I don't know what they would say." And what about his mom? "She'd say I don't listen, don't have any respect for authority. She'd probably say more."

Some measure of defiance is normal during adolescence. In fact, it may actually be encouraged through the natural power struggles that happen as the teen attempts to develop his or her own identity. Dr. Zakreski summarizes the balance of power this way: "Over time, power has to change in a family. Parents have all the power over an infant, which they exercise for the infant's benefit. During childhood, the balance begins to change to include socialization through school, teams, clubs, and other peer contacts. In effect, the peer group becomes the teenager's 'alternate family,' lending support as he or she leaves the biological family. In adolescent years, the power shifts qualitatively because now you have a kid that has his or her own agenda who is socialized significantly by peers. Some teens want to shift that power before they're ready." Many parents tend to worry, perhaps because they view the teen's actions as dangerous or disrespectful. From the teen's point of view, the parents may appear controlling and nagging. There's nothing unusual here.

Jeff's behavior has gone way beyond normal defiance. This teen has a consistent pattern of seizing the power. He breaks or does not follow rules and constantly challenges authority figures, whether at home, at school, or on the job. Jeff's misbehavior is so severe that it led to a placement in a residential treatment center for teens with serious behavior problems whose parents, for the most part, have lost control. This degree of defiance is highly unusual for most teens. Although Jeff has ADHD, oppositional defiant disorder and conduct disorder happen to be his main problems at the moment.

For a number of complicated reasons, Jeff's behavior deteriorated from minor disobedience, or noncompliance, to almost full-blown anarchy. Nonetheless, Jeff is not a bad kid. He does some bad things. He's gotten in over his head. So far he's responded very well to the interventions he's received in his residential program, mainly strict rules, immediate consequences, and frequent feedback. Jeff is learning to follow rules and to use communication and problem solving to deal with his issues.

Typically the youth with ADHD who have behavior problems ranging from noncompliance to defiance are the hyperactive, impulsive, and aggressive type. Over time, a good percentage of these kids show a progression of behavior problems that began in childhood as noncompliance and some degree of opposition. If the problems are left unchecked, by the teen years the children become quite oppositional and defiant.

What's the difference between noncompliance and defiance? Noncompliance has to do with not doing what is asked in a reasonable amount of time, doing only part of what is asked, and failing to follow rules. Generally, the noncompliant teen looks to get out of or avoid something that he or she doesn't want to do. Defiance, on the other hand, has to do with verbal or physical resistance to doing what is asked or following the rules—for example, verbal refusal, temper outbursts, or physical aggression toward an authority. Unchecked defiance often leads to delinquency, which means breaking the law, and to other troublesome acts such as running away, violating curfew, or truancy. There are degrees of noncompliance and defiance. But noncompliant behavior did not land Jeff in a residential school. Defiant, delinquent behavior did. Jeff consistently violated even the most basic household rules.

Roots of Defiance

Defiance doesn't just happen. When a kid gets to the point where he or she hardly listens to a thing the parent says, or has explosions that make the parents shudder or tiptoe around their teen to avoid a land mine, then there's a serious problem that needs careful investigation. This level of defiance probably cannot be lessened without highly skilled outside help.

How does a teen get to this point? There is no simple answer. Oppositional, defiant, explosive behavior has multiple pathways. First of all, as Dr. Barkley points out, "genetics indicate that we are dealing with a monstrously biological problem." ADHD changes the playing field.

A New Look At Oppositionality

A study recently completed by Dr. Ross Greene and his colleagues at Massachusetts General Hospital shows that 80 percent of teens with oppositional defiant disorder also have ADHD. Fifty percent have comorbid depression. Sixty percent suffer from anxiety. Twenty percent are lin-

INFORMATION LINK

> Dr. Greene has written an excellent book about understanding
> chronically inflexible and explosive behavior. Ross Greene,
> *The Explosive Child,* HarperCollins, New York, 1998.

guistically impaired. Nonverbal learning disabilities are also common. Dr. Greene finds that many of the oppositional kids he sees have "a learning disability in the areas of flexibility and frustration."

According to Dr. Greene, "Thinking skills deficits come into play with inflexible, explosive children." That means children who come to their defiance and oppositionality through this main pathway of inflexibility and poor frustration tolerance require a lot of training in cognitive skills. These need to be modeled time and again in order to teach these teens how to use socially appropriate replacement skills. Of course, in order for cognitive skills training to be effective, parents and teachers have to be shown what skills the teen needs and how to model these consistently in the natural setting in order for the teen to bring them into his or her behavior repertoire.

Not all teens with ODD will come by this problem from a skills deficit. As Dr. Greene says, "We have different strokes for different folks. The therapist and parent must figure out how a particular kid got to this oppositional defiant behavior and use the appropriate strategies.

Coercive Interactions

A number of years ago, Dr. Gerald Patterson identified a critical pathway to opposition and defiance known as the "coercive interactional pattern." In this pattern, defiance, like the hurricane that starts with the beat of a butterfly's wings thousands of miles away, begins in early childhood. In most cases, it's actually cultivated unwittingly through parent-child interactions. When the coercive interactional pattern becomes the typical way parents and teens relate to each other, expect trouble.

Coercive interactions often are found in homes where the parents show little acknowledgment when the child behaves well. These interactions usually begin very innocently. Basically, a parent makes a request that the child doesn't want to do. The child doesn't do what is asked upon the first request. Usually the parent repeats the request multiple times instead of giving the child a consequence for noncompliance. At this point, the child sees that the parent's word is not backed up. Even if punishment is eventually received, there's been a period of time where the child has been allowed to do things his or her own way. Without intending to do so, the parent has actually strengthened and negatively reinforced the child's misbehavior.

Perhaps ten or fifteen minutes pass. The parent makes the request again, only this time a threat has been added. The child still doesn't do what's asked. More threats are made. As the child ignores each threat, the parent becomes frustrated and usually makes unreasonable threats. The child knows that the unreasonable threat will be modified in some way. During the threat part of the interaction, the child may yell, cry, divert attention, or ignore, but the point is that he or she doesn't do what's been requested.

At this point in the majority of cases, the parent gives in, which means the demand was not met the way the parent initially asked. Sometimes the parent steps in and performs the task for the child, or the demand is simply not met. In the majority of cases, the child is punished, but it occurs too late in the interaction to be of much value.

Matters are made worse if the parent actually rewards the child for not behaving. For example, the child may lose emotional control, and the parent might hug the child in an attempt to calm him or her. When a child is rewarded for noncompliance, the likelihood of future oppositional behavior increases by 400 percent, Dr. Barkley notes.

What has the youth learned? "I may have to weather the storm, but I know that storm will pass." Or, in other words, "If I put up a big enough resistance, I get my way."

Now let's fast-forward to the teen years. What do you think happens when this pattern of behavior goes on over time? Ten or twelve years of coercive interactions create a pretty defiant teen. Why? Well, the teen has managed to get out of doing unpleasant, unrewarding tasks by being oppositional. Then, the natural order of power in the family flips upside down. At this point you have a teen in charge, and the parents scramble to find bigger and better threats to get simple requests met. They also discipline more harshly and more frequently. The result is greater hostility and highly oppositional defiant behavior.

In an ironic twist, the teen actually contributes to the creation of a more negative, severe, argumentative, and angry parent. The teen's noncompliant, defiant behavior trains the parent to use more coercion and more force.

Is this a matter of blame? No. A trained observer can identify this pattern. But generally, parents are just grasping for what to do. You may wonder why the child or teen doesn't simply do what is asked and avoid all this stuff. Aside from not wanting to follow the initial request for whatever reason, from where the teen sits the parent looks like an incredible nag. The youth may tell him- or herself, "All would be well if only Mom and Dad would get off my back." Also, teens with ADHD live in the now. They don't see the big picture or how an action will lead to a chain of events. If the parents don't give an immediate consequence for noncompliance, the teen simply doesn't get it.

It's important to underscore the point that a fair number of teens with ADHD have oppositional, inflexible, aggressive temperaments. Their defiance may be more a product of who they are "biologically" rather than how they've power-brokered with parents. Parents of these teens will need guidance to learn when and how to insist, when to back off, and when their teen needs coaching in certain skills such as anger management, mood control, or shifting from one activity to another by using steps to ease transitions instead of making abrupt moves.

Before giving a command or making a request, parents need to run a "command check." First of all, think about what you're asking. Does it really matter? Do you have the energy to follow through? Do you have a couple of consequences in mind should the teen not do what is asked? Be sure you don't give commands while the teen is doing something else that's pleasurable and rewarding or is otherwise not available to listen. Give clear commands, and give time limits for the commands to be met.

When coercive interactions become the typical interactional pattern, the results can be extremely destructive. Expect to be visited by some or all of what I call the Seven Miseries:

1. Expect more defiance. The teen's now in charge. Consequences have come too little or too late.
2. Expect to expect less from the teen. Who in their right mind wants to wake a sleeping dragon? Eventually the parent may stop

TRY THIS

Observe what happens the next time you tell your teen to do or not do something.

> *How many times do you repeat your request?*
> *How do you feel after each time you repeat it?*
> *How does your teen react after each time you repeat your request?*
> *Does your teen ever comply?*
> *Do you let it slide? Or do you lose track because you've got other things to do and not enough time to ride the teen?*
> *Do you wind up doing it yourself?*
> *Do you give consequences? If so, how long do you wait?*

To interrupt the coercive cycle, follow the Law of Three.

> 1. *Give a clear imperative command. "Do _____."*
>   *"Do not _____." Avoid indefinite commands such as "Would you please _____?" or "Do me a favor _____."*
> 2. *Give a deadline. "Do _____ by _____." Or "Do _____ now."*
> 3. *Give a consequence. (Positive for compliance. Negative for noncompliance. Give it immediately or as soon as possible.)*

Be sure the teen is paying attention. Avoid giving the teen a barrage of commands at once or in close proximity to one another. Do not allow your emotions into the picture. Pretend you are in a business transaction. However, if it gets heated, walk away—for the time being. It's better to avoid an escalation of anger. Revisit the problem later. Give a consequence. Enforce it.

It's a good idea to tell your teen in advance that things will change. A therapist can be a big help here. Explain why and how. Use a conversational as opposed to a warning tone.

making requests or may keep them to a bare minimum. Dr.
Bumberry finds that "a lot of parents aren't up to the intensity
and duration of the fight that a kid can do, so at some point
their inclination is to give up."

3. Expect learned helplessness, which means coming to believe that
    nothing you do will work. As Dr. Barkley says, "To keep peace in
    the family, the parent quits. You provide food, a roof, say hi
    when you see them, and basically stay out of the teen's life."
4. Expect to feel inept and worthless.
5. Expect to be seen as inept and worthless by the teen.
6. Expect increasingly negative interactions between all family
    members.
7. Expect to become isolated. Dr. Barkley's research shows that
    parents of difficult, demanding, and oppositional teens
    withdraw from a social-support system for a number of reasons.
    Often they feel embarrassed, or other parents want nothing to
    do with them because of their apparent inability to raise a
    "well-behaved" kid. Or they are too depressed to take steps to
    keep themselves plugged into their own lives.

When coercive patterns get mixed with biological monsters, the family gets into a sorry state of affairs. Tina Lyons knows all too well what can
happen. She raised her only son, Eddie, alone since birth. She only took
jobs that would allow her to be home as much as possible. She became
class mother three times. She and her son went on vacations. She fully
expected her commitment and desire to being a good mother would
result in a happy, loving home. When puberty hit, Eddie began to have
lots of trouble in school and also at home. He became very angry and
oppositional. "He was cursing at me, calling me names, and standing in
my face like he wanted to get physical," Tina recalls.

Tina's friends did not believe what was happening in her home. Her
sister would phone and ask her, "What are you doing to him?" But Tina
saw it more as what her son was doing to her. She bought a house and gave
him the best room. He did not take care of it. She bought him a bike. He
lost it. So she bought him another. He lost that one. Then one day she
went to ride her bike. It was gone. "He couldn't understand what the big

deal was. He seems to think he has a right to take things that belong to me," she says, exasperated.

Chores were particularly problematic. One night Eddie decided he wouldn't do the dishes. When Tina insisted, Eddie climbed out the kitchen window and onto the roof. He threatened to jump. Tina says she knew he was bluffing, but he stayed out so long that she began to worry a neighbor might call the police. Eddie had found a way to seize the power, but like a kid playing a game of hot potato, he couldn't find any face-saving way to drop it when he got burned. Tina called her sister for backup. Eddie's aunt convinced him to come inside.

"I looked at him and felt so bad," says Tina. "I knew he didn't want to kill himself. Not for one minute did I think he was serious. It's just that he would go to these lengths for manipulation. He had no boundaries. And I responded in all the wrong ways. I disciplined him harshly," she says as tears well in her eyes.

What's happened in this family is not a pretty picture. Yet even with ugly scenes, some families do not seek professional help. Instead, they may fall into an illusion. After the storm passes, it's easy to lull the self into believing it's not that bad. Usually it *is* that bad. As Dr. Barkley notes, "There's so much disruptive behavior occurring, and the parents only know how to deal with disruptive behavior through discipline. That leads to a spiraling toward even higher levels of harshness as parents try to get control over what has become an out-of-control process." It is possible that Eddie has a language problem that makes it hard for him to verbalize what he's feeling. Therefore he may act out instead of "reason" out.

Other Defiant Pathways

Dr. David Keith, who has coauthored *Defiance in the Family: Finding Hope in Therapy,* believes that worry also contributes to defiant behavior. He finds that while parents tend to be concerned about the teen's choice of friends and how they're doing in school, the teens worry about themselves, their parents, and the union between their parents. According to Dr. Keith, teens worry more with their hearts than their heads. When kids lose faith in the parents' ability to effectively parent them as they grow up, they become defiant. "If you don't have faith in the authority, you are going to have to defy it because your survival is at stake," Dr. Keith maintains. It's as if the youth uses defiance as a smoke screen to hide underlying worries or fear. Of course, some parents do feel helpless and inept. Raising a tough teen can have that effect. Over time, parents may become exhausted and undone by the unusually difficult situations they find themselves in. Demanding, tough, oppositional teens often create white-water conditions and white-knuckle parenting responses.

Sometimes defiance occurs because teens fall into the wrong crowd, as did Marty Prior, who seems to be headed for trouble. He lives in a poor town. His family is better off than most others. They have an aboveground pool, while some of Marty's friends don't have food on the table. His mom has thought about moving to get her kids away from the kids in town.

Marty describes his town as "the smallest town with the highest crime rate, because there's a lot of people here." He says the kids cause the crime, and includes himself in the group. "Me and my friends go out every night. We chase cars on our bikes or they try to catch us, but they never do," he says with great animation. The police have told the boys to stop doing this, but Marty and his friends persist—"because it's fun," he says, and adds, "Getting chased by a car and trying not to get caught—it's a challenge." And so is Marty.

The Lengths Some Teens Will Go To

As the school disciplinarian at a residential center for teens with severe behavioral problems, Jay Hatch sees a lot of what he calls "master manipulators of friends, parents, and other adults." With a soulful laugh, he defines a master manipulator as "somebody who's just very good at it. That kid is able to steer everything their way to meet their end goal, whether it's the conversation or whether it's to get you to do things for them. They'll promise you and sweet-talk you, and then if you say no, they'll turn on you immediately."

Jay's not speaking with any malice toward these boys and girls, either. He knows that they behave in a way that has paid off for them in the past. Thus, they've got a long road ahead. Before they can find other ways to get what they need, the teens must first learn to identify their manipulative behavior. The patterns and ploys become so ingrained, the kids don't see the manipulative methods driving their behavior.

"There's certainly lots of types of manipulation that parents need to be savvy about," says Dr. Robin. Perhaps the teen wants a new bike, or an expensive coat, or to go to a concert that gets out so late that he or she has to miss school the next day. The teen may threaten to defy you by saying he will not do schoolwork or will run away. Or the teen may try to guilt-trip you or make you feel that you are ruining her life. Dr. Robin advises parents to view threats of this nature as choices the teen might make. Of course, choices have consequences, and the teen can be told something to this effect: "You may choose to make that decision. But in return, I will _____." Effective parents establish the consequences before the exchange occurs, and follow through. They also make sure the teen has the skills needed to act in a prosocial nonmanipulative manner.

Dr. Robin trains parents to gradually grant independence as the teen demonstrates responsibility. If a teen threatens to run away, for instance, he coaches parents to pull back on the amount of freedom they allow the teen because the teen is not handling freedom well. He doesn't advise parents to totally restrict the teen. And though many of us may be tempted to say, "You'll never see the light of day again," of course that's an empty threat. You may choose to make the curfew earlier as a way of cutting back on freedom for a period of time. Afterward, the teen is given another chance to prove him- or herself.

Some forms of manipulation can be downright destructive. As Dr. Zakreski explains, "If you define manipulation as trying to get another person to do something you want them to do, that happens all the time. Where it gets destructive, for example, is if the kid plays on the parent's guilt to do something that's not healthy for him to do, or vice versa."

Such destructive manipulation can be considered emotional blackmail, which means using what's near and dear to someone's heart to get your way. Parents whose decisions are guided by their emotions can be easily blackmailed. And, I might say, teens don't corner the market on emotional blackmail. Adults can be quite adept at manipulating each other's hearts and those of their children, too. I want to stress that most manipulative behavior is not premeditated. The teen doesn't ask, "What can I say that will scare my mom or dad into doing things my way?" Manipulation or emotional blackmail happens to be a maladaptive form of behavior. It's something a person latches on to because it gets an immediate result in the short term. Sadly, over the long haul it costs far more than it's worth.

I'm reasonably sure that practically every parent has heard these words at least once: "You don't love me" or "I hate you." When words such as these don't get a rise, kids generally stop using them. However, taking such words to heart happens to be another matter. The teen learns to use love and affection like a master puppeteer. As Dr. Zakreski observes, "If you are prone to that type of manipulation, that's very destructive. Then you've got a very powerful kid who doesn't have the wisdom to manage that power." Parenting can be a lonely job, particularly when teens begin to spread their wings and look at you as an alien of sorts; no one likes to be rejected. But parenting can never be a popularity contest. Saying no despite the venomous words that spew from the teen's lips may make you unpopular. Generally that's only for the time being.

Parents also need to be aware of what Dr. Barkley calls "the social spark." He tells parents, "Your teen is going to say things to you and show emotion to you that could literally be looked at as a fuse. You can light that fuse and follow the interaction where it's going to go. Or you can act like an adult, not take the bait, and see it for what it is." What is the bait? The teen's effort to get his or her way. For instance, your teen cries out, "You're ruining my life. Why don't you trust me? If you don't let me go to the party, all my friends will think I'm a nerd." Knowing that your teen has had years of trouble making and keeping friends, you cave in. You abandon what you know to be good parenting principles for fear that the teen won't love you, or respect you, or approve of you. And in this case, part of you believes you may ruin his or her life. The irony is when you do cave in to emotional blackmail, the teen does lose respect for you. Over time, you may lose love for the teen because you become a victim, constantly giving in to the teen's demands. That, of course, leads to more trouble.

Teens who have become defiant may threaten many things. But the biggest social spark of all is the "I'll kill myself" threat. Teens don't always deliver this threat with words. Sometimes they make suicidal gestures. Of course, suicide threats need to be taken seriously. (See Chapter 3 for a list of warning signs and what to do.)

Dr. Barkley has this caution for parents: "If you allow a suicide threat to coerce you, you will increase the possibility of a suicide attempt." Why? It's somewhat like the boy who cried wolf. After a while, you come to realize the threat is not real, so you stop giving in. Be on guard. Dr. Barkley explains that when parents stop supporting a behavior they have supported in the past, the behavior usually gets worse for a brief period of time. He warns, "Expect the suicide gesture to escalate." Instead of ideation and casual language like "I'd be better off dead," the teen might make a halfhearted attempt. Researchers generally believe that most adolescent suicides are unintentional. They may be cries for help or desperate moves the teen makes to get his or her way.

Don't ignore suicide threats. Don't give in to the demands behind them, either. Should the teen say, "If you don't let me ____, I'm going to kill myself" (or run away, or call child welfare), hold firm on your no. Also, determine whether the threat has any teeth. Most parents know what's serious and what isn't. If you are unsure, err on the safe side and seek help.

With all manipulations and threats, the message to parents is clear. "Don't bite the bait," says Dr. Barkley emphatically.

None of the pathways to defiance exist in isolation. It seems to me a skill deficit can lead to coercive interactions. Manipulation may come from poor language ability, and anger outbursts from poor executive function ability. Clearly, no one should jump to conclusions when faced with a teen who is oppositional and defiant. Instead, great care needs to be taken to accurately identify the causes and interventions must be designed with the cause in mind. Instead of focusing on the outcome you want, spend your energy on changing the pathway. Interventions then become targeted and have a better chance of succeeding.

If you are dealing with inflexible, explosive, oppositional, defiant teen behavior, by all means stop any blaming or witch-hunting. Instead, put this thought into your head: I am not a bad parent and my teen is not a bad kid. Use that belief as the cornerstone for the rest of the interventions and skills you and your teen need.

Anger

Very often families that struggle with oppositional, aggressive, or defiant behavior experience a great deal of anger. In fact, they can become angry systems in which most dynamics and interactions are fueled by this emotion. How does this happen? Dr. Hinshaw notes that there are multiple pathways. It begins with ADHD in the child and quite possibly in other family members. As Dr. Hinshaw states, "Kids with ADHD have been hell on wheels from early ages. They require a lot more time and effort." Parental resources get tapped out. The siblings may grow resentful. Having such a tough time fitting in often hardens the kid with ADHD. Arguments arise easily under such conditions. Usually, the family members feel hurt. As Dr. Hinshaw notes, "There's just enough bad blood that's built up over the years that interactions can get ugly more quickly."

Even if families don't fall into an angry interactional style, many teens with ADHD become angry beings. Dr. Zakreski notes, "In general, adolescents whose ADHD has not been identified or who have not received help have long histories of being punished and rejected, criticized and put down, and have not done well in school. Perhaps they don't get along at home, either. They're more agitated and hurt, and often reject social convention. Anger develops as a by-product. It's a way to protect and defend yourself from further hurt."

That protective armor leads teens to embrace their anger. "It's a coverup calculated to sting you and make you back up," Dr. Zakreski says. It can be hard to reach a teen who is this angry, especially when that teen is a male. "The typical angry male adolescent is not too interested in talking about the hurt," he explains. Over time, kids with ADHD develop a "hostile attribution bias," that is, they come to see most of the people and events around them as intending to provoke them. "They present to the world with an angry, retaliatory stance," Dr. Hinshaw observes.

In addition to the anger pathway that develops from negative effects of ADHD, a small subgroup of kids with ADHD and ODD do not process certain social cues accurately. "They treat ambiguous information in a social situation as a direct indication that something aggressive is going to take place," Dr. Sergeant states. The youth who is not correctly processing social cues will likely jump the gun. He or she may react aggressively to a perceived threat when none actually exists.

According to anger-management specialist Dr. W. Michael Nelson, "These kids with a chip-on-the-shoulder attitude are waiting for somebody to come along and knock the chip off." Can the attitude be knocked off instead of the chip on the shoulder? Yes, with a lot of work.

How Bad Is It?

Emotional outbursts, whether they come in words or deeds, can be unnerving. Parents need to distinguish between provocative and dangerous behavior, whether the behavior happens to be intentional or not. "Managing Anger in Youth" is a chapter in the book *Child and Adolescent Therapy,* edited by Philip Kendall, Ph.D. In it, Dr. Nelson and coauthor Dr. A. J. Finch present a level system to help therapists guide parents about their kid's angry behavior. It is described below. The various levels help the therapist and parents to recognize the differences between anger, verbal aggression, and the different levels of physical aggression. If your teen acts aggressively, you need to be clear about how serious the problem is.

Level 1: the impatient/annoying/irritating child. Such youth control their anger. They may whine, complain, raise their voices, hold their breath, or become enraged when they don't get their way.

Level 2: the stubborn/dramatic child. The youth refuses to do what is asked or follow directions, and shows verbal aggression through swearing, name-calling, making insults, and similar behaviors. Parents may think the teen is on the verge of violence, but the teen is not. This teen expresses angry emotion verbally. As an example, Dr. Nelson refers to "a 15-year-old who takes a few steps toward his mother and calls her a bitch."

Level 3: the threatening child and the beginning of damage. Here you see more anger on a more frequent basis. The youth uses verbal aggression and may make threats to bodily injure another but doesn't act on them. He or she does some minor unintentional damage to objects, such as kicking a chair and putting a dent in a wall. This youth may be angry and combative but knows when to stop. "It should be noted that at Level 3, youngsters have never really injured any human being or living thing," Dr. Nelson clarifies.

Level 4: the "taking it up a notch" child. This youth purposely vents anger by destroying or seriously damaging inanimate objects—for instance, holes are punched in walls, objects are thrown through windows, or valuable objects are broken deliberately. The youth may threaten to hit with an object or weapon but never acts on the threat and usually retreats or storms out of the room, which shows an ability to stop short of physical violence against another. "The parents believe the child is very dangerous at this time and may become quite intimidated by him or her," Dr. Nelson states.

Level 5: the assaultive child. This youth commits acts of physical aggression that cause bodily harm to another, such as pushing, hitting, shoving, or throwing things. Parents are legitimately frightened that the teen may lose control and harm someone by violent means. "Actual physical injuries at this level are minor, and such injuries tend to be more incidental than directly intentional," Dr. Nelson maintains.

Level 6: the violent child. This youth engages in violent behavior that causes serious harm, and may use fists or weapons such as bats, sticks, stones, or worse. This youngster intends to harm. "At this stage, parents feel intimidated, hopeless, and even abused. They may seem shell-shocked or burned out. They may even feel resigned to the violence that has escalated," Dr. Nelson says. This behavior is dangerous.

Parents can usually handle the first two levels alone on a daily basis. When minor, unintentional property damage starts to happen, as in Level 3, it's advisable for parents to seek help. According to Dr. Nelson, these lower levels of aggression can be handled with problem solving, communication, behavior management, and cognitive-skills training. These have been explained in earlier chapters.

Once kids move to Level 4 aggression, where more serious damage occurs, Dr. Nelson finds that parents see their child as dangerous and in need of immediate help. He believes *it's important for parents to distinguish between behavior intended to cause serious damage and behavior that unintentionally results in serious damage.* "It's a distinction parents don't often make," he adds. With ADHD, it's an important distinction. When hyperactivity and impulsivity are present, unintentional damage happens. That's not to say that such behavior should be excused because of ADHD. Giving consequences and teaching the youngster better ways to manage anger are two different approaches Dr. Nelson uses for Levels 1 to 4.

If a youth gets to Level 5 or 6 behaviors, that's a sign of really serious trouble. At these levels, parents often feel helpless and hopeless. Says Dr. Nelson, "They don't have any control and may even feel abused by their adolescent." At this point, the family is dysfunctional. The teen's calling the shots. As Dr. Nelson points out, "Severe aggression is very much a power play about who's in charge." Parents dealing with highly aggressive teens should use professional guidance. Otherwise, they run the risk of setting a match to a highly flammable situation.

Teens who engage in violence seen at Levels 5 and 6 are very rare. I might also point out that this behavior is not considered ADHD behavior. If your situation has gotten to this point, you need to know there is hope. "It's gonna take some work, but things can get straightened out," says Dr. Nelson. Putting the parents back in charge has to be the first step.

Parents have to use harsh consequences. For instance, a therapist might advise them to strip the teen's room to the bare essentials, such as clothes and a bed. Most parents cringe at this type of suggestion. It goes against our sense of normalcy and decency. We don't want to be so tough with our kids. However, power reversals and seriously aggressive behaviors create desperate parents who may need to use tough methods until the situation improves. "Parents have to be two steps ahead of the teen," notes Dr. Nelson. That requires a lot of careful, planned-out, if-then parenting. Parents will need to anticipate problems and be ready for them.

Dr. Nelson strongly recommends that parents of moderately and seriously aggressive teens get help from a family therapist trained in using effective consequences. The therapist also needs to be comfortable taking direct-intervention approaches. Such approaches might include helping parents locate resources outside the home that can be of help. These might include asking a willing relative or neighbor to come over when things start to escalate. This new blood often interrupts the family dynamic long enough to reestablish some cooler heads.

Parents who feel hopeless may throw in the towel. Giving up doesn't work. "The adolescent has to realize the parent can do some things. If worse comes to worst, they can call the police," says Dr. Nelson. He understands that most parents feel reluctant to take such action. The next chapter covers this issue in depth. Meanwhile, if it's gotten this bad in your home, hang on to your hope. With good help, the family structure can be righted.

Once the family order has been restored, a therapist will work directly with the teen in an anger management program. The strategies therapists use fall under the heading of cognitive-behavioral interventions (CBI). The idea behind CBI and anger-management has to do with helping the teen identify the nature of his or her anger and the way he or she reacts.

Nelson and Finch recommend that therapists use this four-part approach:

1. *Assessment.* Identify the triggers.
2. *Education.* Teach about the nature of angry feelings and how aggressive behavior creates trouble.
3. *Skills acquisition phase.* Teach skills such as problem solving, assertiveness training, relaxation training, verbal self-talk, and humor.
4. *Application training.* Give the teen increasingly more problematic situations to practice the techniques.

These techniques "help the teen look at the situations with different-colored glasses," Dr. Nelson explains.

Parents may also need to wear different-colored glasses. Very often they come to view the teen as always angry. Adding some perspective, Dr. Nelson points out, "Even the most aggressive teens I see are not angry twenty-four hours a day." Anger expressed aggressively creates such an intense impression that, understandably, parents see the teen as always angry. As with teen training, Dr. Nelson coaches parents to clear up any misperceptions by identifying the three or four times a day when things fly off the handle. Anger-producing situations, or triggers, need to be identified, too, and then steps to eliminate them must follow. A lot of ADHD management requires running some type of pass interference.

Initially when intervention begins, most teens do not see themselves as the problem. They think it's the other guy's fault. The teen may be partially or totally correct. Nonetheless, the teen has to get the point that he or she needs to learn how to react in a socially appropriate way, as do all family members.

It must be said that effective anger management for people with ADHD can be hard to accomplish. Characteristically, the teens may learn the skill and use it perfectly under training conditions. Once outside the practitioner's office, however, they may forget to use the new skill because they function on automatic pilot. Researchers find that practice in the natural setting helps. Thus, parents usually need to be trained in anger-management approaches, too. Doing that goes beyond the scope of this book. My purpose here is more like quality control. It explains what a good anger-management approach for your teen would look like. From here a therapist can guide you in this approach.

INFORMATION LINK

The American Psychological Association (APA) and MTV have created a Web site for teens who are dealing with anger, either in themselves or in others. It has some excellent information, including warning signs, and some anger-management techniques.
www.helping.apa.org/warningsigns/about.html
As cited earlier, Lynn Clark's book *SOS Help for Emotions*, Parents Press, Bowling Green, KY, is another source.

Parent Anger

While teens with little self-control may pop off, parents and other adults often create a climate that aids and abets these teens to lose their cool. Flappable teens need unflappable parents, teachers, and coaches. It behooves all of us to understand anger, our relationship to it, how we use it, what it does, and how to dump it appropriately.

We may escalate anger in a million little ways. In fact, researcher Gerald Patterson has identified what he calls an "aversive chain." Basically, aversive chains occur when two people attempt to influence each other through a rapid exchange of punishing communication. Some of the communications may be verbal or nonverbal (words, sentences, tone of voice, hand gestures, facial expressions, body movements). Here is an example of an aversive chain:

Parent   *You never do a thing I ask.* (said with emphasis on each word)

Teen   You're always bugging me when I'm busy. (in a loud voice)

Parent   *Who do you think you're talking to?* (with hands on hips, clenched jaw)

Teen   What the hell are you mad at? All I said was . . . (voice edgy, rolling eyes)

Parent   *How dare you swear at me!* (finger-pointing, shouting)

Teen   You call that swearing? You're such a bitch! (body tight,
          foot stomps)
Parent   *That's it. You're grounded.* (finger-pointing, screaming,
          eyes bulging)
Teen   Screw you. (stomps out of house, slams door)

In this example, I've used sentences to make the point. In real life, rolling eyes, a clenched jaw, a slammed door, or a hand that puts a finger in your face are anger escalators that need no words. This entire chain plays out within a minute or so, and often catches us by surprise. Parents need to become aware of how situations get set off.

Have you heard this myth? "When feeling angry, it's good to get it out. You should ventilate." That's like adding oxygen to fire. It makes a bigger fire. Like stress and fear, anger marshals the body into a highly aroused state. The more we allow ourselves to feel anger, the angrier we feel. Experts agree that it's better to know the strength of your emotion and take steps to lessen the degree. Otherwise, your anger may feed on itself and you may erupt. Dr. Curry advises his clients to use a very simple method.

TRY THIS

1. *Create an imaginary thermometer. Determine the point on it when you (or the teen) lose control—the boiling point. Let's say 8 on a scale of 1 to 10. List the behaviors that signify "out of control" to you.*
2. *Identify a point on the thermometer that serves as a warning—let's say 5. List the ways you act and feel that signal trouble ahead.*
3. *Adjust your temperature downward to keep yourself under control. List the things you will do—for example, go for a walk, go to your room, practice deep muscle relaxation, give a silent signal, smile, or think of a humorous image.*

INFORMATION LINK

You might want to read these two excellent books about understanding the nature of anger and anger-management tools
written by Matthew McKay and his coauthors: *When Anger
Hurts Your Kids: A Parent's Guide,* Oakland, CA, 1989, and
When Anger Hurts, New Harbinger Publications, 1996.

Bullies and Victims

Most people consider 12-year-old Marty Prior aggressive. He believes his
behavior toward others results from how others behave toward him. For
instance, he says one boy "started stuff with me the first time I ever saw
him." Now they can't stop getting into fights. Marty acknowledges that
this situation makes his life miserable. "As soon as I fight him, he's dead,"
Marty promises in a somewhat spirited but unconvincing voice. He doesn't
have a well-thought-out plan for this fight. At first, he considered beating
the boy up at school, but a reminder about the potential consequences
changed that notion. In fact, he's reconsidered the entire idea and says a
fight could be avoided "if he stops talking stuff to me."

Is Marty a bully or a victim? He's probably a bit of both. Bullies are
generally viewed as kids who use power to oppress or harass others. They
don't always use fists or physical assaults, either. They may bully through
ridicule, teasing, threats, or property damage. Some bullies see their
actions as justified. They may also feel less anxious and more secure when
they're in control.

There are two types of bullies. "Some bullies plan their actions," says
Dr. Hinshaw. "Others do not." Provocative bullies deliberately aggress
toward others. They tend to be nonemotional and controlled.

Teens with ADHD mainly fall into the type of bully referred to as
reactive. They don't plan their actions. Marty fits this profile. Reactive
bullies are aggressive and emotional, feel threatened a lot, and believe, as
Marty does, that the aggression is justified. "It's one crisis after another for

kids with ADHD. There's so much retaliation. They're always overreacting and explosive," notes Dr. Hinshaw.

Like many other aggressive and angry behaviors, bullies learn how to bully. Though some people may be genetically predisposed toward aggression, bullying is not a "skill" they're born with. In his book *The Lost Boys*, Dr. Garbarino notes that some bullies develop this habit when their naturally aggressive temperaments are inadvertently rewarded by kids who give in to them, and by adults who ignore or encourage their behavior.

Many also interpret facial expressions and bodily movements as aggressive when they are not. Some of these kids are really quite fearful. They develop extremely poor coping skills and pick up a lot of negative baggage. They actually wind up the victims of their own troubles. Of course, it's hard to see an aggressive kid as a victim. As Dr. Hinshaw notes, "Everybody gets teased and hammered, but a lot of kids seem like they have a Teflon coating. Kids with ADHD probably get very emotional. They are both too submissive, which makes them a real target for victimization, and an aggressor."

The shape of bullying tends to change over time. Dr. George Batsche writes that physical bullying decreases with age and grade. However, verbal abuse or aggression and property violations do not change as time goes by. As mentioned in an earlier chapter, girls with ADHD engage in relational aggression, which is indirect. The female may bully one friend into not speaking to another, or tell a certain boy that a girl likes him, or tell everybody that so-and-so had sex with someone.

Victims, too, tend to fall into two basic profiles. Passive victims appear anxious, insecure, and unable to defend themselves, and do not seem to provoke their attackers. They tend to have few, if any, friends at school. Lack of friends may actually set them up to be picked on, since the bully knows no one will come to the rescue. Thus, these kids make easy prey. "Bullies feed on the misery and torment of a passive kid," says Dr. Zakreski. Teens with the inattentive form of the disorder are more likely to fit the passive-type victim profile.

Proactive victims, on the contrary, can be hot-tempered, restless, anxious, and reactive. Researchers have noted that some aggressive kids who are picked on by older bullies turn on younger kids and bully them—often with serious aggression. If your teen has suddenly taken to bullying behavior, you might want to determine if that's a reaction to being bullied. In any case, find out what's causing this behavior.

Parents also need to be aware that many siblings feel bullied by their brothers or sisters with ADHD. They may also mistrust or lose confidence in their parents, believing that their moms and dads do not protect them. This idea may happen in part because often parents will stifle the more easily controlled sibling as a way of de-escalating conflict. Of course, this action makes the sibling feel less supported.

Siblings of those with ADHD need to be taught skills to de-escalate conflict, such as problem solving, assertiveness training, and communication tools. However, they also need parents to intervene in any hostile or aggressive act. Any physical violence on either sibling's part must be dealt with seriously, through consequences given immediately. If sibling conflict continues despite efforts to stop it, get help.

Dealing with Bullies and Victims

Outside the home and before adolescence, most bullying incidents happen around school. I was shocked to learn about the level of violence that goes on in boys' locker rooms during gym and after-school sports. With increasing independence and a social arena that includes malls, parties, sporting events, concerts, and similar venues, it becomes much harder for a parent or educator to intervene. Parents have to watch for the signs of both victimization and bullying, described earlier.

In this book, I can't go into the systemic change that needs to happen to ease the bully/victim situation. Suffice it to say that parents, schools, and other institutions need to follow a few basic guidelines.

For bullies:

- No physical discipline, humiliation, or exclusion. Remember that most bullies come from a wounded place. More wounds make more aggression.
- Give five times more praise than negative feedback.
- Model socially appropriate behavior. (Dr. Hinshaw tells us, "Kids with ADHD need practice, practice, practice reading social cues and approaching social situations without a chip on

their shoulder.") The most effective programs train parents along with their kids in social skills and anger management. This way they practice in the natural setting.

- Be clear that no bullying behavior is acceptable.

For victims:

- Don't ignore the problem. It won't go away.
- Teach the youth to say, "Stop bothering me," and then to walk away.
- Teach positive social skills.
- Give far more positive feedback.
- Help them to see their strengths.
- Come to their aid.

When Law-Enforcement Assistance Is Needed

If a teen is being bullied, Lieutenant Kristie Etue, a section commander for the Michigan State Police in the Prevention Services Section, advises the parents to first bring the issue up with the school principal. However, "if the bully is threatening the kid with great bodily harm, then you have to get the police involved," she emphasizes. Many schools have liaison officers who play a vital role. As Lt. Etue points out, law-enforcement personnel do not tolerate name-calling and threats. If a kid goes to them for help, the law-enforcement officer will in all likelihood speak to the bully. They are trained to first ask the bully if the allegation is true. Then they advise the kid to knock it off or else. That usually works.

Teens, of course, often don't ask adults, especially teachers or lunch aides, for help, for fear that other students may label them as a "nark" or tattletale. With my middle school students, I found that when I made an observation such as "You seem a little on edge when Ralph is around" and follow it with a direct question such as "Is there a problem between the two of you?" generally the student spills his or her concerns. I've also seen that most of these early adolescents welcome the opportunity for adult intervention to get them off the hook. High school students don't tend to be as forthcoming with their classroom teachers. Here, guidance counselors and student assistance coordinators can help. Also, teachers hear a lot in the halls and during classes. They can be lifesavers for both the threatened and the threatening kid. If you suspect your teen is in some sort of bully trouble, you might enlist the aid of a sympathetic teacher or counselor to help your son or daughter. School-based peer mediation programs can be very helpful here, too.

Parents of teens with ADHD also need to listen if the teen complains about being harassed. Other teens may not be the only problem. Some teachers and coaches do harass these teens. When talking about being harassed, some teens speak in code. For example, the teen might say, "I hate Harold. He's a real jerk. I'd like to beat the heck out of him." First translation—"Harold's been harassing me. I'm gonna have to beat him up to get him to stop." Second translation—"Do something to help me."

If you suspect code talk, speak directly to your teen. Calmly ask if there is a problem. Ask what you can do. Be prepared for your teen to answer, "Nothing," or "I can handle it myself." Ask the teen to tell you his or her plan. Then offer some guiding suggestions along with reminders of how aggression will come back to haunt him or her. Think prevention and take these problems seriously. Teens, whether they are bullies or victims, need to feel safe in order to thrive.

CHAPTER NINE

Tough Calls

A small percentage of teens become out of control to the extent that courts view them as children in need of supervision. Sometimes when teens get this out of control, parents have to take severe steps. This chapter explains the pros and cons of various intensive interventions. These intensive interventions, which range from the police and the courts to substance abuse rehabs and residential treatment centers, are among the toughest decisions parents will ever have to make. Of course, sometimes parents receive a call from the authorities when their teen gets in trouble, and then there are few other options. Fortunately, few of you will need the information in this chapter, but for those who do or for those who know somebody who could use it, the information will be helpful. No situation is hopeless.

When Caroline Phelps gave birth to her son, she never dreamed that one day she would have to remove him from the home because he would be that defiant and out of control. From his earliest days, Nat has been aggressive, explosive, and almost impossible for Caroline to handle.

According to Caroline, Nat's father, an alcoholic and drug addict, seldom supported her efforts to help Nat. This lack of support, coupled with the constant barrage of verbal abuse the father spewed at Caroline, taught Nat that he didn't need to listen to his mother or treat her with respect. Though Caroline brought a huge heart and the best of intentions to the parenting table, she also had some problems. In addition, she had few skills to help her raise a son as difficult as Nat. All things considered, the groundwork had been laid early on for the severe defiance that came later.

The problems have taken their toll. "A child like this," she says in a lifeless voice, "he drains you. You are always on edge. You hear an ambulance or a cop car, you just think of him automatically. You think the worst all the time." Nat has a lot of comorbid problems: oppositional defiant disorder, conduct disorder, severe anger-management difficulties, and a substance-use problem that looks as though it may lead to addiction.

Nat began stealing his dad's pot in ninth grade. His smoking coincided with his refusal to take medication any longer. The following year his father was diagnosed with a brain tumor and died within a matter of months. After her husband's death, Caroline tried to take more control and to set limits. Nat flew into rages. He'd punch the nearest wall or throw objects. He'd follow his mother from room to room and constantly badger her, trying to get her to give in to his demands. With an expressionless voice, Caroline says, "It made me very fearful."

Matters came to a head the night she wouldn't let her son have the keys to his truck. He chased her around the house, cornered her a few times, and as she jumped in the car to get away, he almost closed her arm in the door. Afraid to return home, Caroline decided she had to seek help from the police. She describes this experience as "a terrifying, horrible thing to go through. You feel like such a victim, and it's just like experiencing your child dying." Calling the police on a child is among the most traumatizing experiences a parent can have.

Caroline had to press charges. Nat was taken to a juvenile judge, who sentenced him to a thirty-day program designed to encourage teens to change their belligerent, defiant ways. He lived with a foster family at night. During the day he went to a special family crisis center for counseling and such. When Nat came home, he promised to be different. He signed himself back into school after having dropped out months earlier. But within six months, and for much the same behavior, he again stood before a judge who sentenced him to thirty days in the youth detention center, a lockup facility.

"It just kills you as a parent to see your son in handcuffs. I brought this child into the world and gave him such love and support. I was there for him his entire life," she says, still feeling the traumatic aftermath of the hellish situation.

While Nat was in the detention center, Caroline had to face another tough decision. It became clear to everybody that Nat couldn't return home without first attending some type of long-term intervention program. She sent him to a residential treatment center that specializes in youth with severe emotional and behavioral difficulties. Though he complained a lot, he did well there. Unfortunately, he stayed only five out of the twelve recommended months, for a combination of reasons. The monthly cost was very high, and this worried Caroline. On top of that Nat kept begging to come home. Every opportunity he could, he told her he wasn't learning anything. Despite recommendations, home he came. It didn't take long for the circus to resume. Now that he's 18, Mom's wrestling with the decision to kick him out, which is basically a non-solution. Nat has no job skills and no resources to live independently.

Dr. Yellen refers to the type of behavior that we see in Nat as "random emotional terrorism." "Of course," he says, "it tears the parents up. One day they've got this 15-year-old sweetheart who is sorry for everything he or she has done and is leaning against Mom's chest, saying, 'I'm sorry. You're the only one who's stood by me.' Then the next day there's the explosion and the pot that flies across the kitchen. Now the kid says, 'I hate you.' There's no predictability. And it's actually worse in that situation because the parents keep saying, 'Okay. There's hope. See? He was this way yesterday, so he doesn't need to go anywhere. We just need to straighten this out.'

"Well," Dr. Yellen continues, "a week turns into a month, a month turns into a year. And the cycle of this random emotional terrorism continues. It doesn't get any better. The parents become too intimidated to take stronger action." That's a terrible state to get in.

Seriously aggressive teens, regardless of how they got that way, often need intensive treatment and multiple therapies. The toughest calls parents have to make are the ones like Caroline Phelps made.

At a Loss

Tough calls have to do with going outside the home and the weekly visit to the therapist. Caroline Phelps used just about every tough treatment that was readily available: the police, the juvenile justice system (including courts and probation), and a private placement in a residential treatment facility. She might have tried to get Nat admitted as a psychiatric patient in a hospital as Nat had obvious mental health issues. However, it's doubtful that she would have had success.

Psych admissions are usually granted only to those individuals who present an immediate danger to others or to themselves. Even for those who are admitted, once the threat passes, usually the individual is sent back to the home, whether or not the teen or the family has made any important changes. The teen and the parents are referred to outpatient services such as counseling. Many families of teens this problematic have already tried this approach. Drug and alcohol facilities tend to be a little easier to get into. Still, even those are hard pressed to give long-term treatment.

Residential treatment facilities, such as the one Caroline's son ultimately wound up in, fall under the category of mental health placements. Funding for these barely exists. Quite often these are private placements, which most parents can't afford on their own.

I don't want to paint a bleak picture here, because if you have a tough call to make, you need to feel there's hope. There is, but you have to hold on to it as you go through the struggle. In all candor, I tell you that I am frightened by the lack of prevention and treatment services for teens in trouble. When a parent turns to a system for help, if that system does not respond appropriately, the teen actually becomes even more empowered. He or she learns that the parents have few alternatives. Unfortunately, these really tough teens don't have foresight. When they get the power, they run with it until they hit a brick wall, which too often may be a detention center or jail. Parents considering tough calls would be wise to find out in advance what real support the system can and cannot provide.

How does a parent know when to make a tough call? I wish I could give a clear-cut answer. None exists. Teens who become what the courts would deem "persons in need of supervision" present one of the toughest challenges for parents. No decision the parent makes comes with a guaranteed result.

Still, parents can tell if the teen's behavior has reached a point where tough calls may have to be made. Dr. Barkley says, "When you try to set five basic rules for living in your house, and your teen repeatedly violates those rules, then that is probably an indication that you are in need of intensive help. That help may come through a residential school, or a psychiatric program, or a group home for delinquents, or some assistance from the juvenile justice system."

The five rules he cites are:

1. You will not break any laws.
2. You will not threaten anybody.
3. You will not destroy property in this house intentionally—as in fits of anger.
4. You will obey curfews when we apply them to you.
5. If you are grounded, you will not leave the house.

When a teen cannot follow these bare-bones rules, parents often feel like the worst failures. Quitting may seem to be their only option. It's not. As Dr. Barkley says, "The parent can move into a higher level of intensity of intervention. Bring other people into the treatment team as opposed to saying, 'I give up.'" There is hope and help to be had.

If the teen in your life has become this defiant, please don't make decisions without outside guidance from a respected professional, such as a family therapist. Friends and relatives are great for moral support, as are support groups. But these tough calls require objectivity and expertise from those who are most familiar with working these systems. You will need to know which system you are seeking support from and why it seems to be the best choice. Notice the word *choice*. Unless your teen gets arrested and all decisions rest with a judge, you have choices. You want your actions to be planned and well informed. As Dr. Nelson states, "Sep-

---

✐ INFORMATION LINK

Tough Love is a nonprofit organization that provides information and a support network for parents of tough teens. Their Web site is www.toughlove.org.

Families Anonymous, www.familiesanonymous.org, helps parents of teens with substance-abuse problems.

arating the child and the parent is almost taking a surgical approach. It should be done only in severe cases and with a lot of thought."

The following sections take you through each system and the intervention possibilities. Sometimes parents have to make a selection based on finances. Other times, the interventions don't get the desired result, so parents have to try other measures. About the choices that sometimes have to be made, Dr. Jensen says, "We'll do whatever is medically indicated. But understand that sometimes surgery draws blood, and surgery can be harmful in itself."

Parents of tough teens often shut down and lose social support. Networking with other parents in similar situations can be a lifeline.

The Tough Options

The Juvenile Justice System

As a last resort, therapists often advise parents to seek help from the police or juvenile justice authorities, especially under these two circumstances:

1. When the teen's actions threaten the safety of persons in the home. Such actions could involve actual physical contact or rages that destroy property.
2. When the teen, despite all efforts from parents and the mental health professionals, refuses to follow the bare minimum rules.

When the police are called, a few different scenarios can happen. The police determine if the situation is dangerous and if there are legal violations. "Typically it's dangerousness with a teenager," says Dr. Barkley. The police may refer parents to the local social services agency. If it's a matter of safety, they may take the teen into protective custody. "That process will take time. It's not intended to be an emergency service," Dr. Barkley explains. Protective custody means the teen goes to the county juvenile authorities for evaluation—usually done in first-time situations. On the second visit, the teen may be ordered into a detention center or another court program. That's what happened with Nat.

The other option police have is to get the teen to the nearest medical center that provides urgent psychiatric care for an evaluation, which often includes a drug and alcohol screening. They may tell the parents to take the teen, or they may do the transport. "This process may mean being kept overnight in the emergency room. They may even start the teen on a trial of medication," explains Dr. Barkley, who adds, "This intervention is not going to be effective in the long term. It's meant to contain emergencies only."

Here's where a problem arises. If the hospital does not admit the teen until he or she is stabilized, in most situations the teen is released back into the custody of the parents. At that point the parents may be advised to seek outpatient help from a therapist (which the parents may have already done) or from a drug and alcohol counselor, should that be the problem, or to contact the juvenile authorities. That usually puts the parents back where they started, only on a faster track to the juvenile justice system.

Parents need to know that when they contact the court system for help with a troubled teen, they've basically entered into a crapshoot. Most public corrections systems are not designed to handle youth with these types of behavioral and emotional issues. While the system may promise help, more often than not neither the teen nor the parents get the help they need.

Dr. Sheri Meisel, associate director of the National Center of Education, Disability and Juvenile Justice (EDJJ), bemoans the general lack of appropriate treatment services in the community for troubled kids. "The juvenile justice system is becoming much more of a catch-all for kids with mental health issues who do have intensive needs but who do not need that type of setting. It's the only game in town because it's funded," she notes. Dr. Meisel's data show that even though juvenile delinquency rates in this country are decreasing, the incarceration rate is increasing, mainly because other systems such as schools, mental health agencies, and social service agencies are not providing necessary services.

Lili Frank Garfinkel, also an associate director at EDJJ, advises parents and teens who need help from social services agencies for mental health issues not to seek it through the courts. As she explains, "If I thought the kids could get adequate mental health services through a juvenile justice system, I would endorse it." She doesn't endorse it because there's no guarantee. As both Dr. Meisel and Ms. Garfinkel point out, the juvenile justice system has a bias toward punishment and not rehabilitation. "It should be the agency of last resort for kids who truly need secure confinement," says Dr. Meisel.

Parents may be told that the system can help their troubled teen, but as Ms. Garfinkel knows from her experience as a juvenile advocate, "There are so many ifs and maybes." For instance, who's doing the evaluations? Is the assessment comprehensive? Is the family involved? What about the school's input? Understandably, parents may feel that this system will offer some promise for their teens, especially when they find themselves in a crisis situation feeling hopeless and helpless. As Dr. Meisel explains, "The parent is told that this is a situation where their child will be supervised, will have mental health services, and will be going to school every day." That sounds like the answer to a prayer. As Dr. Meisel says, "I don't envy the parent who has to make that very critical decision. The local juvenile correctional facility probably holds as many or more kids with mental health problems than are served through the mental health and public school systems. That was not what juvenile justice was structured to do."

No one is saying that wrong behavior should be excused or ignored. And some teens do need supervision that goes beyond what a parent can provide. Before a parent seeks help through the courts, he or she needs to know whether the system can truly rehabilitate or if it's a punishment-driven model. It may also be a good idea for parents to talk candidly with their local juvenile authorities before a crisis occurs. Find out what help they may be, and what help might be found outside the courts. There are other alternatives, as you will read. Have a plan—just in case.

When a Parent Approaches the System

Parents who have "children or youth in need of supervision" (that's a juvenile justice system term) need to know how this system operates. Procedures and laws vary from state to state, so parents must find out the specifics for where they live. As explained by Judge Gerald Rouse, past president of the National Council of Juvenile and Family Court Judges, here's what typically happens when a parent approaches the juvenile system for help with a minor in need of supervision, as was the case with Caroline Phelps. "First," he says, "the parents would contact their local human service agency or its equivalent to get some advice. Then, the parents would contact whoever has the authority to file a juvenile petition." That may be a family court crisis center, a county social worker, the local police, or, in some states, the school district.

Once a petition is filed, many states automatically appoint a lawyer, or guardian ad litem, who represents the youth. "I do that because the child's interests and the parent's interests may be at odds, so you want a third party who is going to look at the child's best interests," Judge Rouse explains. Representing the child's best interests does not necessarily mean advocating what the child wants. The guardian is supposed to gather information, give advice to the youth, and make a report to the court. Depending on a given state's law, the youth has a right to tell the judge that he or she does not like what the guardian has to say and request his or her own lawyer. Then the judge appoints a lawyer for the youth.

In situations where the parent approaches the court either because the youth needs supervision or because the youth may have committed a legal violation against the parents, the parents are considered parties to the action in most states. Thus, in some states they don't have a right to a lawyer to appear in court for them. Parents can get information about their rights by consulting with an attorney, or through a local law school that has a practice clinic, or by contacting the state bar association for references. They can also read the juvenile statutes.

Once a petition is filed, that youth is entitled to a hearing, and in some cases a jury trial. Judge Rouse says, "What I see a lot is the kid who's out of control and punches Mom. Mom goes to the county attorney, who then files an assault charge in juvenile court." At the hearing, the juvenile has a right to have an attorney, the right to remain silent about the issue, the right to testify, and the right to confront witnesses who testify against him or her. Generally, Judge Rouse says, most states require a standard of proof that's beyond reasonable doubt. Most courts seek a lot of parental input when they gather information and when they make a ruling.

After reading about how this process generally works, if it seems to you that parents have little or no control once the courts get involved, you are correct. That's the problem with going to the courts. It's not a team approach. Matters are taken out of parental hands. According to Judge Rouse, "Usually a juvenile court judge has a lot of options: group homes, the family home under intensive supervised probation, which means under bracelet or other conditions [mainly for law violators], foster homes, therapeutic foster homes, and residential treatment centers such as a ranch or a 'boot camp.' The options progress into what would in essence be a juvenile locked facility, usually for the most habitual and violent offenders." The point is, parents may have no say in the placement. Some of the court's alternatives may be a poor match for the youth's needs.

Furthermore, some of these options do not address the needs of the whole family. It's ridiculous to think that just sending the teen away solves the problem. When the teen returns home, chances are he or she returns to the same family system problems and dynamics. The teen may have a few more skills but usually not enough to sustain a permanent change.

Judge Rouse strongly believes that all judges need to know a lot about the institutions where they send kids. That includes knowing what the institution can and can't do, including providing for the unique needs of a youth with a disability. Juvenile justice is supposed to be a model that focuses on rehabilitation. But with disabilities, he finds, more than rehab is needed. For instance, does the facility properly monitor and dispense medication? Also, does the facility have room? Judges often find that the programs they want to use (because they seem the best match for the youth) have long waiting lists.

The ideal system of matching teens to the program just right for them that Judge Rouse espouses is a "best of all worlds" system. Juvenile justice systems often fall short of the ideal. Before you go to the juvenile authorities, know the other available alternatives. For instance, if Caroline Phelps had known about the residential school where she ultimately sent her son, she could have skipped the entire juvenile justice loop and gone directly to the program that suited his needs.

Regarding Teens of Legal Age

As most parents of teens with troubles know, age 18 doesn't bring any magic changes in behavior. It does, however, have a huge impact on considering help from the law as an option. An 18-year-old cannot be forced into treatment by a parent. A call to the police that results in charges means a court appearance and the possibility of a record. That seems to leave no alternative other than to kick the teen out.

"I don't often advise parents to throw the kid out at 18," says Dr. Robin. He will do so in cases where the teen will not—no way, no how—adhere to the five minimum basic rules on page 194. However, he finds more often than not that when parents expect just those minimum standards and nothing else, the youths don't cross that line. "The parents have to reconcile themselves to the idea that right now this is the best they can hope for, and that they have to try to find islands of strength and focus on any positives," he counsels.

If the Teen Gets in Trouble with the Law

Teens and young adults with ADHD do not have to be defiant and out of control to get in trouble with the law. It's commonly known that teens with disabilities wind up in the justice system much more often than teens who do not have disabilities. This disorder plus its related disorders definitely adds risk. Poor attention to details, acting without thinking things through, poor problem-solving abilities, being mouthy to authority figures, speeding, poor mood regulation, weak anger-management skills, hanging with others who have poor self-esteem—these set up the teen for potential trouble. Other risk factors include family problems, poor parental supervision, poor school performance, the wrong peer group, and involvement with drugs and alcohol.

How schools deal with behavior problems is another area of major concern these days. Schools often refer difficult-to-serve youth with attention problems and other emotional mental health problems to the police. As Dr. Meisel states, "There is a lack of ownership in the public school system to follow through and be responsive to that child within the system itself. There's no disincentive for them to refer disciplinary issues to the police."

If a teen winds up in the police station, parents need to know what to do. First of all, be courteous to the officers. Parents must listen carefully to what the police say about why they have detained or apprehended the teen. Some parents get angry and may verbally (or even physically) attack either the teen or the police. It's important to stay in emotional control.

Attorney Janice Miller advises parents to be careful about what they say to the police. Some parents, in an attempt to be cooperative, may be inclined to tell the police more information than they need to know. Though many juvenile authorities want to help the teen, their job is to get information. The parent's job is to protect and advocate for the teen. Ms. Miller advises parents to get an attorney immediately, because once the police have been notified that an attorney is on the case, the questioning stops. It may not be necessary to get an attorney in circumstances where no charges are being filed and the teen is being remanded to the parent's custody to seek further help.

Often the local juvenile authorities can be helpful to parents of troubled teens. Still, it helps to understand the role of the law-enforcement personnel and their perspective. Lt. Kristie Etue of the Michigan State Police Prevention Services Program explains, "Just having a learning disability does not provide children with an excuse to go steal or hurt somebody else. Police deal with the letter of the law. That's pretty black-and-white." Thus, if a youth or young adult breaks the law, the police have to apprehend or arrest him. Minors get apprehended. Young adults age 18 or over get arrested.

"Our job requires us to enforce the law," says Lt. Etue. However, in her state, police can divert a minor if it's the first offense, which basically means the youth is turned over to his or her parents with the understanding that the parents will get the help the teen needs. "We always looks at juveniles as a work in progress, particularly if they do something based on their age," says Lt. Etue, and she adds, "We need to recognize that some kids really need help."

When Dealing with the Courts

Judge Rouse offers the following suggestions for parents whose teens have to go before a judge:

1. Get legal counsel as soon as possible. The judge suggests parents use an attorney knowledgeable about children with disabilities, especially those who represent parents and children going through conflicts with the school district regarding special education.
2. Notify the intake officer about the teen's disability and any medications he or she takes. When a teen is apprehended or

arrested, the police determine whether or not that teen receives a warning or is released. If they decide to keep the juvenile, then the teen is taken to a detention facility; a petition is filed, and the teen sees the judge, usually within twenty-four hours. On weekends, the judge often speaks to the intake officer and parents by phone to determine if the youth needs to be kept. Parents should give the intake officer and the judge as much information as possible about their teen's special needs.

3. Work with the teen's court advocate or yours to document mental health issues, including substance-abuse issues or unaddressed special education needs, so that the courts can make the appropriate rulings. "Make sure you keep your records," says Judge Rouse, "but bring copies of documents—if they've been to doctors, had past hospitalizations, that sort of circumstance. Those are great things to provide because that gives the court system an idea of whether they are going to need further evaluation. They will know what to look for."

4. Supply the court with school records, including those concerning unaddressed special education needs; if the teen has been identified as a special education student by the school district, supply the court with a copy of any relevant documentation, including any IEP, that is, Individual Educational Plan. (See Chapter 11 for more information about IEPs.)

5. Make your concerns known to the court if you disagree with the plan put forth at the ruling, especially if the ruling is something that's already been tried and failed. Parents cannot speak directly to the judge outside the court. However, they can provide him or her with written communication that gets entered into the record.

6. Be respectful and don't be emotional unless emotion is called for. "The place where we don't have a democracy is in court, because the court is an instrument of the government that is set up to do a certain thing, and that is to respect people's rights," says Judge Rouse. Most judges understand that people are upset when they are in court. However, the judges have a process they

must follow. Thus, if anyone disrupts that process, they've got to be removed or sanctioned by the court.

7. Advise the teen to be respectful in both appearance as well as behavior.

Parents need to understand that many judges have very little time to actually hear a case. Also, many judges have little knowledge about mental health issues. They rely on the public defenders, probation officers, and court social workers to give them a clear picture of the youth before them. As a parent, you want to help the judge in any way you can. So be calm and reasonable. Show that you are a thoughtful individual. Supply the judge with as much information as possible to help him or her make the best possible ruling for your teen. While there's no guarantee, it's worth the shot.

A Matter of Substance

Very often teens who wind up in trouble with the law are involved with drugs and alcohol. In fact, as Ms. Garfinkel reports, "Over half the crimes committed that result in a teen being incarcerated occur while the teen is under the influence." That's bothersome because, as Dr. Meisel notes, "Too often the youngster who is caught up in this delinquency system because of substance-abuse issues will then be incarcerated for those issues and not receive treatment."

Not all teens who use drugs and alcohol wind up in legal trouble. However, when a teen's behavior becomes very problematic, that's a reason to suspect substance use or abuse. Many people draw a distinction between alcohol and drugs, the idea being if someone is drinking and not taking drugs, then it's not that bad. Alcohol is a drug. And, according to one substance-abuse Web site, it's the number one drug problem in our country.

If your teen has a problem that's affecting his or her life, it doesn't matter whether the substance is a drug or a drink. Either one takes the youth and his family to the same miserable place. Parents need to keep their eyes wide open on this issue. If you detect a problem, talk openly and candidly with your adolescent about his or her substance use, but not while the teen is under the influence. Go to the emergency room if you suspect an overdose or alcohol poisoning. Don't accept rationalizations such as "Everyone does this." Understand that the more the teen resists, the greater the likelihood that substances have become very important to him or her. If you think your teen has a problem, chances are you are correct. Talk less. Take action. So what do you do?

There are a number of places you can call for more information—for instance, a drug hotline, the local hospital, a school counselor, Alcoholics Anonymous, Narcotics Anonymous, Al-Anon, your family physician, or a counselor that specializes in substance-abuse problems. Your teen will need an assessment to determine the extent of the problem and the appropriate treatment approach. A professional will make this determination.

A range of treatment options exists. The following information on the types of programs came from the Prairie Center for Substance Abuse Web site.

Outpatient Counseling Centers—treatment programs that provide planned and structured individual, group, and/or family counseling for abusers. This type of program allows people to work or attend school while recovering and learning to live drug-free. Some programs require only a few hours of counseling a week, while others are more comprehensive, with attendance required seven days a week.

Residential Centers—supervised, twenty-four-hour programs where clients live in a professionally staffed facility with others in recovery. This modality is appropriate for clients who need a highly structured, secure environment to resist substance abuse. These treatment facilities provide assessment, diagnosis, and comprehensive treatment for clients. The period of treatment in this environment varies and may last anywhere from thirty days to a year.

Therapeutic Communities—full-time, residential, drug-free treatment programs that are highly organized and use peer support, confrontation, counseling, and residential jobs to rehabilitate clients. This type of treatment lasts longer than other modalities, from six months to over a year. It emphasizes self-help and often uses recovering addicts as staff counselors.

Inpatient Centers—programs usually last three to five weeks, are generally located in a hospital, and provide a structured, supportive environment.

Methadone Maintenance Centers—outpatient programs that offer treatment for dependence on opiates (usually heroin), in which addicts take oral doses of a synthetic opiate called methadone. Methadone is administered once a day, and by eliminating the craving for heroin, it permits physiological stabilization without withdrawal symptoms in order to make rehabilitation easier. It also frees the clients' energy and attention to address personal problems and behavior related to their addiction. Referrals for treatment and vocational training or rehabilitation are available.

Halfway Houses—peer group–oriented, residential treatment facilities aimed at helping clients gradually adjust to independent living in the community. They provide food, shelter, and supportive services, including vocational, recreational, and social services, in a supportive, drug-free environment. People generally stay in halfway houses less than ninety days.

Many parents find that getting treatment is almost harder than facing the problem, particularly because of insurance practices. Make sure you know what your insurance policy covers, especially if admission to an intensive treatment center is in order. Some policies cover only hospitalizations for certain types of mental health problems so the admitting diagnosis can be critical for reimbursement. Length of stay is often an issue, too.

Unfortunately, insurance companies have a lot of input into how thorough the evaluation is and how extensive the treatment is. The parent in search of inpatient treatment will likely hear the words "medically necessary" over and over. So, even if you get your teen into a standard twenty-eight-day program, you may find that your teen is released sooner because the teen's problem no longer meets the insurer's definition of "medically necessary." You can take a proactive approach with your insurance company and insist on any benefits due your teen. It may not be a bad idea to tell them you would like a letter stating that they will assume full responsibility should anything happen to your teen due to an early release against professional advice. They won't write the letter, but you may see a change of decision.

At world-renowned Hazelden, Dr. Montgomery says, the facility is frequently full and has a waiting list. That's true for other places as well. Though Hazelden, like many places, will take a teen right away if it's a really critical situation, parents need to be aware that they may reach a breaking point and see the situation as dire, whereas the facility may feel the teen can wait for a bed to become available and use outpatient help in the interim. The wait can range from a day or two to a week or so.

In determining where to send your teen, Dr. Montgomery advises parents to look for programs that have licensed staff who do the jobs for which they are licensed. Of course, the staff should include chemical-dependency specialists. It also should have a psychiatrist well versed in adolescent and dual disorders.

Parents should understand that no teen sets out to become dependent or addicted. If you have to make this tough call, make it. If you don't know how to pay for the help, ask questions. Call community mental health centers, local charities, or places of worship. Treatment centers run into parents with this predicament every day. Call them and ask for guidance. Persistence pays off as the following anecdote shows.

"I had a lot of problems with drugs and lying," 17-year-old Jesse Olmstead readily admits. His first marijuana experience was in fourth grade. He didn't smoke pot again until sixth grade, at which time he started more-than-occasional use. Though it gave him a headache, he persisted. "You try to look and act older at that young age," he explains. Jesse's playing grown-up led him to be sexually active early on.

In ninth grade, he and his best friend went to a girl's house to smoke pot. The details of Jesse's story get a little sketchy here, but it seems her father caught the three of them in bed and threatened to press rape charges against the boys. Jesse hadn't raped the girl and was able to explain that to her father the following day.

Heavy pot smoking brought him many other troubles, for instance at school. "I used to go to school and tell myself I would go to every class. In first period if someone asked me to go smoke a joint, I'd go. Then I wouldn't go to class." He missed many days. Jesse's parents knew he had a problem and tried to convince him to go to rehab. But Jesse told them, "No, I don't need it." So they wouldn't allow him to get his driver's license until his school grades improved and he could pass a drug test. "I couldn't do both," he says. Little did his parents know that he drove anyway.

One day he took his friend's car and got into an accident with a school bus. "The bus driver said we had to call the police. I went back to the car to get my stuff. Then I just took off because I didn't have a license and I was scared." After a while he returned to the school to pick up his friend and tell him what happened. The police stopped him on the way. Naturally, he was arrested. His parents asked the police to hold him for the day, which they did. When his parents picked up Jesse, he told them, "Put me in outpatient treatment," but his parents had made other plans. They felt Jesse needed a long-term intervention. So far, that placement has worked out quite well.

As Jesse talks about his preplacement days, he speaks in a barely audible voice. But when asked what he would tell parents of kids like him, he's loud and clear. "Never give up on your kids," he says without a moment's hesitation. "When my parents sent me away, there was nothing else they could do. They had tried everything. Don't wait until it's too late."

Residential Placements

Jesse's parents did not send him to a rehab that specializes in substance-abuse issues. Instead, they opted for an out-of-home placement in a highly structured, supervised environment to help their son learn how to control his behavior. Jesse learned a lot more: "I used to hide what I had to say, but the staff here showed me that I don't have to be afraid."

Most of the kids who wind up in residential placements are headed down the juvenile justice path or have already been there. Though to outsiders it may seem like a relief when a parent can turn over a seriously disruptive teen into someone else's hands, it's not.

Jay Hatch, of Sorenson's Ranch School, says, "I see how hard it is when parents come in and leave their kids—the tears they shed, because they love this child so much and they want him or her to succeed and be happy and healthy. It takes a great commitment and a great love to actually place a student in a residential center where he or she can get help."

There are many residential schools and treatment centers for emotionally and behaviorally disruptive youth. Program approaches vary. Most are expensive. There are no guarantees that the youth will transform into a totally changed, well-behaved young man or young woman. Those centers with good school programs usually help the teen receive an education.

If one of the tough calls you have to make is to place your teen in a residential school or treatment center, here are some thoughts to consider. Teens, even troubled ones, are individuals. No program is good for all teens. The teen's needs must be matched to the program the facility has to offer. Even if you are not sure you will go down this road, it's better to have a plan than to wait for a crisis. Seek guidance from a counselor or an educational consultant to select some possible placements. Once you have a list of options, visit the places if at all possible. Plan to spend a day there. Talk to staff. Talk to residents. Call parents whose teens are there and who have been there. Ask what they think of the program. It may also be helpful to speak with teens who have finished the program and returned home.

Find out about the counseling services. Is there a clinical team? What types of counseling services are offered? Do they have a licensed psychiatrist either on staff or as a consultant? Is the facility equipped to handle teens with multiple needs? Regarding counseling, it should be noted that many teens who get to these types of programs have not been responsive to talk therapy approaches. Usually teens who get in trouble this deep benefit from a very structured cognitive-behavioral approach, plus some peer-group work and some one-to-one therapy.

Education is also a main consideration. For long-term programs, make sure the facility has an accredited school. Find out what types of courses they have and whether or not those course credits are transferable. Speak to the staff member in charge of the school. Hard as it is to believe, a good number of teens with these severe problems do go on to college or vocational training schools once they get back on track. Find out if the facility has vocational classes as well as academic ones.

What type of aftercare program does the facility have? What does it do to help restore the parent-teen relationship? Do the parents get any training in how to manage the teen when he or she does come home? Generally, programs provide some coaching, but often the parents get this type of help from a local professional. The main point here is that parents also have to make changes.

There are a number of different program styles, geared to different student profiles. Shane Sorenson, the director of a residential school, explains, "The parents have to figure out what they are looking at. Are they looking at shorter-term recovery or are there longer-term pervasive behaviors that need to be addressed?" If the teen needs what Mr. Sorenson calls "a clinical screw turned," then the youth probably needs a less-intensive intervention such as home therapy or a day school close to home that offers treatment as well. Some residential schools are actual lockup facilities for teens that need a total clinical environment; others are not. There are also wilderness programs. "If Tommy is just being a brat and needs direct feedback, a wilderness program is not a bad option, because the teen can get intense work, it's practical, and the child is home in two months," he explains.

Parents need to proceed cautiously before making a placement decision. Program referrals can come from a variety of sources. Educational consultants tend to be a good starting point, although they charge fees, which can be expensive.

Attorneys who specialize in special education usually know about or can refer you to people who know about good programs. Substance rehabs sometimes refer teens to longer-term facilities, so they, too, may be a good referral source, as might the local school district.

 INFORMATION LINK

For referrals, contact the Independent Educational Consultant Association at www.iecaonline.com or (800) 808-IECA.

A Model Program

I visited Sorenson's Ranch School, a residential treatment center located in a remote area of Utah. This program has a unique setup for the teen population it serves. Jesse, the boy you just read about, went there. My purpose in describing this program is to give you a closer look at this type of placement should you need some guidance. While there are numerous residential programs, it goes beyond the scope of this book to review them all. I chose Sorenson's because it came highly recommended, and it serves mainly students diagnosed with ADHD, plus ODD, CD, sometimes depression, and often substance-abuse disorder. Many other programs also serve this population. Of course, people need to be matched to programs, so Sorenson's is not a recommendation for every teen with these diagnoses.

Burnell Sorenson, the founder and director of admissions, has been an educator for forty years. Fifteen of those have been with the tough kids that come to Sorenson's. "The typical child who comes here has ability [meaning intelligence] and has gone completely off track and is out of control," he explains.

Sorenson's is a family-owned, licensed treatment facility with an accredited school. The program is geared to help students develop behaviorally, emotionally, socially, and academically. Sorenson's also happens to be a working cattle ranch. That makes this program unique. In addition to classrooms, counseling services, and recreational activities, the teens work on the ranch. Ranch work is paid unless the teen receives it as a work detail consequence for breaking rules or other defiant acts. As Burnell says with a laugh, "It's a real deterrent to them getting in trouble when they have to spend the day hauling horse manure."

The ranch work is much more than a deterrent, though. It's a hands-on activity that provides a physical release. For many of the teens, it also provides a sense of accomplishment and of contributing to a community. "What really makes a difference in a human's life," says ranch director Shane Sorenson, "is if they can experience worthwhile mastery of a skill. Those are the events that change our lives and help us feel feelings of self-worth. In addition to a textbook, if a youth can go out and by their hands build a fence, see something they've done, see quality in what they've done, that's a wonderful learning experience."

The ranch is a 24/7 program, meaning the teens are there and supervised twenty-four hours a day, seven days a week for however long the stay. Twelve months is recommended. "There are no casual admissions," notes Shane Sorenson. "It's well thought out ahead of time." Before sending a child, he finds, the parents "must come to peace with the consequences of making the decision versus not making the decision." Typically, parents who bring their teens here have been depleted of personal resources. They're usually at their wits' end, exhausted, and frightened.

Parents need to understand that residential placements, by and large, are not country clubs. The living quarters may be spartan. That's all part of the treatment. As Pete Smith, a mentor/case manager who supervises the night staff and student activities, says, "We don't want them too comfortable here. If they like it here, then we're probably not doing our job."

Upon arrival, many teens are uncertain as to why they've been sent here. Burnell Sorenson, who usually interviews each resident at admission, finds that after the first week, 90 percent come to see that they "earned" their way there. In fact, practically every teen I spoke to told me that "not respecting my parents, not following the rules, and not doing what I was supposed to do" got them there.

One of the girls, Lisa, was a bit more specific. She landed here because her parents kept finding boys in her bedroom and she ran away multiple times. Lisa tries a bit to minimize her behavior. "I wasn't really gone probably more than three days. I called them to say I was okay—from a pay phone. I'm not that stupid to call the house 'cause my parents have caller ID. I'd tell my mom, 'I'm okay. I have clothes, food, a place to sleep.'" Fifteen-year-old Lisa also had her mom's car, which she'd taken more than once to chauffeur the friends her parents forbade her to hang with because they were on drugs.

Through his years of experience, Burnell Sorenson has found the girls to be more challenging than the boys. Generally, he says, "A girl that comes to us is a harder case. They've been in more trouble, and they've been defiant longer." He adds, "A girl has to be pretty much out of control before her dad will kick her out or place her out of his control." He finds the ranch environment really helps a defiant girl because "that same girl will take responsibility for a horse, take care of the animal, and revert back to being a little girl."

The girls tend to defy the staff at Sorenson's more, too. According to Burnell Sorenson, when given a work task for inappropriate behavior, a resistant boy may put up a fight for an hour or so. Many girls resist all day. Regardless of gender, the staff uses a one-on-one approach and stays with the teen until the work detail is complete.

Burnell Sorenson's attitude about all the teens that he sees carries throughout the ranch: "Most of them are bright, beautiful young people that just need to be structured." Of course, he means a far more intensive structure than parents can provide at home. Sorenson's has a staff of 107 people who manage the 100 or so residents. "If I was the parent of one of these kids, I couldn't do it alone. We've set up a system and a group of individuals that can take turns trying to help the youth realize the consequences for their behaviors and modeling more appropriate behaviors," Shane Sorenson explains.

Pete Smith says, "Our main issues are safety first, and secondly to create a learning environment." Safety comes first because of the nature of the students. "A lot of times they don't want to be here and their emotions run high," he explains. "They lash out at times, say things like 'I hate this place,' attack your character. Basically, they try to pass some of their misery on."

What the staff attempts to do is turn that misery into a life map. To do so, the program sets firm rules and limits and consistently gives feedback and consequences. Many teens come in balking at this structure. But, notes Mr. Smith, "They figure out that if they follow the rules and do everything they're supposed to be doing, they get rewarded. After a while, they really start to internalize and see that the program is for their benefit, not for their parents, not for the courts. It gives them a foundation to go home and work on so that they can make the right decisions."

The daily program uses a behavioral/level approach. Every day each student receives or loses points for behavior. Once a week, the teen's counselor tallies the points. The teens are placed on levels depending on how many points they earn or lose in a week. Each level has certain privileges. Teens can earn the right to go on a camping trip or to a movie in a nearby town. They also earn housing upgrades. Students who reach the highest level, Level 5, live with key staff personnel and their families. Most Level 5 students are nearing the end of the program, and family life and more freedom help them transition to the return home. Modeling appropriate social and life skills is another main thread used in the daily program.

Since Sorenson's is a treatment center, it also offers a wide array of psychological services, from cognitive-behavioral to group counseling and one-to-one therapy. A consulting psychiatrist manages medication therapy for those teens who may need it. No medication is prescribed or discontinued without parental input. Each teen is assigned a counselor who serves as case manager. That person has frequent communication with the parents. Intake coordinator Phyllis Bagley notes that these students can become emotionally needy in a matter of seconds, and so in addition to formal approaches, they get a healthy dose of some "mothering," as she calls it whenever the need arises.

In addition to their social, emotional, and behavioral needs, most of the teens here are way behind in school, often by as much as two or three years. Sorenson's uses a mastery approach to education. There are classrooms, but the teens work individually, receiving instruction and support from teachers certified in regular and special education. Class sizes are under ten. The school's guidance counselor, Betzy Cazier, finds that most of the students excel because "independent study is exactly what they need instead of classroom lecture."

After mastering 80 percent of the curriculum in a given subject area, the student moves on to the next level. It takes students a little over two months to complete a course credit, which allows them to complete two years of high school (and more, in some cases) in about a year. The guidance counselor works closely with the student's home school to keep each teen academically on track as much as possible. "The mastery-based program inspires and motivates the kids so they go faster," says Burnell Sorenson. It also helps the student who would normally drop out of school to finish a high school diploma.

The learning at Sorenson's goes far beyond the classroom. The staff truly understands the social, emotional, and behavioral aspects of education. "School is a privilege here, and good behavior has to be on line to attend school," Ms. Cazier explains. "For the most part, they're learning the proper way to behave." The social learning focus also includes how the residents interact with peers and authority figures. "This is a really hard thing for some of them," Ms. Cazier says with a smile. "They get lots of chances to practice with authority figures."

Another type of learning Sorenson's tries to impart has to do with success. "We try to teach the kids that success is waking up every day, taking care of your family, taking care of yourself, being responsible, being an active member in your community," says Mr. Smith. Defiant as they may be, the kids who arrive at Sorensons' have been fairly wounded by life. Many think they are worthless and believe that they can't break out of the being-bad mold. Some are belligerent and take the "you're not going to change me" stand. To that, Mr. Smith says, "You're right. But I'm going to be here for you. I'm going to extend my hand, and I'm gonna help you see that you can make the right choices in life. You can be yourself and still follow society's rules, or your parents' rules, or your own rules if and when you leave here you're on your own." Though most kids who leave Sorenson's return home to rebuild their lives and family relationships, some choose not to go home. And some parents refuse to let the teen come back.

Not every parent who sends a kid to the ranch will be happy with the program. Sorenson's, like any program, does not boast a 100 percent success rate. One follow-up of a hundred kids showed that eighty were doing great. The program aims to get kids through school and on to college, the armed forces, or a vocational training program. Burnell Sorenson estimates that about 50 percent of the students go on to college. But he feels their success rate is a lot higher in terms of influencing the students and helping them feel good about themselves: "We think we can help every child understand work, responsibility, and get pretty much drug-free."

Many teens who need this level of help either don't get to places like Sorenson's or, if they do get to come, have to leave before they should. As Burnell Sorenson says ruefelly, "The biggest bug in my program is that every day I get someone who calls and can't afford it. We can't afford to take them tuition-free because we need to make payroll." Shane Sorenson echoes this sentiment and also points out that the middle class really suffers the most, because they can't get state benefits and they don't have enough money to provide for a program. There are loan systems and charities that might help. Some health insurance policies pick up part of the tab. Of course, the school districts are another source, especially if the student needs such a placement to get an education. But most of these school placements don't happen without a legal action.

Parents need to hang tough when it comes to tough calls. Dogged determination and a drive to help a child often open doors that look nailed shut. Many parents have weathered tough times and seen their teens turn around. As Jesse Olmstead says, "My parents never gave up on me, and hopefully when I go home, I can show them I've changed, thanks to them."

PART THREE

Outside the Home

CHAPTER TEN

Grades to Graduation

Secondary-level education can present a huge challenge for many students with ADHD. This chapter explores the nature of the ADHD-related difficulties in the school setting and how attention, memory, and executive function problems contribute to difficulties. A close look is given to the reading problems associated with ADHD. Other typical problems are described, and strategies for coping with many common problems are presented. The chapter also looks at after-school hours as well as some medication considerations.

I f secondary schools could advertise for pupils, a typical ad might read:

Got smarts? Like to work hard? Great at problem solving? Self-aware? Seeking highly motivated self-starters willing to work in crowded rooms. Must be a true eclectic, able to stay focused and interested regardless of task, teacher, love interests, or other social concerns. Requires emotional control, flexibility, and the ability to work for and with many personality types. Must be able to fulfill each teacher's agenda. Good planning and organizational skills are necessary. Must take work home. Salary not guaranteed. Offers potential for future benefits. Interested candidates should show up before daylight. No food or beverages allowed on the job. Twenty-minute lunch or brunch based on work schedule.

Doesn't that make you want to just beat the doors down? In essence, students with ADHD tend to be weak in most of the areas that middle and high schools require for success, be it academic or social and emotional. Let's look at what major changes happen at the magic time of sixth, seventh, and eighth grades: multiple teachers, more independence, more responsibility, and ever-increasing demands for time management, organization, and planning. Add to that the requirements for listening and note taking, continuous concentration, and super study skills, not to mention self-control, the ability to think things through, and the need to stay energized throughout the day.

Then there are the intellectual challenges. By middle school, higher-order thinking skills come into play. Students begin to analyze complicated text and problems. They now have to synthesize this complex information and use it to make predictions, solve problems, and create products. They also have to evaluate information. They must be able to give opinions, make judgments, and support their conclusions with evidence. All this goes on while their bodies are changing rapidly and as they are making the shift from parent/teacher control to greater independence.

By high school, ninth and tenth graders see a huge shift in expectations. Even greater independence and self-direction are required. The reading and writing load increases. Midterms and finals enter the picture. Then the upper-class years come. Now there's lots of reading, lots of writing, lots of research, and very complicated subject matter that builds upon previously learned material.

On top of academics, many students live busy lives. Between extracurricular activities, jobs, and social life, the day doesn't leave a lot of free time. Prioritizing takes on new importance. The student who's not great at delaying gratification or who procrastinates quickly finds him- or herself left behind in the chalk dust.

Consider Ted Harris. Ted's school-related problems are typical of those seen in many teens with ADHD. He's all over the academic road map. One day he performs; the next, he forgets. It's as if his body is a full-time student but his mind attends part-time. He knows enough to ask for help but doesn't always use it. He's been humiliated by a rigid, nonunderstanding teacher and buoyed by one who took the time to care and try some strategies to help him do better.

Ted's really quite innovative and loves to learn, especially when "you're not trying to make thoughts and they just come to you." That happens to him a lot, usually when he's supposed to be concentrating in a class. Instead, Ted's in his seat mentally designing Web pages, which has become his new favorite pastime.

As a recent high school graduate, he looks back and says, "School was painful and a challenge most of the time." He doesn't remember any successes in middle school. "I do remember I was terrible at reading. I got F's all four marking periods. I would see a whole book. I wouldn't see each word. I'd think, 'I have to read this whole book!' and I wouldn't read it." His one positive reading experience happened in his senior year, with a teacher who used a lot of open discussion. Ted likes those because he's good at rolling from topic to topic, and if he doesn't have to answer specific questions, he does better.

His participation in band and on the cross-country team required Ted to keep his grades up in high school. "The best way to learn something is to teach it," says Ted, who found a clever way to study the detailed information he had to learn. "I would sit with my notes or review sheets and act like I was on talk radio and people were calling in asking me questions." Ted would page through the notes or the book to find the answers and then he would recite them "on the air." His technique had only one drawback, as he explains: "I didn't always use it, and I should have. If I just sit there and look at a book and read, the information goes in my eyes and out somewhere else. I have to talk it."

Ted describes one of the typical problems for teens with ADHD—unless someone supervises them, they often don't use the tools that help them perform. By high school, many teachers expect students to be self-initiating. Many see themselves as helping students in that process by insisting that standards be followed precisely. They may make an accommodation or two, but some are inclined to believe that they're harming the student by not insisting on personal responsibility.

In high school, Ted might have benefited from some of the reasonable accommodations that have helped many students with ADHD:

- understanding, supportive, flexible teachers
- a schedule better suited to the teen's personal time clock, such as academics during the student's best hours, breaks during the day, and similar strategies
- direct instruction and cues to use learning strategies
- a lot of structure within the classroom
- consistent feedback
- courses that stimulate but don't overwhelm

As the parent of a teenager with ADHD, by now you've seen your son or daughter have some degree of difficulty at school because of this disorder. By the time many of these kids get to high school, they've amassed a significant amount of failure and frustration. Their true talents and abilities may have gone unrecognized or, even worse, been devalued. Many have wounds and a poor self-concept. They may see themselves as stupid, lazy, incompetent, or bad. And you may be thinking, "What happened to that little kid who used to be so interested in everything?" After all, your teen may resort to causing disruption in school or be like Neil Farnsworth.

This is what Mike Farnsworth wonders about his son, Neil. "Neil will go to the back of the classroom, not cause any problems, and just fail. He's the sort of invisible kid in the class who is just not performing up to par. It takes an extraordinary teacher to recognize him and bring him back. His high school has two thousand students, and his guidance counselors have four hundred kids each. He's got two guidance counselors. Neither one knew about his ADHD. The school is geared to helping kids become adults. In their minds, that means helping them become independent, successful kids. So they're not doing the interventions that are necessary to treat a kid with ADHD. That's my feeling. Their perception of Neil is that he's bright, talented, he could do it if he really wanted to. And even if he has ADHD, he's going to have to figure out how to deal with it sometime, and he might as well do it here in high school." Of course, all eyes focus on what Neil does or does not do, when the essential question is really this: How does ADHD affect his learning?

The Brain at School

Secondary school curriculums require students to have great attention, memory, and executive function skills. These, as you will recall from Chapter 2, happen to be brain-based functions that seem to be compromised in ADHD. The school environment, with all its performance demands, doesn't allow much wiggle room for the teen who's got some functional problems in these brain-based areas. They simply have a hard time meeting the situational demands and the requirements of academic tasks.

It's not that people with ADHD do not have ability. They have performance problems. Remember, teens with ADHD tend to be "younger" than their years and uneven in their skills. Attention, memory, and executive function happen to be processes that become refined with age. So students with problems in these areas will have trouble meeting demands for more sophisticated levels of thinking as well as doing tasks in planned, orderly, complex ways. As the school years advance and the demands come faster and harder, the gap widens between what is expected and what these teens produce. Of course, I'm speaking in general terms here. Clearly, the degree of difficulty experienced has a lot to do with the severity of ADHD, the level of previous intervention, the individual's strengths and weaknesses, and each individual's attention, memory, and executive function efficiency.

Students who don't do well academically often don't behave well. Many students with ADHD are considered discipline problems, and they may be. But learning problems are a cause of behavior problems. My teaching experience leads me to this conclusion: Entirely too much school-based intervention focuses on controlling or "fixing" poor behavior instead of understanding how the learning process is affected by ADHD and taking steps to change instruction and task design so that students with the disorder perform better academically. When they do, they tend not to disrupt or act out.

Let's look closely at attention, memory, and executive function to examine how they affect learning and performance. Though I discuss them separately, it's important to remember that they are interrelated. For example, an executive function problem affects long-term memory, attention, and other executive functions.

Attention

We often say, "This student doesn't pay attention." Do we really know what we mean? *Attention* happens to be a word used to label a brain system that has many subsystems or components. For instance, we imitate, or direct, attention to where it is needed or desired at a given moment. Then we *sustain* or *stick with* the object of our focus. To do so means we have to *inhibit* or overlook distractions. We may *shift* our focus back and forth, or from one thing to another, for instance, listening to a teacher and taking notes.

Of course, each of these components develops at different times. We don't expect little children, for example, to stick with a focus for hours on end—although some do when they're involved in something that turns them on. But the development of these processes is not the only issue here. As Dr. Freund explains, "It isn't that you just get more attention as you mature. It may be that particular components have not developed completely so that other components could come in. Or it may be that different components aren't functioning together efficiently." As 16-year-old Drew Rothman describes it, "I definitely have trouble keeping my attention and listening. I just keep drifting off. At points it gets almost like trying to keep yourself awake."

Many people with ADHD can stay tuned to things that really turn them on. The reason we pay attention has to do with the stimulus, or potential focus, of our attention. Stimuli arouse us, especially novel and significant ones. When a stimulus presents itself, our brains go into a response mode. They release neurotransmitters that activate different cells, and thus systems and subsystems. So when we say a student doesn't pay attention, do we mean he or she isn't aroused or doesn't stick with a task? There are a number of possibilities for why a student doesn't sustain attention. That's the information we need before we decide how to help the teen pay better attention.

Executive Function

"The difference between child and adult resides in the unfolding of executive function," writes researcher Martha Denckla. Executive functions are like overseers or corporate bosses. They keep the workers in order, the products on schedule, the budgets in check, the stockholders happy. Students with executive function problems basically have difficulty in these areas:

- getting done what needs doing
- doing it in an orderly, consistent manner
- using problem-solving strategies
- taking time to use skills
- prioritizing
- delaying today's payoff for a better tomorrow
- staying on task
- emotional self-control

As students hit their teen years, we expect more from them in terms of executive functions. Ultimately, by the time of high school graduation, we expect students to be totally independent in terms of these types of skills. The problem areas that stem from poor executive function are discussed later in this chapter. For now, understand that the better students aren't necessarily the smartest students. In part, they're better because they have good executive function abilities. Fortunately, we can help people with ADHD to use scaffolds to manage the external problems caused by poor executive control, and thus minimize the negative effects. That requires a lot of direct instruction and practice. Many of these organization and study skills need to be practiced repeatedly, until they become second nature. Cram courses don't work. Good skills are built over time and through consistent use.

Memory

The problems students with ADHD have with working memory affect reading, mathematics, and language, which of course means everything having to do with learning. There's only so much information a student can keep in working memory. In a sense, the disorder causes difficulty in making memories and retrieving them. As Dr. Barkley explains, "Working memory is like the chalkboard in your head where you write things down and keep them in mind so you remember them. Kids with ADHD have a problem with the mental blackboard." For instance, they frequently have difficulty doing mental computations in math, because they don't keep the necessary information in mind through the multiple steps. For instance, the student may forget the sum of two numbers he or she just added as a step to complete a multistep problem.

Working memory also seems to play a role in the types of language difficulties many kids with ADHD have. They may make off-target verbal responses or have poor topic management. Expressing thoughts in language, whether written or spoken, requires the ability to organize bits and pieces of information rapidly and efficiently and keep them on the mental chalkboard. Then these must be put together in order and converted into phrases, sentences, paragraphs, and so on. Writing especially requires a lot of going back and forth and picking up previous pieces to weave them into a new design. People with ADHD seem to have little problem speaking what's on their minds. Problems arise when they are put on the spot and asked to speak to a specific topic or make an on-demand response.

Working memory also allows us to call to mind information from long-term memory that may be necessary for the task at hand. It's an active and interactive process. In addition to there being only so much information a student can keep in working memory, retrieving information also poses a problem. So often these students understand the material as it is being taught. They know they know it. Then test time comes. They stare at the question, hold their heads, maybe even give the skull a tap or two as if this slight jar might dislodge the knowledge. Still the answer doesn't come, or what does come to working memory arrives in dribs and drabs or out of order. Furthermore, for some students with ADHD, time constraints add additional pressure. Time becomes one more thing to think about, except of course for the teens with this disorder who are naturally inclined to rush through. Rushing causes mental chalkboard errors and poor mental filing of information.

Traditional evaluation methods, such as tests and quizzes, don't always allow students with ADHD to show what they know. Perhaps the questions have been asked in a way that doesn't allow these students to tap into their memory stores. Or maybe the student needs a key to open the door—a word prompt or some such thing.

Teachers may need to use alternative evaluation methods—perhaps by asking the student orally, and allowing the student to respond in a roundabout fashion. For instance, students with ADHD commonly can supply lots of examples that show they understand a main idea, yet may be unable to define that main idea in precise terms. Students with ADHD tend to do better if they are orally pulled through a question in a dialogue with the teacher.

Reading, ADHD Style

Generally, reading is a huge area of weakness for most students with ADHD. As practically every aspect of the secondary school curriculum requires a good deal of reading comprehension (math included), reading problems have a far-reaching effect.

There's a difference between reading problems that stem from a learning disability or lack of appropriate reading instruction and the types of reading problems that ADHD causes, although certainly your teen could have both problems. When someone has a reading problem, we need to know what part(s) of the process are involved. That is, can the reader get the data in? That's basically decoding. How does the reader get the data in? That has to do with fluency, meaning speed plus accuracy. These are the biggest predictors of reading success. What does the reader do with the data? That's comprehension. As Dr. G. Reid Lyon explains, "Comprehension is extraordinarily complex. It integrates so many different types of things: data in, speed, accuracy, understanding of terms, relationships among the terms (the syntax, the grammar). Then it has to integrate how the person uses it with respect to preparing it or relating it to their own knowledge. It integrates instructional stuff and motivation."

When middle school begins, reading emphasis shifts from simple topics to more complex comprehension. It doesn't help to say a student isn't reading. You need to know why. I want you to have some understanding of the types of problems your teen with ADHD experiences, along with possible explanations for them, so the following is an oversimplification of the complex subject of reading.

Reading comprehension has three basic levels. We read "on the lines," which means the literal text. What information is provided? "On the lines" means the basics: who, what, where, when, and how. Vocabulary enters in at this level. What do the words mean?

We also read "between the lines," which means we make inferences. That requires problem solving. We look to answer the question of why. What inferences or conclusions does the author want us to draw? Or what conclusions can we draw from the facts? To an extent, that's a matter of judgment. Readers can draw faulty conclusions, for example, because they do not consider the evidence presented. Like poor detectives, they miss the obvious and the not-so-obvious clues. And vocabulary figures in as well. Can I figure out the meaning of a word by looking at the words around it? What are their relationships to the other words?

Finally, we read "beyond the lines," which means we interpret the information, apply it to our own lives, and try to make worldly meaning of it. To do this, we need to draw on past knowledge. That requires organizing ideas, seeing how they relate to one another, and picking up on the subtle nuances of language—the tone, for example.

These levels don't happen in a step-by-step or linear way. We constantly go back and forth between them, much like a master weaver. We take a thread here, another there, knot them, and then build until eventually we have a tapestry. The tapestries of secondary school students with ADHD often have holes in them. Why? It goes back to performance and capacity. Many miss connections and essential information because they constantly lose track as they read.

Dr. Lyon explains, "Typically, they have the vocabulary. That's not the culprit. They can usually see the relationships at some level. That may be some of the culprit. Syntactically and grammatically, they're probably pretty good in a lot of ways." Dr. Lyon thinks a big part of the problem has to do with understanding the purpose for their reading and then altering the way they read to fit that purpose. For example, he says, "Are they reading for sequence, or main idea, or the tough one, inference? What does it mean to me?"

There are numerous purposes for reading that students encounter within the course of a school day. For instance, if the students have to read the science text to get background information for the next day's lecture and lab, then they might scan for the general idea of things. But if they have to know what to do in that lab, they need to read for detail. There's a big difference between "looking over the material" and "reading to be prepared." By the way, teens with ADHD may be inclined to overlook an assignment to "look over," which can be a problem, as the homework usually give the students a framework for the next day's information.

Another problem readers with ADHD experience has to do with cognitive energy. Dr. Lyon notes that good readers do not use a lot of cognitive resources to get the printed word from the page. Though they're reading each word, they don't have to labor over them to decode them or to determine how the words are strung together to form ideas. That gives them "cognitive energy left over to really absorb and relate," says Dr. Lyon. "Kids with ADHD are really spread out all over the place in terms of how much they give here and there. They only have so much resource for attention. Often as they read along, their minds drift, and they lose the train of thought. So they have to go back and reread to try to pick up the flow again. That becomes a tedious turn-off."

Also, such interruptions in concentration cause another problem from a memory standpoint. "Information comes in but decays very quickly. What holds it in working memory is relating it to the known," says Dr. Lyon. Readers with ADHD typically are all over the place when the information comes in, and so often it's out of context. Or, it takes too long from when they've started reading, and by the time they return to the working memory drawing board, the information on it has been erased.

Then there's the whole time and interest factor. With an "I'm sure you find this unbelievable" type of laugh, 17-year-old Adam O'Leary admits, "I've really never actually finished a whole book." He means a schoolbook. "If the book is cool, then I'll read it and understand it. But if something is really boring, something I hate, I'll never finish the book," he explains.

Adam is not unusual. As Dr. Lyon notes, "The text doesn't feed back to them." That may have to do with a number of possibilities, including slow, inaccurate reading, an inability to build relationships within the text, or not knowing what to do with the material. And, says Dr. Lyon, "Maybe it just doesn't grab them. I don't know how you increase someone's motivation and desire to continue unless we hook what is new to what is known in a way that's compelling." The classroom teacher of students with ADHD has to make the text interesting and meaningful to the student's life. Otherwise, forget it.

Also, the degree of difficulty must be taken into account. As Dr. Lyon notes, research shows that in any situation, at any age, when novices are presented with new things that are made extremely difficult, they quit. Many teens with ADHD have quit years before they come into high school. Turning on this turned-off kid who's fallen behind makes for a monumental task. Giving him or her a text that's too difficult is bound to backfire.

So what can be done to help teens with ADHD better comprehend what they read? First of all, give much more direct instruction. These teens need to be led through the text by the nose. They need guiding strategies. Also, "You basically need to teach the skills in every setting where they are going to apply, because students with ADHD don't generalize well," says Dr. Lyon. Not being able to take a skill learned in one setting and apply it to another follows the basic ADHD characteristic of "out of sight, out of mind." Thus, for example, if strategies to identify the main idea and supporting details are taught in reading class, the students with ADHD also need to be shown how to use these strategies in science class for that type of text.

Second, active reading strategies must be taught and reinforced through frequent and consistent feedback. Researchers have been working on how to use computers as a way of helping teens to develop reading strategies. Until that technology comes on line, active reading strategies can be taught and the students prompted to use them as they read along. The typical active reading strategy has four parts:

1. Ask questions.
2. Make predictions.
3. Clarify the answers to questions and predictions while reading.
4. Summarize periodically, depending on the type of text.

Of course, note taking helps, too.

Finally, consider the method of delivery. Some kids learn better by hearing rather than seeing. Some learn better with movement or a combination of delivery styles. By the middle school years, your teen's preferences should be very apparent. Play to these. That's what Connie Maresca did with her son throughout all of his years of English class. Jim is not a visual learner. He needs to hear to learn. So his mom made the accommodations. She proudly tells me, "I would read out loud all the assignments, so that he could get them. We spent a lot of time together. I think that helped him not go down the road of behavior problems, because he had a lot of support."

Many teens won't stand for that level of parental involvement. If your teen does and you are helping with reading comprehension, use active reading strategies, which basically means that you guide your teen to stop periodically to ask, predict, clarify, and summarize the text.

Adding the Executive to Executive Function

Many ADHD problems require consistent management. That means parents and teachers need to prompt interventions often, on a daily basis, until the student is able to use them on his or her own. That may not happen fully until after college and beyond. Before discussing those strategies, let's look at a few critical elements that can make them successful.

The Teacher/Student Match

By middle school, and usually way before that, most parents know that the relationship between the student and teacher can make or break the year. In the elementary grades, it's much easier to have a say about who teaches your child. The complexity of the schedule in secondary school makes that much harder. Also, secondary school educators tend to be highly curriculum-focused. That's not to say they don't care or take an interest in their student's personal lives. Many do. Many are also coaches and activity advisers. They get to see these kids outside the academic world, often in a setting where they excel. A good coach or adviser can often be a major life influence. In addition to providing help to the teen, they often encourage staff to provide more care and support for a teen in trouble.

To the extent possible, I suggest trying to be actively involved in teacher and course selection. For teens who can't exercise control, it also makes sense to separate kids who set each other off. In general, students with ADHD do best with teachers who are structured and orderly in their presentation of information, yet able to cut some slack. A sense of humor is a necessity. Their teachers need to be well suited to students with special needs. They also need to know how to use incentive, reward, ritual, and direct instruction to make learning interesting and accessible.

With multiple classes and teachers, it's seldom possible to get the ideal match in every class. So you may have to make some quality-of-life decisions. Is it better for your teen to have the best teacher in the subject he or she does worst in, or would it work better if the best teacher teaches the subject that comes easiest? That's a highly personal choice. It must be answered with the student in mind and with the student's input. If there is a staff member about whom the teen absolutely says, "I better not get so-and-so," respect that statement and try to have the teen assigned elsewhere. What's the best way to alleviate problems? Prevention.

Generic Versus Brand-Name

Educators and parents need to look carefully at the individual student's performance and determine specific areas of difficulty before deciding what needs to be done to help an individual. It's easy to say that a student has ADHD and then use a list of one-size-fits-all suggestions to meet the individual student's needs. However, that can backfire. For instance, a common recommendation is to have the student sit closer to the teacher. But that may or may not be helpful. Some students become very nervous if they have to sit in front of the class, where everyone else can see them. They'll spend more time trying to be invisible than staying on task.

Another problem with ready-made "here's what you do for ADHD" lists is that the items may not apply to the student in question. For instance, a teacher may be told to allow the student more time to take tests. Yet experience has shown that this student usually finishes before many others, so allowing more time is not likely to improve matters. We need to be sure the accommodations actually bring gain from the effort. Otherwise, and understandably, teachers—and the student and the parents, too—may come to see these interventions as either failures or too much effort for too little gain. So they stop doing anything to help because it seems like nothing works.

That's why it is extremely important for school personnel and the teen to sit down and identify areas of strength and those that need improvement. Furthermore, it helps to define the student's problem in specific terms along with its causes. For instance, it's easy to say, "The notebook is messy," but that observation doesn't really help with what to do.

Here's a quick problem-identification process that teachers, parents, and the teen can use to pinpoint difficulties.

1. Describe the problem in specific terms. For instance, if the notebook is messy, is it that the papers are flying around? Or is it handwriting? Or is it that the student rushes and doesn't put things where they belong? Or all of the above?

2. List all the difficulties it causes. For instance, does the messy notebook prevent the student from getting started on time, or does it interfere with test preparation? Perhaps work gets lost and thus credit is lost.

3. Brainstorm to identify possible interventions for the difficulties. Notice that the goal is not just to have a neat notebook, but rather to address the cause or the effect of the underlying problem. If the problem is rushing, then the student might need to have time to organize notes each class period.

4. Try solutions and evaluate them. Quickly discard those that don't work.

If the teen is not on board, even the best programs may not be so successful. Understand that many of these students resist help, especially school-based help. That usually has to do with self-esteem, not wanting to look stupid, peer criticism, disinterest, not grasping that there's a problem, or a combination thereof. Also, many teenage students need to mature into accepting help for their deficiencies. That comes, as it does for all of us, when we realize that no one is perfect and mistakes are okay.

Of course, teens' resistance doesn't mean you want to leave them to their own devices. Engage the school personnel as best you can. A tutor can also be helpful here. You can follow some of the recommendations made in Chapter 4 for treatment-resistant teens, plus consider using the communication, problem-solving, skills training and contracting methods mentioned in earlier chapters. Also know that extracurricular activities that require your teen to keep a certain grade average and attendance record can be quite powerful motivators for accepting help.

As parents, you are in a unique situation when dealing with the schools. They are the experts on the curriculum. You are the expert on your teen. It's important for you to know what types of strategies and learning techniques will help your teen. But it's up to the school to deliver them—at least during the school day. They have the primary responsibility for identifying problems and devising solutions. With luck, school personnel will welcome your expertise and input. Do be careful how you give it. Courtesy and respect for school staff are necessary. It's probably not a good idea to tell teachers how to teach. Most of them like to problem-solve, so if you talk about your teen's difficulties and ask the teachers what can be done and what they think about some of the suggestions you've heard about, chances are your input will be better received.

Generally Helpful and Necessary

Now that I've stated the importance of using interventions specifically designed for your teen, following are some typical problems experienced by students with ADHD and some generic solutions to guide you. These should be custom-fitted to your teen.

As you read through this list of many of the typical problem areas and their generic solutions, remember to keep your teen's age and maturity in mind before you try or suggest any of them. They may not be age-appropriate, or they may further stir up an already stirred-up teen. You decide what would be best for you and your adolescent—in the best case, with teacher input. Ideally, your teen will learn to identify his or her needs and interact with school staff on his or her own to find ways to meet those needs. Your parental role will change to that of a guiding observer when the teen demonstrates the capability to live with less scaffolding.

Organizing Materials

"How do I help myself stay organized? Do you mean now or when I still cared?"

—Hallie Banks, 15

The constant effort to keep organized can defeat teens with ADHD. Materials get disorganized usually because the teen rushes or because he or she can't figure out or follow through on a system to keep things in their place. Establishing routines helps. If the teen doesn't have to think about where to put what and when, and can do it on automatic pilot, that saves time.

Most teens will need help selecting workable organization systems. Frequent straightening up and out will be needed. At home, parents can set up a weekly schedule for straightening the backpack and notebook, but it's better if that happens in school under the supervision of a staff person. Home workspace needs to be free of clutter, with bulletin boards, desktop organizers, and storage space to keep supplies in place. Give lots of incentive to encourage good organization. You may also have to pitch in.

Time Management

"He showed up for the SAT—on Sunday." (SATs are given on Saturdays.)

—*Dan Primavera, father*

If there was a credo for the ADHD time-management problem, it might be this: Time—there's never enough and always too much, and no time is the right time. I call kids with ADHD "last-minute learners." Often they are last-minute about everything—that is, if they make it at all. People without ADHD usually don't understand this behavior. It's not intended as disrespectful. Sometimes those with ADHD need the pressure to get aroused and activated, so they wait until the last minute. That's a biochemical issue. Sometimes they don't take the time to plan in advance or write things down. Thus, they remember haphazardly, like when they get to sports practice and suddenly realize they don't have the equipment they need. That's an organizational problem. It's not a lack of caring.

Sometimes they put things off because the tasks are unpleasant. That could be a motivational problem—one that usually stems from a fear of failure, which is anxiety, or boredom, which comes from underarousal. And sometimes they're so busy thinking ahead that they miss the present. That may be an anxiety issue, which usually comes from too many bad experiences, or a problem with working memory, which allows for only a little bit to remain on line at any given time.

Time management is a fairly sophisticated skill. You can start by training aspects of it, for instance, setting a watch to come home on time, or monitoring the use of a homework assignment pad, or making a schedule of daily activities. Eventually teens should keep a daily to-do list in a schedule book or notepad and write down everything, including phone calls that must be made and leisure activities. They need to learn to accurately estimate the amount of time needed for each. Timers and wristwatches with alarms can be very good prompts.

Microsize

At a workshop I gave, a mother asked, "My son's school makes every junior do a U.S. history term paper. My son can't do that kind of project. The school insists that he do it. Don't you think he should be allowed to skip this requirement?" I answer, "Your son has the right to learn how to do a term paper. Is he truly incapable of the task, or does he need help in structuring it into a more workable series of small tasks?" The answer in this case: task structure.

Many students quit before they start because of the immensity of the task. They simply don't know where to begin. Or they may go from part to part without ever completing a section. Why? Sequencing is often a problem for people with ADHD, as is prioritizing. Many large tasks get left until the last minute. And let's not forget the emotional side of looking at something that's no fun to begin with, not having the vaguest idea of where to start, and then seeing how much effort it will take. What can be done? You and the teacher can help the teen microsize. Break the task into smaller, more manageable segments. Schedule a deadline for each segment. Plan a celebration or reward ceremony after each completed segment. Monitor progress and have your teen use a checklist.

Note Taking

"I have trouble taking notes and listening at the same time. So I would get the notes, but I wouldn't understand them. I found a student who had really good notes and asked if it would be possible for me to photocopy her notes. It wasn't cheating or anything. I still took notes, just not as in-depth. I'd look at her notes and that way I'd see what I missed out on."

—*Drew Rothman, 16*

Note taking presents a unique challenge to many students. In secondary school, it usually requires the student to listen to a lecture; identify main ideas and important details; write while listening, thinking, and paying attention; and use a system of key words rather than a word-for-word lecture transcription. All of this requires efficient selection, working memory, concentration, and the ability to shift attention between two or three tasks. Throw in difficulty with penmanship and the student has an almost impossible task.

It's an important skill to know, so I don't favor simply giving the student the notes. The approach that Drew described earlier is quite good. In addition, ask the teacher to teach various note-taking strategies. If you can arrange for your son or daughter to organize notes and study them each night, then that will keep the information clear and fresh.

Test Taking

"I fail tests. Sometimes it's because I don't study, and sometimes I just don't understand them. And that's what's really bad—when I think I do well and then I realize that I did badly. Then I get so upset."
—Hallie Banks, 15

This skill can be a problem for three reasons: (1) poor test preparation and test-taking skills, (2) difficulty retrieving what is known, and (3) running out of time. Meet with the teachers, guidance counselor, or, if your teen is classified, the child study team to find out the problem's cause and to get some strategies in place.

Task Completion

"I fight myself every minute of class. My brain wants to think about sports, girls, and all the other fun stuff. I have been very ignorant in my studies. I still throw myself to the ground for not doing assignments. I want to do them. I need to do them. I have to pass, but I always screw myself over. I have to put up with my brain always trying to rush me."
—Brian Ballard, 16
(excerpt from a letter written to his teacher)

Most of these problems have to do with being underenergized, underaroused, disinterested; not knowing what to do; or the level of difficulty.

If teachers say, "Your teen never does his or her work," find out exactly what that means and what the conditions are. Is it a problem of starting? If so, that's usually an arousal problem. Or is it not knowing what to do, doing something else and not being able to get to the task, or task avoidance? Maybe directions need to be made clearer. Maybe the teacher needs to give a cue that it's time to start work. Maybe incentives are needed. Maybe the task needs to be broken down into easily completed parts. It depends on the cause of the problem. Is it a problem of sticking with it? If so, that's usually a problem with not enough interest (too boring), or too much frustration (too hard), or having other things on the mind (competition). Ask the teacher to give more incentives, break tasks into easily completed parts, or give less work. Also, your teen can be taught to build in break time and prioritize, and you can give more incentives.

Memory Problems

"The first three years of high school, I got mostly C's in English. I have a C as a final grade and I'm convinced it's because vocabulary is a major part of the course. All the teachers expected us to memorize it and spit it out on a test and that's it. This year I haven't had any vocabulary and I have an 89 average right now, so I may even finish the year with an A. If the teacher teaches it, I can spit it out on a test. If it's just memorization, I have trouble. Now I have to take history. I'll get through it, but I don't know how I'm gonna do."
—Paul Enright, 17

We've talked about memory before, particularly working memory. In Paul's example, the type of memory he refers to is long-term memory, or our brain's storage system. Paul could have several possible problems with his memory. Either he doesn't do enough with his vocabulary words as he inputs them to remember them, or he can't find them because they were stored inefficiently, or he's got a combination of both problems. Remember that Paul said he has a problem when teachers don't teach the information. That means his problem stems from not doing enough with the conceptualizing and contextualizing of the material on the data entry side.

Not surprisingly, a study found that children with ADHD had more difficulty memorizing material than a control group without ADHD.

Even when the group with ADHD was given metacognitive strategies, which are techniques to aid thinking and learning processes, they still did worse than the other group. However, when given strategies plus guidance in actual learning situations, they did as well as the controls. Thus, we see the need for deliberate and supervised instruction.

Handwriting

"I've taken keyboarding classes. I don't type as fast as my parents, but I type enough to where I can do a report. If I have to hand-write a report, it probably would take me two hours. On the computer, it takes me half an hour."

—*Becky Needham, 15*

Dysgraphia is the major scholastic shortcoming of kids with ADHD. It is often the reason that they resist doing written work, and if they do written work, the process is often laborious, time-consuming, and the final product comes out messy.

You might have a shot at working on handwriting in the early middle school years. By high school, that probably won't happen. Poor handwriting may be the result of many factors. You can find out why, or treat the symptoms. The computer is a great solution, but students who have to hunt and peck for letters lose their train of thought, so keyboarding skills are a must.

Problem Solving

"I jump into things without thinking twice about them. I always have."

—*Lucy Lovitch, 22*

One of the best problem-solving approaches is trial and error. On the surface, students with ADHD look like trial-and-error learners. Actually, they tend to problem-solve haphazardly: "Let's try this. Let's try that. Let's try anything, including acting out in frustration when problems aren't easily solved." Poor problem solving is the result of a lack of planning and not taking time. This skill has to be over-trained. Students need to be taught to talk themselves through each step over and over. Here a coach, tutor, or teacher can help the student by providing structure and prompts to use problem-solving strategies.

Inconsistent Performance

"In terms of academics, he does very well in what he's most interested in. If he's not interested in it, he doesn't do as well. He pays attention, but he just can't give it back to the teachers. He can't synthesize a lot of the information. So he doesn't do well on exams, but he can discuss world events or literary concepts with you—and at a very high level."

—*Grace Enright, mother of Paul*

Inconsistent performance is the bane of existence for students with ADHD. Advanced schooling affords students such as Grace's son an advantage. In college they can focus their energies on the areas where they excel. Inconsistency results from many possibilities: underarousal, frustration, task preference, type of task, method of presentation, impulsivity, difficulty sustaining effort, or any combination. It's helpful if teachers play to your teen's learning strengths, accept variation, and analyze places where performance dips to find solutions. Also realize that in "real life" very often we stick to our areas of strength. Sometimes a parent will need to allow for these inconsistencies.

Attitude Problem

"I'm incredibly lazy. I have nothing to look forward to really. All you get is school and then more school. And it's winter. I can't do many of the things I like."

—*Joel Milstein,13*

By middle school, many students with ADHD have amassed quite a history. Often their school lives have left indelible marks of failure and frustration. These kids don't turn off—they're shut off by years of negative return on investment. Cognitive energy problems lead to making less of an effort. There's a sensitivity to criticism. Constant put-downs and poor grades create not thicker skins, but painful layers of scar tissue. Students in this situation easily become emotionally overwhelmed. Often, they express feelings such as anger or apathy. The prescription for this problem is to find and build on strengths, help the teen set small goals that can be achieved, use extracurricular activities or work to motivate, and help the teen find a passion.

Homework

"We had regular homework time every night and reading time. We had the little rules—homework first. In junior high school, I could provide some of that, but no longer could I provide all of it, and it got even worse in high school. He couldn't sustain that focus. And it kind of creeps up on you as a parent when you see him doing very well and you're proud of him. Then all of a sudden he's missing assignments, or doing assignments and not turning them in. What he discovered about himself was that he could not do all the assignments, no matter what. Even with his best efforts there would be some work he wouldn't be able to hand in."

—Maggie Prescott, mother of a 17-year-old

Most unsuccessful students don't see their role in their lack of success. They'll say things like, "The test was too hard," "The teacher doesn't like me," "She never explains the material," "He sits on his butt all day and never teaches." In short, they see external conditions as the cause of their woes. Better performance requires sustained effort. Generally, straight-A students in middle school work between one and two hours a night on homework, which includes studying. In high school, it's estimated that students need around half an hour per academic subject each night. Of course, that changes with the type of assignment, and other factors. In general, if a student has a normal load of six classes, that is three hours.

The following guidelines need to be considered in light of the individual teen and his or her extracurricular activities or part-time work. Most of these will fall upon your teen's shoulders to do.

- Never do the teen's homework.
- Provide assistance—when asked.
- Monitor completion. Don't correct.
- Keep an extra set of books at home.
- Set up a schedule and a place to work, and help the teen keep the workspace clutter-free.

- Allow regularly scheduled breaks. Use a timer for these.
- Determine preference for beginning work—immediately after school, or after dinner, or some before dinner and some after?
- Provide incentives—privileges, goods, but not money.
- Use a schoolmate to check on assignment particulars.
- Develop a system to get completed work back to school.
- Store completed homework in binders as opposed to folding papers into book pages.
- Write down all assignments on an assignment notepad or in an electronic organizer. For assignments not immediately due, write them down day by day until they're completed and handed in.
- Consider a home/school report or contract system.

Tutors

"We asked Kevin what we could to do to help him get through math. It was the eleventh hour. He said, 'Get me a tutor.' We got someone I knew. She saw him two to three hours at a clip. She told us his processing speed was slow, but that he was determined to get through his final-exam packets. He got an 'A' on the exam."

—*Jill Gillingham*

Many of the above strategies, along with assistance in tackling hard-to-understand material, are best accomplished with the use of a tutor. I don't suggest parents be tutors to their teen unless they get thrills from conflict. For parents who have the financial resources, Dr. Jensen finds tutors to be "a powerful, interpersonal human stimulus to work with them, and to coach them. Tutors help them learn and overlearn the things that might otherwise be very tedious and difficult to learn off the page."

If you can't afford a tutor, tap into other resources. Talk to the school's guidance department to see if they have any services to offer. Perhaps the school can pair your teen with a mentor student. Sometimes local colleges have a bank of students learning to be teachers who might be interested in some special practice. You might also try to "tutor-share"—find students with similar problems and try to get a tutor to offer a group rate.

Extracurricular Activities and Part-Time Work

These life areas may provide the most reward for many teens, not just those with ADHD. Extracurricular activities have been known to entice a poor student to meet minimum grade requirements in order to maintain eligibility. They help the marginal students become part of the school community in a positive way. They can help students get a free ride to college, as football did for 18-year-old Jim Gunther. They've also been known to keep an at-risk teen away from troublesome behaviors. I strongly urge parents and educators not to take away extracurricular activities as a punishment for poor behavior or poor school performance. If a sport, for instance, is the only circumstance in which the teen excels, to eliminate it may be to take away the teen's last saving grace.

Some schools have rigid policies regarding participation in extracurricular activities. If your teen falls short of expectations and the school administration adamantly refuses to bend the rules, find another way to fill this gap, perhaps through a local club. It's so important to keep a teen engaged in what he or she does well.

Having made these suggestions, I also need to offer two cautions. First, sometimes some teens need to experience the loss of privileges, especially when they're not doing their part. If you and the school have struggled to create a reasonable program with supports and services for the teen and he or she refuses to take that help or blows off these efforts, then you may have no alternative other than the hard lessons of life.

The second caution has to do with priorities and overdoing activities or part-time jobs. These may also a pose a resource problem. Consider Mark Prescott, an eleventh grader whose mother hates hassles brought about by the academic part of school. She became hopeful when Mark started his junior year off with great enthusiasm. Then he fell apart. As his mom explains, "This fall he was really into school. He loved his teachers, was playing soccer. He joined the drama club and got a part in the play. He tried to juggle work, school, soccer, and play practice. That was just way too much for him to handle." Mark's school, like many schools, has a mandatory attendance requirement. By the middle of fall, he either missed too many days or too many early-morning classes because he had overslept. He couldn't meet the attendance requirements and had no way of passing. He had to enroll in an alternative program, where he's been ever since. Because he could not regain any momentum, he's now considering getting his GED rather than returning to the formal program.

Were his activities the culprit? It's quite possible that Mark needed to prioritize and determine how much he could reasonably handle. It's also possible that extracurricular and work activities were the only areas where he experienced success. Thus, his natural inclination would be to seek refuge and personal development in his areas of strength. Because he has ADHD, it's not surprising that he overdid it. His mom might have intervened and insisted he take on fewer after-school activities. But she didn't, possibly because she had been so overjoyed to see her son positively engaged in teenage life that she did not think about whether he had too much on his plate until that became glaringly clear.

It's hard to convince a teenager with ADHD to put aside pleasurable and rewarding activities for the academic grind, especially when that's not going well. Here's where schools need to work with the teen and the parents. Mark should not have been placed in an either-or situation. Perhaps he could have forsaken work for soccer. That might have been wise. Perhaps the school could have allowed him to take fewer courses or use his work experience for school credit.

For the many teens with ADHD who don't fit the mold, schools need to offer more alternatives. According to Richard Horne, a senior policy advisor with the Presidential Task Force on Employment of Adults with Disabilities, kids with disabilities who have access to work-based learning opportunities are more likely to stay in school, achieve more, go onto postsecondary education, and graduate with a diploma. Work-based opportunities don't just mean going out and getting a menial job. In fact, researchers Ann Masten and Douglas Coatsworth report, "Too much work, particularly in stressful, dead-end jobs is associated with worse academic achievement, misconduct, and the use of tobacco, alcohol, and other substances."

Speaking personally, Dr. Horne says, "When I talk to young people and their families, they are crying for access to employment and training as well as a good education." Unlike in days of old, work-based learning doesn't mean tracking students into vocational rather than college prep classes. Rather, it means giving the youth an opportunity to sample from a wide range of life opportunities. For kids with ADHD who have trouble with an entirely academic-based school program, work-based learning offers the types of alternative approaches students such as Mark need. There's a lot more on-the-job learning to be had from real-life experience. The problem is how to design flexible schools so that this type of learning factors into the high school student's total program.

As schools currently operate, generally parents have to push hard to get the type of alternative schedules that would benefit kids like Mark. In the next chapter, you'll read about the laws that govern your teen's rights. Without their protections, unless you happen to live in a very progressive and supportive school district, you may not find much help for custom-fitting your teen's school program.

Social Considerations

The whole social side of education often gets overlooked. Yet key areas of life success are social and emotional intelligence. So much of teen life has to do with social acceptance. Those teens with ADHD who have poor social skills have usually been taught the appropriate skills, but generally they have not become second nature. Furthermore, these teens may get derailed by emotional hijacking when frustration, fear, or anger overtake cool, calm, collected behavior. Teens with ADHD don't always read social cues correctly, either.

Tenth grader Hallie Banks has a terrible time fitting in. "I'm like one of those people who have a lot of weird views about stuff. The teacher will be saying something and I'll make some sort of comment on it because I'll think what she's saying is wrong. Or I'll want to add to it and everyone will start saying, 'Shut up, Hallie.' And then there are some other kids in that class who constantly bug me. They come right up to me and sit right next to me or something and start trying to talk to me. And this might sound like they're trying to be friendly, but trust me, they are not. You can tell because they sit way too close to me or they ask me stupid questions. When I say, 'Please go away,' they say, 'What's wrong? You're not my friend?' or something like that. They are trying to set me up. And when I tell the teacher, they'll say, 'We were just trying to be nice to her.'

"I don't want to be popular, but it kind of upsets me that I don't fit in. I'd like to fit in for a while, but I guess I'm at the stage now where it's like no way am I ever gonna fit in, so I may as well have fun with my life. My problem now is mainly if there's a school project and the teacher says, 'Pick a group and start.' No one wants to be in my group. I usually end up working alone."

Clearly, from what Hallie says, teens with ADHD aren't the only students to suffer from poor social skills. Her classmates could certainly use some help in the empathy department. Hallie could benefit from learning to handle frustration better and not always saying what she thinks. These skills, along with basic manners, knowing when and how to pay compliments, respecting others' boundaries, and being able to share, help, compromise, and use good conflict-resolution tools are often taught through peer mediation or conflict-resolution programs.

Guidance counselor Marsha Bartolf runs this program for her middle school. "What we've done is train these kids with ADHD and special education students to be the mediators. That's made a big difference for a lot of the kids. They may never get to do a mediation, but they're at least being taught the skills," she notes. In one fortunate family, Mrs. Bartolf trained both children. They, in turn, trained their parents. That's excellent, because research literature shows that youth with ADHD have a better chance of using good skills when these are practiced in everyday life. Though school-based conflict-resolution and peer-mediation programs have great use and promise, the skills learned don't spill over into the other settings unless they are used consistently and frequently. Social skills need to be taught throughout everyday life and practiced over and over again until they become the first response the student makes, rather than one they have to be reminded about after the damage is done. Social skills must be overlearned.

Cooperative learning can be fraught with problems for students with ADHD. Guidance counselor Eileen Vogel says, "As soon as you get an unstructured setting, I think that's more of a distraction to a student who has ADHD. Many times in these cooperative lessons, the students aren't on task part of the time. Now they're in a situation where there are built-in distractions."

Even the most highly structured cooperative lesson can be a problem for certain students. That doesn't mean such lessons need to be abandoned. With students who have ADHD, an extra pair of hands helps. A classroom aide can keep students on track while the teacher assists those with learning needs. Also, cooperative learning can be structured to meet individual needs, for instance, by using pairs instead of groups or making mentor relationships. Ask the teacher not to give responsibility for materials and work produced to your teen if he or she is likely to lose them. Also, if finding a group is a problem, ask the teacher to set up the groups ahead of time.

Medication and School

The story of the student with ADHD in secondary school is a sequel to what happens in the elementary years. These students have more suspensions, poor academic achievement, greater off-task behavior, more fidgeting and out-of-seat behavior, and generally less productivity than their peers. Despite all the troubles that may occur at home, most parents seek help because of their teen's school-related issues.

In one of the largest medication trials done to date on adolescents and education, SUNY Buffalo researcher Dr. William Pelham along with other researchers note that stimulant medications definitely improve behavior. This multisite study looked at note taking, scores on study hall assignments, quiz scores, essay grades, and disruptive off-task behavior. In addition to teacher ratings, the researchers used direct observation and achievement measures to determine the results.

Participants in the study attended a school with highly structured classrooms. Students were well supervised in class, in study hall, and during recreational activities. They received intense supervision, consistent and immediate feedback about behavior, immediate consequences, and a lot of incentive. In this laboratory setting, the researchers found that the beneficial effects of stimulant medication clearly outweighed any risks. This study supported the findings of an earlier one of Dr. Pelham and colleagues, which found that stimulant medication had clear positive effects on behavior, academic performance, and social performance.

Regarding academic performance, not only did the quantity of work increase, but the quality improved as well. The students did better with written expression and with quiz and test grades. After the students were taught note-taking skills, these also improved. That's important to note. Pills don't teach skills. Rather, medication helps the brain's efficiency. That's why performance improves. Medication cannot make up for skills not learned in earlier school years. If your teen goes on medication, that's the time to teach previously unlearned or poorly developed skills. Here's where a private tutor or a school-based support teacher can be very helpful.

Because medication usually has such a dramatic positive effect on misbehavior, unlearned skills can be overlooked. Don't be fooled or caught up in what I call the "no trouble" dismissal. You may receive positive reports because your teen isn't aggravating staff and peers. That's super. But that's not all that's involved in education. Be sure that true academic progress happens. If the teachers tells you, "Rob's doing so much better," ask for specifics. What does "so much better" mean? Find out what needs to be done to beef up the areas that still sag. Don't accept less than your teen can do simply because everyone is happy that he or she is no longer a disturbance.

For more detail about medication, see Chapter 4. Meanwhile, with regard to medication in the school setting, consider these key points:

- ADHD is a medical diagnosis.
- Medication recommendations come from doctors, not school staff. However, school personnel should tell parents when they suspect medical problems.
- Pills don't teach skills. They do help the brain function more efficiently.
- Keep medication a private issue. School staff should not publicly ask a students if he or she has taken medication.
- Follow the school's rules for dispensing medication. Most schools do not allow students to carry their medications with them. Thus, the student will have to visit the nurse for a dose during the school day. If this is the case, the nurse can be a good information source regarding compliance.

INFORMATION LINK

This book will be very helpful for school practitioners: George DuPaul and Gary Stoner, *ADHD in the Schools: Assessment and Intervention Strategies,* Guilford Publications, New York, 1994.

CHAPTER ELEVEN

Special Needs and Special Education

A critical issue for many parents is the difficulty ADHD creates for their teens in school. Many teens struggle and fail in school districts that are unresponsive to their needs. This chapter explores special education laws and parent and student rights under these laws. It's a long chapter, but a must-read for parents who need to know and understand the key provisions of special education law, including the new discipline regulations. It also offers glimpses at placement options outside the school district and guidance about seeking such options.

Many teens with ADHD will need educational services above and beyond what students without disabilities receive. In other words, they'll need special education. Becky Needham is one of those students. Her needs might have been easily overlooked because Becky is neither hyperactive nor impulsive. She zones out. Her mother, Cindy, recalls how bad things were before Becky got help: "I knew something was wrong in second grade when it took her three hours to get her homework done every night. At a lot of different points I would be crying. My husband tried to help when he got home from work. We were starting not to like each other."

Cindy's recollection reminds us that ADHD-related school problems can and often do spill over into the home front. Parents who try to make up for their child's learning problems and what's not happening at school run a relationship risk with their sons and daughters. That makes life especially hard. Often, schools view children with learning problems as not having enough support from the parents.

Fortunately, Becky's early identification as a student with special needs along with some excellent intervention helped to prevent her from going down a problematic path. Getting that help took some doing on her mom's part. Cindy sought to have her daughter classified for special education services in second grade. The school's child study team evaluated the then 7-year-old girl. They didn't feel she should be classified. Their reasons? The team found Becky to be in "a very gray area." She had some weak areas, but she also had some strengths. From their point of view, this little girl was simply not bad enough.

Cindy still remembers the teacher who came into the meeting and said, "She's just like my daughter, and she doesn't need to be classified." Then there was the school psychologist. She put her hand over Cindy's and commented, "We don't have a problem not classifying Becky because we know you are such good parents. You won't let her fall through the cracks." Cindy tells me, "It took everything I had not to reach across the table and pummel her. I wanted to tell her it was her job to make sure my daughter didn't fall through the cracks."

Cindy Needham didn't get into a battle at that meeting. Instead, she contacted other parents who had children with special needs and learned about the laws and procedures that govern the education of students with disabilities.

Cindy went back to the school as her daughter's advocate. She was able to convince the school to classify her daughter as a student with a disability in need of special education and to have a program put in place.

Today Becky is a high school sophomore getting A's and B's. She gives much of the credit for her school success to the special education teacher she had during the elementary grades. "In the beginning, I was very disorganized," Becky recalls. "I couldn't find anything. I was put on Ritalin to help organize me and keep me focused and everything. I was able to be on that long enough for my resource teacher to help me get an organized situation."

Though special education has helped Becky immensely, she does have some complaints. In high school, as in the elementary years, she spends most of her day in the same classes as students without disabilities. That makes her feel good, and she does get good grades. There's another problem, though. In some classes, she has in-class support, which means a special education teacher stays in the class and assists her and other students with disabilities. "Sometimes that gets annoying because I get babied by the in-class support teacher," she says. Becky believes this teacher thinks she can't do anything on her own. "If I get a bad grade, she'll come up to me in class and say, 'Did you not have enough time?' I have classes with most of my friends, and it can be so embarrassing."

The teacher often tries to have Becky do things over. She resists. As Becky explains, "Sometimes I don't want to, because maybe I deserved what I got and they don't understand that. And if we are doing group work, they'll ask who I want to go with instead of putting me with someone like they do with the other kids. Just little stuff, but it can be annoying, and nobody else gets that. It's almost like being treated specially when I'm not that different."

So what's a teacher to do? As Becky approaches late adolescence, she's more aware and opinionated about the services she receives. Interestingly, she prefers to receive her extra help in a resource room rather than the regular classroom. That's a change from middle school. "When we were younger, we just knew we had special classes that we went to instead of being with everybody else. But when I got to fifth, I didn't really like it because we got pulled from our classes, so everyone in the class knew that you were being taken and brought to special classes. The classes helped, but it could be a little embarrassing. The other kids teased us, but not me really. Mostly they picked on the boys, because you don't think of boys as having trouble. When I got older, I didn't really like it. Now it's better because it's just another class that you go to."

Clearly, the logistics of special education are not problem-free. A benefit of in-class support is that the students get the same instruction that all the other students receive. You should know that many special education teachers at the high school level do not have subject matter training in the curriculum areas. When they have to be subject matter replacement teachers, the lack of expertise may place them and the students at a disadvantage.

Obviously, more sensitivity needs to be given to students with special needs. Individual strengths, weaknesses, and social concerns must be considered with all students. We also need to listen to their feelings about service delivery and creatively find ways to help them save face. I don't have a cure-all here. Answers have to be found on a case-by-case basis.

What the Laws Say

Over a quarter of a century ago, the U.S. Congress enacted legislation to protect the rights of children with disabilities in schools. Those laws are presently known as IDEA, the Individuals with Disabilities Education Act, and Section 504 of the Rehabilitation Act. Section 504 is part of a civil rights law. It protects each student with a disability from discrimination on the basis of the disability. Like the IDEA, it requires state and local educational agencies to provide a free, appropriate public education (FAPE) to all students with disabilities.

In addition to the many jobs you do as the parent of a teenager with ADHD, you have to add education advocate to your list. Because ADHD is a disability, your teen may be protected under Section 504 and may also be entitled to special education under IDEA. As Cindy Needham discovered, the best way to ensure that your teen gets all that he or she needs to receive a free, appropriate public education is to know the laws, which can be difficult.

Heaven knows I field way too many phone calls from distraught parents of students with ADHD who fall through the system's cracks. Their stories do not come as a surprise to me. I have been on the inside of that system. I know firsthand what happens. At times, even I have been confused by the school's version of the law I thought I knew pretty well. I don't believe most schools deliberately shirk their responsibilities to students with disabilities. I do find that often they're not sure what those responsibilities are. They also become overly involved with bureaucracy.

As I prepared to write this chapter, I wrestled with how much I should go into detail about the law. It can be boring reading. And yet I came to conclude that parents need to know this information in simple, black-and-white terms. The reason why you need to be familiar with the law is that, like it or not, as long as your teen is in school, you are an education advocate—probably a tired one, too, as dealing with school systems can often be exhausting, especially if your teen doesn't fit the mold. The more you know, the better the chance you have of getting necessary services for your son or daughter.

You might want to use the bulk of this chapter as a working checklist. Any time you have contact with the school regarding special education, read the appropriate subsection to be sure the school's doing what they must.

IDEA

Under IDEA, special education and related services, including supplementary aids and services, must be provided to each student who (1) has a disability and (2) by reason thereof, needs special education and related aids and services.

The law entitles all students with disabilities to the following basic rights:

- A free, appropriate public education (FAPE)—at no cost to the parents
- An appropriate evaluation to determine eligibility and need
- An Individual Educational Plan to meet the unique needs of the individual student
- An education in the least-restrictive environment, which includes a range of placement options depending on the needs of the individual student
- Parent participation in decision making
- Due process, which is the right to a hearing before an administrative law judge or hearing officer, dependent on your state's procedures

We will go through each of these rights in more detail elsewhere in this chapter.

Section 504

This law covers students who meet the definition of a person with a handicap: someone who has a physical or mental impairment that substantially limits a major life activity. Learning is considered a major life activity. Therefore, students with ADHD may or may not be eligible for Section 504 rights and protections. It depends on the severity of their disability and how it affects their learning.

Section 504 entitles the student to certain rights protections, and freedom from discrimination for reasons related to the disability.

- When parents believe their child has ADHD, the youth must be evaluated.
- Eligible students are entitled to an individual education program. (An IEP can be used.)
- The school district must provide reasonable accommodations and related aids and services.
- The quality of the services must be equal to those provided to students without disabilities.
- Appropriate materials and equipment must be made available.
- Education must be provided in the regular class unless it cannot be satisfactorily achieved without the use of supplementary aids and services.
- Schools must have a system of procedural safeguards, including hearing procedures related to resolving disputes, should schools and parents disagree.

Perfect Together

Section 504 and IDEA complement one another. IDEA covers students until the receipt of a high school diploma or age 22, whichever comes first. Section 504 covers students throughout the life span, including post-secondary education. It covers people in every area of life, including work and recreation. Section 504 is a broader statute meant to provide access for people with disabilities to life's major activities; it's not just about school.

Since these laws were first written, Congress and the U.S. Department of Education have made serious efforts to marry these laws even further through similar procedural regulations. Therefore, the procedures used in IDEA for identification, evaluation, and placement may also be used for Section 504.

About the words *disability* and *handicapped:* Basically, these words mean "a lack of strength or ability." They do not mean "worthless" or "incapable" or "stupid." Yet teens often translate these words as such. Remember, the teen years, especially those up until mid- to late adolescence, are the years when fitting in counts the most. Naturally, teens may balk at being labeled with words such as *disabled* or *handicapped*. Hell, even adults may find these labels offensive. For the purpose of receiving services, these labels happen to be necessary evils. However, let's not lose sight of the fact that we don't have disabled teens. We have teens who happen to have a disability or simply may learn differently. I strongly encourage you to be sensitive to the teen's feelings. As parents, we have to make safe harbors. We need to build on and remind our teens of their strengths way more than we remind them of their limitations.

 INFORMATION LINK

Special education rights and protections can be very confusing. In addition to my explanation, following are some excellent resources to help you understand the law.

National Information Center for Children and Youth with Disabilities. (NICHCY), www.nichcy.org or (800) 695-0285: "Briefing Paper on Individualized Education Plans," "Basics for Parents: Your Child's Evaluation," "State Resource Sheets," "IDEA'97 Regulations."

Robert Silverstein, "A User's Guide to the 1999 IDEA Regulations" and "Overview of the Major Discipline Provisions of the 1999 IDEA Regulations." Silverstein is director of the Center for the Study and Advancement of Disability Policy. The documents are available from www.c-c-d.org (click "Legislative Issues/Announcements").

Peter W. D. Wright and Pamela Darr Wright, *Wrightslaw: Special Education Law,* 1999. Visit www.wrightslaw.com for ordering information. This site has many other publications available for download free of charge. Their advocacy guide will also be helpful.

Ask Reed Martin is a Web site that offers information on various special education topics and a place to ask specific questions of a noted professor specializing in special education law: www.reedmartin.com.

I'm going to focus most of this chapter on IDEA as the main vehicle to enable a student to receive a free, appropriate public education (FAPE). That does not mean you should discount Section 504. It's a strong piece of legislation. It's just that my school experience shows me that students classified under IDEA command more recognition and their programs receive more serious attention from school staff. I've taken what I see as the practical route based on my past experience in the field.

FAPE

FAPE is the heart of IDEA. It means that the education provided to a student with a disability must be meaningful. *Meaningful* is a vague term. Basically, it means that schools need to provide whatever special education and related aids and services are necessary for students with disabilities to be educated in the same general curriculum as students without disabilities—and these need to be provided at no cost to the parents.

Unclaimed Freight

Many schools in this country have a long-standing, unwritten policy when it comes to providing special education to students with ADHD. I've translated all that doublespeak into one short and not-so-sweet sentence: "Students with ADHD need not apply." For too many years, parents of students of all ages have been told that the laws that govern students with disabilities do not apply to students with ADHD.

As a layperson, and later as vice president of government affairs for CHADD, I was one of the principal people who went to Congress to advocate for an amendment to the Individuals with Disabilities Education Act. Since I worked the issue of ADHD and IDEA at the national level, I know what the laws require. You may find this sadly ironic, but when I returned to the classroom as a teacher, in two of the four schools where I taught, I could not get services for students with ADHD. Why? Because I was told, "We don't cover that."

In 1991, the U.S. Department of Education made sure that schools knew their obligations regarding students with ADHD through a policy statement that it sent to every state director of special education. It then added new teeth to that policy in the 1997 amendments to special education law. As part of the department's regulations, ADD/ADHD was listed under the disability category of "other health impaired." Those regulations were finalized in 1999. That means practically a decade passed since the U.S. Department of Education let every school in this country know its obligation to students with the disorder. In the commentary accompanying the 1999 regulations governing IDEA, the U.S. Department of Education wrote, "It is important to take steps to ensure that children with ADD/ADHD who meet the criteria under Part B receive special education and related services in the same timely manner as other children with disabilities."

If you are the parent of a student with ADHD, you may still be told that special education does not cover your student. Guess what? You are not alone. School personnel may also be given the same information.

Millie and Tom are middle school guidance counselors. In the schools where they work, ADHD presents a challenge to the guidance department. Both counselors are in school districts that don't understand their obligations to find and serve the needs of students with ADHD. They've both been told that ADHD is a "medical diagnosis" as opposed to a "learning diagnosis." Thus, if a parent comes to them with the suspicion that his or her teen has ADHD, the parent is told, "We don't test for ADHD." As Millie says, "Parents have to be wise enough to take their kids on their own for that kind of diagnosis."

"That's one of the problems we face as guidance counselors," Tom adds. "We don't test for ADHD." When I tell the counselors that this practice appears to be a legal violation, they're shocked. "Who is supposed to test?" Tom asks.

IDEA has "child find" provisions. Special education law makes it crystal clear that each public agency (the school district) must seek to locate, identify, and evaluate all children within the district, including those attending private schools, who have disabilities, to determine their need for special education and related aids and services. Furthermore, "child find" requires schools to locate, identify, and evaluate students who are *suspected* of having a disability to determine the need for special education and related aids and services. Since ADHD is a medical condition, parents may be confused as to whether or not schools can make a diagnosis of ADHD. Only licensed medical practitioners may make medical diagnoses. However, schools may evaluate students they suspect of having a disability for the purpose of determining if the student has a disability and to determine if the disability's effects require the student to receive special education and related aids and services under IDEA. However, the federal law does not require schools to provide a medical evaluation, per se. Rather, in its comments about the regulations, the DOE clearly states that "if a determination is made that a medical evaluation is required in order to determine whether a child with ADD/ADHD is eligible for services under Part B, such an evaluation must be provided at no cost to parents." That means that unless your state requires a medical evaluation, the decision must be made on a case-by-case basis.

The law also requires the school to review existing data on the child. This data includes any parent-provided evaluations and information, current classroom-based assessment and operations, and observations of teachers and related service providers, which often includes a school psychologist. On the basis of that data review and with input from the parents, the parties in the evaluation process (which include the parents) determine what, if any, additional data are needed to determine whether the child has a particular category of disability such as other health impairment, which includes ADHD. The DOE states, "Part B does not require that a particular type of evaluation be conducted to establish these regulations; rather the evaluation requirements [in 300.530-300.536] are sufficiently comprehensive to support individualized evaluations on a case-by-case basis, including the use of professional staff appropriately qualified to conduct the evaluations deemed necessary for each child." Of course, as mentioned earlier, schools are required to consider parent-provided information, which would include any medical evaluations and diagnoses your child has received from outside medical professionals.

For parents, the legalese can be confusing, but it's important for you to be aware of what the regulations say. Here's the bottom line: If you go to the school and tell them your teen has ADHD and the disorder causes problems with his or her educational performance, *which includes social, emotional, and behavioral aspects as well as the academic ones,* the school must consider doing an evaluation. They cannot tell you, "ADHD is not covered." Furthermore, if your teen is having trouble socially, emotionally, behaviorally, or academically, the school must consider doing an evaluation if you or they suspect that the teen has a disability. So even if your teen doesn't have a diagnosis of ADHD, the local school district is responsible for finding out if a disability exists and if it is interfering with the student's education. Don't let school personnel tell you otherwise. Make a *written* request to them for an evaluation.

Both Millie and Tom were suprised to learn that ADHD is specifically covered under the law. As Millie says, "When we sit down with the child study team, the minute they hear ADD/ADHD, they say it's a medical diagnosis and not something they do. And that's when I go, 'Okay. That's the way it is. Let the parents handle it on their own.'" She's not being callous. Millie knows that the child study team will not do an evaluation of the impact of ADHD on the student's performance until the parent has a diagnosis. Even then, most of the time they forgo IDEA. On rare occasions they'll develop a very minimal 504 plan. This practice is wrong and does not meet the requirements of the law.

Unfortunately, I've seen cases where districts provide the student with a 504 plan that doesn't really provide the appropriate services. As explained earlier, 504 plans can be extremely beneficial and this law actually offers great legal protections for students with disabilities—when the law is practiced as written. Under 504 regulations, a school system must provide the student with reasonable accommodations and any supplementary aids and services necessary for that student to receive a free, appropriate public education. Unfortunately, 504 plans are not often done that way. They often miss the student's needs and the teacher is not given the necessary support. Furthermore, schools often do not do thorough evaluations to determine all the student's disability-related needs. Also, when the school system implements the plan correctly, the classroom teacher receives necessary support and training to implement the plan.

Many teachers of students with ADHD and 504 plans do not receive this training. While they may make reasonable accommodations, such as preferred seating and less homework, they generally don't use specialized instructional methods that might be necessary for this specific student. That's often due to a lack of training, not a lack of concern. Teachers cannot do what they don't know how to do. Like Millie and Tom, guidance counselors and even some child study team members may be well-meaning but nonetheless in the dark.

Tom believes part of the problem serving students with ADHD has to do with funding. "We have a child study team that is overworked and understaffed. They are not full time in our school, and we could sure use that," she explains. The law does not allow funding to be an issue. If a student has a disability and special education is needed as a result, the school must provide the necessary services.

In Millie's school, she finds that special ed seems to have preferential groupings of who they serve and don't serve. "Kids with ADHD are low on the totem pole. It's the group that isn't claimed by anybody unless you have a parent who is somewhat of an advocate," she explains.

Kids with ADHD appear to be "unclaimed freight" in Tom's district, too. As he says, "We don't have a choice. If the parent mentions ADD, the first thing I do is recommend that they go to their pediatrician. We can do a PAC [pupil assistance committee] referral, which is our first step down the classification road. It's just more paperwork, but we don't have a choice in our system."

In the state where I live, schools have pupil assistance committees (PACs). I believe use of these committees is common practice in most states, although they may have different names. PACs can be very helpful. For instance, they may be used to address some of a student's specific needs, such as peer problems. The PAC team might meet and decide that the student should be invited to become a peer mediator, where he or she would be trained in mediation and conflict-resolution skills. Or the PAC can be another level of bureaucracy that delays the "child find" process or the provision of special education and related aids and services. Legally, PAC cannot be used as a first step on the special education evaluation road. If you believe your child has a disability and therefore requires special education, you can request that the school start a special education evaluation immediately and not delay that process by having to go through this other step first.

ADHD Is Specifically Named as a Disability Under IDEA

The IDEA has a section of the law that defines disabilities. It then goes on to list categories of disability types. Within each type, there are specific disorders listed. One of those categories is "other health impaired." It is located in Section 300.7(c)(9), and it specifically mentions ADHD within this cate-

THREE KEY IDEAS OF IDEA

1. ADHD is covered under the category OHI—"other health impaired."

2. To be covered, ADHD must adversely affect the student's educational performance.

3. Parents and teachers have the right to request an evaluation. (Always put requests in writing.) The school must evaluate the child or put in writing why they refuse to evaluate.

gory: "*Other health impairment* means having limited strength, vitality or alertness, including a heightened alertness to environmental stimuli, that results in limited alertness with respect to the educational environment, that—(i) Is due to chronic or acute health problems such as asthma, *attention deficit disorder or attention deficit hyperactivity disorder* . . . [and] (ii) Adversely affects a child's educational performance."

With this information, no school can tell you that they don't cover ADHD. What they might tell you is that your state does not have the same law. While the words in the state law may differ from those in the federal law, the coverage does not differ. States must follow the federal law. Call the special education department of your state and ask them to tell you where your state regulations coincide with the federal regulations on ADHD. Then ask for a copy and bring that copy to the school.

The school may agree with you that ADHD is covered but disagree that your child needs help. They may say your teen's problems aren't severe enough. That's a no-no. They have to evaluate your teen to determine how the ADHD affects his or her educational performance *or* put in writing why they refuse to do an evaluation. Remember, educational performance includes social, emotional, and behavioral learning—not just academics.

Appropriate Evaluation

When a student experiences difficulty with any aspect of the school program, be it academic, social, emotional, or behavioral, the law requires an evaluation to determine the need for special education and related aids and services if the student is known to have or suspected of having a disability. That includes students in private schools, too. Many times when parents request evaluations, they run into some typical scenarios. School personnel advise them to take a wait-and-see approach, as happened with Becky before her mother spoke up. Schools may also refuse to evaluate because the student is advancing from grade to grade. Or where ADHD, oppositional defiant disorder, or conduct disorders are concerned, the schools often label the students as "disciplinary problems" instead of "disabled." If you believe your son or daughter needs an evaluation, *put your request in writing*. For kids who keep getting into disciplinary trouble, insist upon an evaluation. If the school refuses, you can use mediation or get a lawyer or advocate to help you convince the school that an evaluation is probably necessary. Your request should include:

- your name and the teen's name and address
- school attended and grade placement
- reason(s) for request
- date

Teachers may not be aware, but they too have the right to request evaluations or changes in the classified student's educational placement. Sometimes schools see problems where parents don't. Parents, if the school tells you they think your teen may have problems that contribute to poor performance or behavior, please listen. Work with them. Your teen's future may be at stake.

Following are special education procedural guidelines, some of which I've excerpted from NICHCY's "Basics for Parents: Your Child's IEP," and "The NICHCY Briefing Paper on IEP's," Robert Silverstein's "A User's Guide to the 1999 IDEA Regulations," and the federal regulations for the law. These documents are available on the Web. See the information link on page 255.

- Schools conduct evaluations to find out if your teen has a disability, and if so, what kind of special help he or she needs to progress in the general curriculum. Either you or the school may request the evaluation. The evaluation is done by a group of people consisting of school personnel, the parents, persons with specialized knowledge of the child, and where appropriate, the child. *Parents, you are a full-fledged member of this team, with the same rights as anyone else to give input.*

- Evaluation is essentially a four-step process. Steps 1 and 2 are like screening processes. Information gained from them helps the team determine if further evaluation is necessary. Steps 3 (page 265) and 4 (page 267) establish eligibility and an education plan.

Step 1: *Review existing data*, which include but are not limited to your child's school file, recent test scores, private evaluations provided by the parents, current classroom-based assessments, and teacher observations.

Step 2: *Collect more information.* After the initial review, the team must decide if and what additional information may be required. Before this additional information can be acquired, the school must give you *prior written notice* and obtain *informed parental consent* to an evaluation. The written notice must include a description of the evaluation procedures the team plans to use. Once you have given consent, the additional data is collected.

You may be a bit confused at this point. Perhaps you find yourself asking why you need to give consent for the evaluation when you are on the team that decides whether or not additional information needs to be collected. IDEA is loaded with protections for parents and their children. This part of the process is a bit like going to the doctor and discussing the need for an invasive procedure, for example, surgery. You and the doctor agree the surgery needs to be done, but you still sign a consent form agreeing to the procedure on the actual day of the operation.

The additional evaluation data collected will come from a variety of sources, including:

- appropriate school personnel (e.g., regular and special education teachers, a school administrator with knowledge of the general education curriculum)

- a person who can interpret test results, usually the school psychologist
- other individuals recommended by you or the school who have specialized knowledge about your child
- representatives from other agencies who may be responsible for providing transition services (for teens age 16 or above)
- you, the parents
- the teen, where appropriate

The additional data might include:

- norm-referenced testing such as I.Q. tests, child-behavior checklists, reading tests, etc. (tests must assess specific areas of need and not just I.Q.)
- in-depth observations
- functional evaluations of academic and behavioral performance
- your child's medical history when it is relevant to school performance
- your ideas about your child's strengths, needs, feelings about school, and behavior in and out of school
- observations by professionals
- information that relates to helping the child be involved and progress in the general education curriculum—which is the same curriculum as that of the other students

Evaluations must also follow these guidelines:

- be conducted in the child's native language
- be comprehensive enough to identify all the child's special education and related needs—not just those of the disability in question
- be conducted by trained evaluators
- be conducted under standard assessment conditions or contain a statement as to why that is not possible (e.g., the child may be hospitalized and therefore unable to come to school for psychoeducational tests)
- consider *present levels of educational performance* (PLEP)

WHAT EVERY PARENT SHOULD KNOW ABOUT EVALUATIONS

Please know that no single test or measure may be used to find a youth eligible or ineligible for services.

Also, your teen cannot be found ineligible simply because he or she is advancing from grade to grade.

Congress never intended IDEA to be a law that required the student to fail first before receiving services.

Step 3. *Determine the youth's eligibility.* After collecting all the data, the team meets to determine elgibility. You are a member of that team. In some areas, it is referred to as the Eligibility Committee. In others, the team meets in an ARD meeting (Admission, Review, Discharge), the name of which varies around the country. The determination of eligibility is based on the results of the evaluation and the policies in your local district about eligibility for special services. (State and local policies must conform to federal regulations.)

The eligibility determination must be made in a reasonable amount of time from the time you sign consent for the evaluation. The federal regulations recognize that some cases go faster than others. Many states have set timelines, which you can obtain from your school's child study team or your state department of education. You need to consult your state's regulations to know what these are. *However, in general, the process from when you sign consent to evaluate to the development of an IEP should take about sixty days. IEPs must be completed within thirty days once the student is found eligible.*

Also, the law requires eligible students to be reevaluated if conditions warrant or if the child's parents or teacher requests it, but at least every three years to determine the need for continued services. The triennial evaluation should also look for new problem areas that may arise due to increased demands on attention, memory, and executive function. It does not merely need to determine if the disability is still present.

At the meeting to review the data and determine elgibility the following should happen:

- Evaluation results should be explained to you in a way that's easy to understand. For instance, the meaning of test scores should be explained to you. Be sure to ask any questions you may have. If the results don't make sense based on what you know about your child, share your insights and information. (See "Understanding Tests and Measurements" at www. wrightslaw.com.)

- Results should also point out your teen's areas of strength and competence.

- You have the right to be part of the group that determines eligibility.

- You have a right to a copy of the evaluation report and the paperwork regarding your child's IDEA eligibility.

- If the school determines that your child is or is not eligible under IDEA, it must tell you in writing. It must also tell you what to do if you disagree with this decision. You have the right to disagree with the eligibility decision and be heard in a due-process hearing. (See procedural safeguards later in this chapter.)

- If you disagree with the school's findings, you have the right to request an *independent educational evaluation* (IEE) paid for by the public agency (school district). If the school district disagrees that an evaluation is warranted, it must explain to you why they believe their evaluation is sufficient. If after hearing its reasons, you still disagree with part or all of the school's findings, then they must provide the IEE or start a due-process hearing to show that its evaluation was appropriate. By the way, a hearing officer can also request an independent educational evaluation. If you request one, the public agency must give you information about appropriate criteria for such an evaluation. It's a good idea to have the IEE as soon as possible as some judges have imposed timelines stating that the parents delayed too long.

- If you agree with the school's eligibility determination, then you will be expected to sign a document noting that your rights have been explained to you and that you consent to your child receiving special education services.

Again, you may find yourself confused. How can you be part of the team and then walk into a meeting and be told your child is eligible or ineligible? Since you have previously given your input, technically it's possible for the team to determine that your input has been considered. Of course, as part of the team at the eligibility meeting, you have the right to disagree. You should also know that it is common and acceptable for the eligibility meeting to turn into an IEP meeting. Then the program is developed that day with your participation.

> Step 4: Once your teen has been found eligible under IDEA, the team needs to write an Individualized Education Plan. The evaluation serves as the basis for developing your child's educational program. When the school-based participants come to the eligibility meeting, often they have an idea of what they think is necessary or of what they want to offer in the way of services. A good evaluation would reveal that information. You may not be as far along as the school. Or you may disagree with parts of the plan. Schools often try to wrap up IEP business quickly. They may even come with a draft IEP in hand. However, they may not come to the IEP meeting with a finalized IEP. *Parents, know that you are allowed time to think about the IEP plan and to make recommendations.* Before any services can be given, the IEP must be in effect. However, schools may try a trial placement before finalizing the IEP of a student who has been found eligible, to determine if that placement would be appropriate for the youth. That temporary placement cannot become a final placement until the IEP is finalized.

Individualized Educational Plan (IEP)

The evaluation contains a statement about your child's present level of educational performance (PLEP). PLEP tells everyone how the disability affects the child's involvement and progress in the general education curriculum. The evaluation also uncovers areas where your teen needs help. Therefore, the purpose of the IEP is to provide your teen with the special education and related aids and services including supplementary aids and services needed in order for him or her to progress in the general-education curriculum. The IEP team develops this very important document.

Who is on the IEP Team?

- The parents. You are equal partners. And Congress has made that intent clear.
- At least one regular education teacher. (Input from all the child's regular education teachers is encouraged.)
- At least one special education teacher.
- A person from the school with authority to allocate school resources, who is knowledgeable about the general education curriculum and the school's resources. Usually that person is the director of special services or the building principal. *Note: Schools may not consider cost when deciding on necessary services.*
- A person who can interpret the instructional implications of the evaluation results, usually the school psychologist or learning consultant.
- Others who may be invited by you or the school. Such persons must have specialized knowledge about the child and may include therapists or advocates.
- If appropriate, the teen. Some teens welcome special education services. Others resist. Although it's preferable for a teen to be an active member of the IEP team, some teens may not handle this responsibility in a way that's in their best interests. In fact, the teen may resist special education. By law, teens do not need to be at IEP meetings except under the following circumstances. For teens age 14 and above, if the IEP team will be discussing what the teen will do after high school graduation (transition, see pages 272 to 274), then the student should be invited to *that portion of the meeting.* Some teens may refuse or may be unable to attend. The decision to have or not have the teen at the entire meeting should be made prior to the meeting. As the parent you have the final say on this point, except for the transition planning, or if your teen has reached the age of majority, at which point all of special education IDEA rights *may* transfer to the teen depending on your state's law. The IDEA authorizes but does not require states to transfer rights to a teen who has turned 18. Thus, if your state requires rights to be transferred at age 18, the school district will do so.

I can't tell you how best to handle the inclusion of your teen at the IEP meeting. You know your child. You know the law. So you must decide what's in the teen's long-term best interests. I hammer this point because I have seen school personnel insist that the student be at meetings to determine eligibility—which usually turn into IEP meetings. Instead of offering necessary services, I know of cases where schools have attempted to discourage teenage students from their special education eligibility and rights by appealing to the teen's sense of needing to be like everybody else. One young lady was even told that she was too smart to be with the other "special ed kids."

We know that teens generally resist unilateral decisions that affect their daily lives. So you have to find a way to be sure your teen has a say in his or her school life. If not, the best-designed IEP may fail. What then might you do? If you think your teen will be resistant to special education services, you could have the meeting without your teen. Develop the IEP. Discuss it with your teen after it's developed. (You could also use a treatment professional, especially if you and your teen have been receiving this type of help.) Then negotiate with the teen about how best to meet his or her special education needs while at the same time taking into account the teen's concerns. With teens, the IEPs require creative planning. *Obviously, the best scenario would be to involve the teen as much as possible and help him or her to become a self-advocate.* You may also use some of the suggestions from Chapter 4 about treatment resistance to encourage your teen's participation. There's no doubt about it—for teens with ADHD, the appropriate school program becomes a needed management tool.

Note: Some parents need an attorney when they and the school district disagree. Attorneys are generally strongly discouraged from attending IEP meetings. Of course, their attendance depends on the case. Unless your attorney is present, the school will not have a reason to have its attorney at any meetings.

IEP Development

The IEP is the document that determines how the school will deliver a free, appropriate public education to the student. It is a both a plan and a program. As a plan, it may need revision or updating as circumstance changes. In order to revise an IEP, the IEP team must meet. You, the parent, as an IEP team member, may request a change or approve a proposed change.

When developing the IEP, the team must consider the following:

- the strengths of the student
- parental concerns for enhancing the education of the child
- results from the most recent evaluation
- if appropriate, state- or district-wide testing results
- whether behavior gets in the way of the student's learning or the learning of others; if so, the team must consider developing plans, including positive behavioral strategies and supports, to manage that behavior
- whether the student needs assistive technology devices for school or home
- input from regular education teacher, if appropriate, regarding positive behavioral interventions and strategies, and supplementary aids and services or supports that school personnel will provide for the student

IDEA promises an appropriate education, not the "best" education. Be careful how you refer to the placement and the goals of the services you request.

What Are the Major Requirements for IEP Content?

The IDEA makes it clear that students must be given the help they need to make progress in the general education curriculum, which is the same curriculum used by students without disabilities. It also recognizes that some children have other educational needs resulting from their disability, for example, social skills deficits. With the full range of the student's needs in mind, the IEP must have the following components:

1. A statement about the student's *present level of educational performance* (PLEP).
2. *Measurable annual goals, including benchmarks and short-term objectives.* The team must:
   a. Develop measurable annual goals.
   b. Develop strategies to meet those goals.

    c. Develop measurable intermediate steps to meet those goals (short-term objectives). These generally break the skills described in the annual goal into their separate parts.

    d. Develop major milestones (benchmarks) that help to monitor progress throughout the year. (These can replace or supplement short-term objectives.) These reports generally are given at the same time as the school's general interim progress reports and marking period reports.

3. A statement of *the special education and related services and the supplementary aids and services to be provided* and a statement of *program modifications and supports* that will be provided to the child. Such services might include psychological services, medical services for diagnostic and evaluation purposes, occupational therapy, academic coaches, aides, and so on.

4. A statement about the *extent to which the student will participate with other students* who do not have disabilities. This includes academic and extracurricular or other nonacademic activities. The law makes it clear that each student must be educated with students who do not have disabilities to the maximum extent appropriate.

5. A statement about what modifications for district-wide assessments, if any, will be made for student achievement tests.

6. A statement of transition services.

For some students, especially those with many comorbid conditions, the appropriate program may not include any regular education classes, or the local school district. It depends totally on the individual child's needs. This concept is known as *least restrictive environment.* Some schools misapply this part of the law. They think the student must proceed through a series of placements beginning with those that appear to be the least restrictive and "fail" their way into the appropriate placement. That is a mistaken notion. A student with significant emotional and behavioral issues, for instance, may need to be placed in a highly structured school with small class sizes, a lot of one-to-one attention, and intense behavioral and emotional strategies in order to progress in his or her education. The local school does have to explain in the IEP why such a placement is necessary. (More information about placement follows in a separate section.)

Transition

There has been a major change in the IDEA. Its purpose used to be to ensure that all students with disabilities had access to a free, appropriate public education with special education and related services designed to meet their unique needs. Now, in addition, the FAPE *must also prepare these students for employment and independent living.* Following are some very important transition guidelines.

The current IDEA emphasizes improved results for students with disabilities in three main life areas: postsecondary education, employment, and independent living. That's because findings have shown that students with disabilities have less favorable outcomes. Many do not go on to college or vocational training. They have trouble with gainful employment as well. Thus, the 1999 IDEA amendments require schools to have transition programs for eligible students in order to help these students achieve their postsecondary school goals.

According to Dr. Horne, a senior policy adviser from the Presidential Task Force on Employment of Adults with Disabilities, after twenty-five years of IDEA implementation, the expectations of families and young people are changing. Dr. Horne says, "They want to achieve those post–high school outcomes, but they don't always get the tools and skills they need as part of what they learn in school. Under the current IDEA, we are looking at standards, tests accountability, and access to the general curriculum, believing those pieces will improve outcomes." Dr. Horne believes a broader and critical look into the quality of the secondary school experience is needed for all kids, but particularly students with disabilities. "Where in the secondary school experience are there opportunities for young people to gain the knowledge, skills, and experience that lead to these positive outcomes?" asks Dr. Horne.

Schools now are supposed to have a school-to-work initiative. From early on, students with disabilities, their families, and teachers are supposed to receive training and support to understand the importance of work-based learning. Some people have criticized this idea as being a way to track kids at very young ages into menial jobs.

Dr. Horne sees school-to-work initiatives much differently. He says that the research shows that students can meet high expectations when engaged in work-based learning and a hands-on curriculum relevant to their interests. So many young people with disabilities fail at their first jobs. "We've got to do career-awareness pieces and interest inventories early on to prepare them to be successful," Dr. Horne comments.

That doesn't mean that students with disabilities pick their future careers at age 14 or 16. Rather, Dr. Horne believes, good transition programs help students explore the larger universe of work. Activities such as job shadowing, mentoring, internships, apprenticeships, and part-time employment prepare students for full-time work. (By the way, these types of activities can also be part of a college program.)

There's no reason that students can't be afforded this wide range of possibilities as part of their education, either through school or after-school programs. What types of things might we be talking about? Formerly, Dr. Horne taught students with emotional disturbances. Many of them had an interest in basketball. He used that interest as a job-shadowing experience. "Students went to the local team and investigated all aspects of that industry, not just what a player has to do," he explains. They learned about merchandising, ticket selling, how a team is run, how to design a stadium, and how to create a schedule. These opportunities opened teens to a varied world of work opportunities. Dr. Horne always had the players ask the students how their grades were, too.

Under the IEP transition plan, school-to-work opportunities can be part of the student's school life. The IEP team should do the following regarding transition:

- Help the student and parents think about the student's future goals.
- Identify the student's needs, interests, and preferences.
- Know how the student presently performs.
- Identify what the student will learn and do throughout the school years to achieve future goals.
- Ensure that the student learns to the maximum extent appropriate within the general curriculum and environment.

INFORMATION LINK

For further explanation of transition, see "IDEA '97 Transition Requirements: A Guide," www. nichcy.org.

The transition requirements are that, beginning at age 14 (or possibly younger), the IEP shall contain a statement of the transition service needs and the courses of study necessary (such as participation in advanced placement courses or vocational training); this must be updated annually. Also, beginning at age 16 (or younger if appropriate), the IEP shall contain a statement about transition-related interagency responsibilities, or any other needed linkages (such as community experiences, necessary courses, graduation requirements, etc.). Appropriate linkages to services and supports the student might need after he or she finishes school should be in place before the student leaves the school setting. These should be documented in the IEP. These might include a connection with the student disabilities office of the college the student plans to attend, or a meeting with an armed forces enlistment officer, or a vocational training consultant.

Once the IEP is developed, the local education agency (school) must do the following:

- Ensure the IEP provides for FAPE.
- Provide a good-faith effort to help the student achieve the IEP goals.
- Ensure all IEP services are provided.
- Have the IEP in place before the school year begins.
- Provide transportation if it is required as part of FAPE.
- Reconvene the IEP team and review the IEP every twelve months.
- Revise the IEP when necessary.
- Make the IEP accessible to each teacher and service provider.
- Inform each of the youth's regular and special education teachers about their specific responsibilities under the IEP, including any special accommodations, modifications, and supports that must be provided to the student.

Transfer of Rights

In many states, once students reach age 18, the age of majority, they are considered adults and thus are given the rights their parents once had on their behalf. IDEA now authorizes (but does not require) states to transfer parental rights to the students who reach that state's age of majority. The IDEA requires that students be notified a year before they reach the

IDEA RIGHTS OF STUDENTS AND THEIR PARENTS

1. The opportunity to participate in meetings with respect to the identification, evaluation, and educational placement, and the provision of FAPE

2. To be part of the group that determines what additional data are needed to evaluate the eligibility for services

3. To share information and concerns that must be included in the IEP development

4. To regularly be kept informed about the educational performance

5. To be equal participants in the development, review, and revision of the IEP

6. To be informed about who will be at the IEP meeting along with the purpose, time, and location of meetings with enough advance notice

7. To receive a copy of the IEP, the evaluation data, and all school records (there may be a copying charge for school records only)

8. To file for due process in case of disagreements that cannot be worked out between the parents and the public agency

9. To invite other individuals with special knowledge or expertise regarding the student

10. To the protections under FERPA (Family Educational Rights and Privacy Act), Section 504, and the Americans with Disabilities Act (ADA)

age of majority that the rights will transfer to them. *This statement must be included in the IEP.*

Once the parent role changes as a result of the transfer of rights, the parent can continue to be involved. However, that involvement is not legally required. Instead, parent involvement is at the discretion of the school or the student. There are two exceptions to this rule. A special rule can be made if the student is proved not competent to give informed consent. The student may also decide to appoint his or her parents to represent his or her educational interests. To do so, special education attorney Pete Wright advises the student to make the following *handwritten* statement: "I hereby appoint _____ to represent my educational interests." That statement must then be signed and dated by the student. (While not necessary, it may help to have the signed statement notarized.) Following is a summary of what rights will be transferred to the student.

Placement

Special education is not a place. It's not a room in a building or a special teacher. It is a right granted to students with disabilities who are in need of an IEP. As previously explained, the IEP is the plan designed to provide the services necessary for the student to receive a free, appropriate public education, to make progress in the general curriculum, and to prepare for postsecondary life. Yet parents often are told that if their teen needs special education, he or she will have to spend a part of the day in the resource room. Why? Well, from the school's perspective, they must provide a service and that is where they provide the service to a lot of "special ed kids."

Too many parents have been told that if they don't allow the school to provide the service, by which the school really means put the kid in the special place, then the student cannot receive special education. If you have been told that, then you have been misinformed. I'm not saying the school has behaved maliciously. Schools are institutions, and the nature of institutions is to categorize and cater to programs instead of individuals. Schools have a very hard time addressing individual needs or adapting programs to fit students. Instead, they try to fit students into programs. Of course, the IEP must be an individualized plan, not a general program.

IDEA requires that a student with a disability not be removed from the regular education environment if that student's education can be achieved in that setting with the use of supplementary aids and services. Many students with ADHD will be able to achieve in this regular education setting. But others will not. *IDEA understands that the setting is determined by where the student can receive appropriate education. Thus it allows for a range of placement options.* "The IEP forms the basis for the placement decision. A student need not fail in the regular classroom before another placement can be considered," states Robert Silverstein, J.D., director for the Center for the Study and Advancement of Disability Policy.

There are some basic types of placement options. These can be mixed and matched depending on the individual student's need and the goals and objectives of the IEP. For instance:

- Regular education classroom with modification, supplementary aids and services, in-class support teacher, modified curriculum, or other assistance.
- Partial pull-out program—have some classes with a special education teacher and others with regular education teachers.
- Full-day program within the home school in a self-contained classroom.
- Out-of-district day placement—where the student attends another school but returns home every day, or may return to the home school for extracurricular activities. It includes transportation.
- Residential placement—which is a twenty-four-hour, five- or seven-day-a-week program. This placement includes all non-medical care, room and board, parental travel to and from the placement, and parent phone calls to the placement at no cost to the parents.
- Extended school year—often a twelve-month program, possibly residential.

As you can see, there are a wide variety of options. Placement decisions must be made on the basis of each child's abilities and needs and not solely on factors such as the category of disability. That means the school cannot say to you something to this effect: "We cannot place your child into a residential program unless we change the classification from 'other health impaired' to 'emotionally disturbed.'" The school also cannot make the needed special education and related services contingent upon cost or administrative convenience. Furthermore, placements do not have to remain the same for the student's entire school career. Let's say a student is in a more restrictive placement, but later, thanks to the help received there, the student's IEP can be carried out in a less restrictive setting. IDEA *requires* that the placement setting be changed to the less restrictive setting.

Graduation from high school with a regular high school diploma is considered a change of placement under IDEA. The law does not require a reevaluation prior to graduation, but it does require schools to give written notice prior to changing the student's placement through graduation. Of course, IDEA rights end when a student receives a regular high school diploma. It's important to know that students who receive any document other than a regular high school diploma are still entitled to FAPE if they are in the eligible age range, which is through age 21. Also, as graduation is considered a change of placement, you have the right to challenge whether or not graduation with a high school diploma is appropriate for your son or daughter.

Temporary Placement

If a youth has been found eligible for IDEA services, the law allows the school to place the child temporarily—before the IEP is finalized—to determine if that placement is appropriate for that student. It can do so only if these guidelines are met:

- An interim IEP must be developed.
- The parents must agree to the temporary placement.
- A specific timeline must be set for completing the evaluation, finalizing an IEP, and determining the appropriate placement.
- An IEP meeting must occur at the end of the trial period to finalize the IEP.

Private School Placement

Students in private schools are entitled to FAPE. However, determining if schools are responsible for the costs of private school placements can be complicated. Clearly, if the public school decides such a placement is warranted, then it understands its responsibility to pay the education costs for the out-of-district or residential placement. When parents place the student in a private school without the prior agreement of the public school, the financial responsibility becomes less clear. If you are considering placing your son or daughter in a private school because you do not think the public school can provide FAPE, consider doing some or all of the following:

- Get a copy of the particular statute, 20 U.S.C. § 1412 (a) (10), and also read section Subpart D—Children in Private Schools—carefully. You can obtain this by contacting NICHCY or www.wrightslaw.com/law/code_regs/20USC1412. Attorney Wright also has a commentary about the unilateral private placement issue at this link.
- Contact the parent training and information (PTI) center in your state. It can answer questions about special education, help you work with your school, and put you in touch with parent groups. To locate the PTI in your state, call NICHCY or visit their Web site and click on "State Resource Sheet."
- Contact your state director of special education, who can also tell you about state policies and guide you about what steps to take.
- Contact a lawyer or advocate who specializes in special education to guide you.

Disagreements and Procedural Safeguards

Parents and schools can disagree over many elements of the special education process, not just whether or not the student needs to be in a private school placement. Actually, very few students will need to be removed from the local school district. Still, should your son or daughter be one of them, it's nice to know your rights.

The more common disagreements between school personnel and parents of teens with ADHD usually have to do with schools refusing to evaluate or find a student eligible under IDEA. Beyond these, disagreements usually arise over the IEP and the student's placement. Fortunately,

IDEA has procedural safeguards that protect both parents and schools when disagreements arise.

I've already discussed one of these safeguards, informed parental consent. Another safeguard has to do with *Content of Notice*. Whenever the school proposes to initiate or change the identification, evaluation, or placement of a student, it must send written notice to the parents. That notice must contain a description of these items:

- explanation of why the school proposes or refuses the action to initiate or change the identification, evaluation, or placement of a student
- any other options the school considered and why these were rejected
- each evaluation procedure, test, record, or report the school used as a basis for making its decision
- any factors relevant to the school's proposal or refusal of an action
- a statement informing the parents of the protections and procedural safeguards they have under the law
- sources for parents to obtain assistance to understand these safeguards

If you or the school disagrees about the proposal to identify, evaluate, or change the placement of your son or daughter, then both you and the school have the right to *due process and/or mediation*. Due process is basically a legal court proceeding. Cases are presented before an impartial hearing officer or judge, who then hands down a ruling based on the facts. Rulings are considered binding and must be followed. Most parents and schools want to avoid due process if at all possible. It can be a gut-wrenching process that costs a lot of money and often leaves both parties bruised and at odds. However, when necessary, it's a great right to have.

Mediation

Obviously one would prefer to work out differences without going to court. Therefore, IDEA has a *voluntary mediation* procedure. The procedure is as follows:

1. Either the parent or school can request mediation. However, the parent can still file for due process before, during, or after the mediation process. Schools may not use mediation as a way to delay or deny the parents their rights to a due-process hearing. Schools also cannot require that a parent use mediation, although they can establish procedures to have the parent speak with a disinterested party about the benefits of mediation.

2. The state pays the cost of the mediator. Mediators are trained in methods of mediation and conflict resolution and in special education law. They are also impartial. Mediators are selected from a list.

3. Any mediation must be scheduled in a timely manner and held in a convenient location.

4. Any agreement reached must be placed in writing and signed by all parties present.

5. Mediation must be confidential and not used as evidence in a due-process hearing.

Due Process

Suppose you and the school district try mediation without success. Or suppose you don't try mediation. You might then need to proceed to due process. The law carefully explains due-process procedures. I don't advise parents to handle due process by themselves; I strongly urge them to hire an experienced special education attorney. Fees can be costly. However, if the hearing officer or judge decides in your favor, he or she may order the school district to reimburse your costs, including reasonable attorney's fees. Your attorney will know the procedure required by the courts to request reimbursements. Trained advocates may also serve as advisers or representatives, although their fees are generally not reimbursable.

To file due process, the parent or the attorney should provide written notice to the school. That notice must include:

- the name of the child
- the child's legal address
- the name of the school

- a description of the nature of the problem, including facts that illustrate the nature of the problem
- a proposed resolution of the problem to the extent it is known and available to parents at the time

The public school may not deny a due-process request if the parents file with state but fail to file a notice with them. Five business days prior to the hearing, all parties must disclose their recommendations based on their evaluations along with all other evidence and the names of witnesses who will testify. Any party has the right to prohibit the introduction of evidence at a hearing that was not disclosed five days in advance.

Naturally, you will want to avoid such serious disputes and actions, but you may not be able to. Your child comes first. Do what you have to, but try to be reasonable. If the school gives you a runaround or refuses to budge on something that you know your child needs in order to receive FAPE, you must fight for your child's rights.

The Discipline Regulations

Students with ADHD, oppositional defiant disorder, conduct disorder, or other comorbid conditions may get caught up in a disciplinary track because these disabilities cause behavioral, social, and emotional problems as well as academic ones. I probably don't have to tell you that under zero-tolerance policies, many schools expel much more readily than they used to. Part of that has to do with concerns about school violence and making the school a safe atmosphere for all students. Also, there is a sort of backlash against students with disabilities who do not behave. In some cases, school administrators want to relieve themselves of the burden of difficult students. As you read about discipline issues, remember that these regulations are always subject to change, and judicial interpretations around the country may conflict with each other. The law is always changing and subject to different interpretations.

Child advocate Lili Frank Garfinkel notes that when schools eject "problems," often they don't want the kids back. She says, "There are two ways to look at this situation. You can shove the kid down their throats and say, 'You have to take this kid back,' in which case they may set it up so the kid will fail." That shouldn't be the case, but these days many school administrators are under pressure to enforce zero tolerance. They may be reactive, which doesn't help. If the student does go back to the school, be sure the necessary supports are in place to help him or her succeed in maintaining appropriate school behavior.

Given the behavioral problems that go along with ADHD and related difficulties, you really have to know what the schools can, can't, and should do regarding discipline for students covered under IDEA. These regulations are described below.

Basically, the law divides discipline problems into two distinct areas: those that result from the disability (viewed as manifestations of the disability) and those that are not manifestations of the disability. The law does not excuse misbehavior. Rather, it specifies what has to happen when a student with an IEP misbehaves. You need to know a few terms to understand the law.

Functional behavioral assessment (FBA). When creating an IEP, the IEP team must look at the student's behavioral difficulties and determine those that are most likely to occur on a repetitive basis—in other words, the student's typical misbehaviors. With ADHD, those can range anywhere from calling out in class to calling others names, being disrespectful, blowing up, storming out of rooms, and many others. Obviously, no one wants to ignore such behavior or say, "The student has ADHD so what do you expect!" Instead, the IEP is supposed to address interventions for these commonly occurring misbehaviors.

Behavioral Intervention Plan (BIP). In developing the IEP, the team must consider, if appropriate, the development of strategies to address the behaviors likely to manifest as part of the disability. These should include positive behavioral interventions and other strategies and supports that address the behaviors. *The team should have a BIP for behavior that could violate the school's code of conduct.* I advise parents to review the school's code of conduct carefully prior to going to an IEP meeting. Circle all the areas that may be problematic for your teen. You might also ask the school personnel to do the same. This way you have a good idea of where your teen will likely run into trouble. You want to avoid behavior problems if at all possible. When students with ADHD are handled well, much misbehavior can be avoided. Also, the law makes it clear: "*A failure to, if appropriate, consider and address these behaviors in developing and implementing the child's IEP would constitute a denial of FAPE to the child."*

It is very important that the BIP be implemented by individuals who are trained to do so effectively. Ask how the school will train the building disciplinarian. Ask to see their written teacher in-service training plan so you can determine whether school personnel are trained to recognize the characteristics of ADHD and in the educational management of students with this disorder.

The BIP should contain specific regular or alternative disciplinary measures. It could allow for denial of certain privileges or it could include short suspensions that would result from particular infractions of school rules, in so far as the school's policy would be the same for the students without disabilities. It should also contain positive behavior-intervention strategies and supports as part of a comprehensive plan to address the child's behavior. The BIP may also be reviewed and revised under certain circumstances that are described in this chapter under the section, "What Is a Manifestation Determination Review?"

There are certain circumstances under which the school may remove a student from the regular education placement or change the student's existing placement. These are listed in the next section and are fairly clear, especially regarding a student who has brought a weapon or controlled substance to school, or if the school believes a student is likely to injure self or others.

Putting these two circumstances aside, one muddy area surrounding removal has to do with whether the student can behave appropriately. If a student can behave appropriately with the right supports and interventions, then the school cannot place the student in a more restrictive setting. However, if the student's behavior, even with appropriate interventions, significantly impairs the child's learning and the learning of others, the school can remove the student from the regular education placement. (Such an action is subject to parental approval, which means that parents either have to agree to the change or file for due process. If they file for due process, the student stays in the placement under the provision known as "stay put.")

This placement issue can be very complex. In exceptional cases, some students might need to be in a special school where they can be helped to work on their behavior as part of the general education curriculum. If that's the case for your student, get professional help, because you do not want the school to come up with a plan that will not work, that will only delay your teen's progress, or that may put the teen at risk for dropping out or being expelled. Don't wait until it's too late.

Following are some key points of the discipline policy under IDEA. See the information link at the beginning of this chapter for where to find further information. As you know, though laws may be written in black and white, they are subject to interpretation. If your son's or daughter's behavior leads to the types of actions described below, seek advice from a professional with expertise in school discipline.

When removals are allowed:

1. Short-term removals—of not more than ten *consecutive* school days—to an appropriate interim alternative educational setting, another setting, or suspension are allowed (a) to the same extent as school policy applies to students without disabilities, and (b) as long as such removal does not constitute a change in placement. Multiple short-term removals are permitted.
2. A removal of more than ten consecutive days is considered a change of placement.
3. A pattern of short-term removals is considered a change of placement. To determine if a pattern exists, these factors must be considered: length of removal, the total amount of time the child is removed, whether or not the type of misconduct differs in each incident, and the proximity of the removals to one another.
4. Whenever a child is removed, the IEP team must meet to decide if the behavior was a manifestation of the disability. If not, then the student is subject to the same rules as other students without disabilities. However, after the tenth consecutive day, services must be provided to help the student progress in the IEP goals and general curriculum.
5. Schools can remove a student for up to forty-five days at a time for bringing or having a weapon at school or a school function. The forty-five days removal also applies to possession, use, sale, or solicitation of illegal or controlled substances at school or school functions.

6. If the school believes a student presents a danger to himself or others, the school can file for an emergency order to remove the student. An impartial hearing officer can order a student to be removed to an interim alternative educational setting for up to forty-five days if he or she finds by *substantial* evidence that the child is *substantially* likely to injure self or others; that the child's current IEP is appropriate; that the school has made reasonable efforts to minimize the risks of harm; and that services have been provided to keep the behavior from recurring. They can also ask for subsequent forty-five-day removals for the same causes. In cases where the evidence is not so clear, a hearing must be held before an administrative law judge.

7. Schools may report crimes to law enforcement personnel to the same extent they do so with students without disabilities. (Consult the IDEA regulations for information about students with disabilities within the juvenile justice system or adult prisons.)

When services must begin:

1. After the student has been removed for more than ten consecutive school days in a school year, or if nonconsecutive removals constitute a pattern exceeding ten days.

2. Services must be given to students with disabilities to the extent necessary to allow them to progress toward the goals set out in the IEP, and must include modifications designed to address the problem behavior. The IEP team determines the extent of necessary services.

3. When the student is placed in an interim alternative educational placement whether or not the behavior is a manifestation of the student's disability. Regarding weapons and drug removals, along with appropriate IEP services, services and modifications must be designed to prevent the behavior from recurring.

About the Alternative School

I have noticed a somewhat disturbing situation in which students who are not classified have been removed from the regular school program to a program within the school district that the school calls an "alternative school." Many of these students have disabilities but have not had the benefit of an evaluation or of an IEP. I also know of cases where parents have informed the school that the student has ADHD and related disorders, for example oppositional defiant disorder (ODD). Still, the school has not followed the child-find requirements to locate, identify, and evaluate any student known or suspected to have a disability.

Parents, if your teen has so much trouble with behavior and performance that school personnel find it necessary to remove him or her to an "alternative school," your child should be evaluated. Your teen may be "a discipline problem," but find out what's behind the behavior. Do not accept arbitrary removal. If you think your child should not be removed and that he or she has a disability that is not being diagnosed or for which services are not being given, request that a functional assessment and evaluation be done. Now, it may turn out that the alternative school happens to be a good placement for your son or daughter. If you agree that the alternative school is a good place, you can allow the school to place your teen there, *but* still insist that a special education evaluation and assessment be done. No matter what the placement, if your son or daughter has a disability that requires special education, then he or she should have an IEP with measurable goals, benchmarks, and short-term objectives. Also know that if your teen is not labeled under IDEA and the school did not know or has no reason to believe your teen has a disability, then they can place your teen in an alternative school program. Of course, under these circumstances you can still request an evaluation and file due process should you and the school continue to disagree.

What Is a Manifestation Determination Review?

A manifestation determination review is a formal process for determining whether a child's behavior is related to his or her disability. Federal law requires this review whenever an eligible child's special education placement is changed for disciplinary reasons. The following material is from the PACER newsletter, fall 1999.

In a manifestation determination, the IEP team must first consider the behavior subject to disciplinary action in relation to all relevant information, including:

- evaluation and diagnostic results, and information supplied by the parents
- observations of the child
- the child's IEP and placement

The team is then required to look at the child's behavior and determine:

- whether the child's IEP and placement were appropriate and the special education services, supplementary aids and services, and behavior-intervention strategies provided were consistent with the child's IEP and placement
- whether the child's disability impaired his or her ability to understand the impact and consequences of the behaviors
- whether the child's disability impaired the child's ability to control the behavior

If the team determines that the behavior is unrelated to the child's disability, the school may use the same discipline that it uses with all students, except that it must continue to provide FAPE. (From PACESETTER © 1999. Used with permission from PACER Center, Inc., Minneapolis, MN; (952) 838-9000; www.pacer.org. All rights reserved.)

Whenever your child has a serious behavior problem, the IEP team must meet to consider how to teach new behavior skills, not just how to punish inappropriate behavior. Part of the discussion should focus on alternatives to suspension, and part should be directed to developing a positive approach to intervening with the behavior.

From my point of view, many suspensions are unnecessary. I believe a good deal of misbehavior happens when the student's teachers are not trained in methods of handling student behaviors, including those things that set the stage for the behavior to occur (antecedents) and those things that keep the behavior going (consequences). If you change the set of the stage, the action changes. If you change what happens after an action, the action changes. That says to me that we have to change what we do with these students rather than expect them to change on their own. That's the old "an ounce of prevention is worth a pound of cure" saying.

Suspension may actually worsen the student's behavior. After all, it takes a student usually already struggling with the curriculum out of the instructional loop. Missed days usually mean the student falls behind. The more the student falls behind, the harder it becomes to catch up, and the greater the likelihood that poor behavior will result from a greater skill deficit. It also means the child has significant unsupervised time on his or her hands. While supervision or the lack thereof is not the school's responsibility, I believe that it should be considered. After all, we want to consider what's in the student's best interests. I see suspension mainly as a reaction and not as a plan. I'm sure there are education colleagues who would argue this point with me. I understand, but I have also taught in tough schools with kids who have a lot of behavior problems. Rarely did suspension change a student's chronic misbehavior for more than a short period of time.

Schools must consider a manifestation review:

1. whenever the school proposes to remove a student for weapons or drugs
2. whenever the school seeks an order from a hearing officer for an interim alternative educational placement
3. whenever the school seeks to change the placement of any student who has violated any school rule or code of conduct

Whenever any of these occurs, the parents must be notified no later than the date of the proposed action, and they must be given the procedural safeguards notice. The manifestation determination review must be conducted immediately if possible but no later than ten school days after the decision to take a removal action. Finally, the IEP team and other qualified personnel must conduct the review in a meeting.

Family Educational Rights and Privacy Act (FERPA)

FERPA ensures confidentiality to parents and their children. Schools may not disclose your teen's special education or disciplinary records to any outside agency without your consent unless a subpoena or court order

FERPA RIGHTS

- Parents are to have access to educational records.

- Consent is required to release records to a third party.

- Parents may challenge information in records.

- Parents must be notified of privacy rights.

- These rights apply to all educational institutions that receive federal funds, and they are designed to prevent curious faculty, administrators, students, the press, or anyone without a legal reason from seeing the records.

has been issued. If a court order has been issued, the school must make an attempt to notify you (or your teen, if he or she is of age). It seems to me that if someone outside of authorized school personnel requests to see your teen's records, that you might consider withholding consent until you get a lawyer. If the disclosure is in connection with an emergency and the knowledge is necessary to protect the health or safety of the student or other individuals, then disclosure can be made without parental consent.

FERPA also allows parents the right to inspect and review their teen's school records. You may seek to have them amended if you think they are misleading or a violation of your student's privacy. You also have the right to file a complaint if the school refuses to make amendments to the records. They must notify you about the procedures to do so.

Parent Advocacy

As you can see, parents and their children have many rights, though sometimes parents have to work hard to get those rights into action. If you are the parent of a child with a disability, you are also an advocate.

Effective advocates know how to work the system, but to do that, you need to know it inside and out. That's why I've explained the rights under IDEA, Section 504, and FERPA.

Effective advocates are informative, credible, polite, persuasive, and know what they're talking about. They use their knowledge to help. They are politely assertive but seldom aggressive. They don't get into "pissing matches" with school personnel. If disagreements arise, they problem-solve and take appropriate action. They believe in collaboration and partnership.

Partnership implies that the purpose of everyone in a certain relationship is a mutual interest or commitment. Partners may not always see things the same way, but they usually do have the same intention. Individuals in partnerships may have different belief systems, so that parents and the school personnel need to keep their eyes on the prize—the student's education. To do what's necessary to enable the student, partners have to give and take. They need to use the principles of communication and conflict resolution.

You can agree to disagree, but you want to avoid power struggles. Pamela Wright, a licensed social worker, has published "Seven Steps to Effective Parent Advocacy" on the Wrightslaw Web site. You might want to download this document (it's free) and keep it in your child's school file. Following are her seven steps:

1. Join disabilities organizations such as CHADD, ADDA, LDA, and NCLD.
2. Organize your child's file, which should include copies of all evaluations, IEPs, correspondence, medical reports, and so on. File documents in reverse chronological order.
3. Learn to measure educational progress. (See www.wrightslaw.com/advoc/articles/tests_measurements.html.)
4. Chart your child's test scores. This helps you to see what progress is being made.
5. Learn about your rights and responsibilities.
6. Learn about assistive technology.
7. Become an educated consumer. Visit Web sites that provide good quality educational and legal information.

The Web site, www.ldonline.org, also offers good guidelines for parent advocacy:

- Know the rules.
- Get to know the people who make decisions about your child.
- Keep records.
- Gather information.
- Communicate effectively. (See Chapter 6 for good communication guidelines.)
- Know your teen's strengths and weaknesses. Share them with educators.
- Emphasize solutions.
- Focus on the big picture. (Keep your eye on getting the best educational experience for your child and involve him or her in decision making early on.)

Every time you meet with the IEP team, they write a summary. They may also do so every time you call. You must do likewise. You want to keep a clear record of who said what, what agreements or disagreements (if any) occurred, who would do any proposed action, and when it would be done.

Always write a follow-up and send a copy of it to your teen's case manager. Request that it be placed in the file. I know this is a lot of work when you already have so much on your plate. Still, should a dispute arise, you will be thankful you've taken the time. In your letter, be sure to give the date of the meeting, your child's name, who attended, and what you agreed or disagreed about. Stick to the facts and be businesslike in the tone. Of course, keep a copy in your records. You may fax such letters or send them by registered mail, return receipt requested. However, if you do fax, be sure it does not go to a general office where students or other staff who don't understand confidentiality have free access to your communications.

With your child's records, also keep a contact log. Every time you call or meet with someone, be sure to have a record. Your state parent training and information center can give you a form for this purpose. Following are a telephone log and guidelines for establishing a record, which may be helpful.

TELEPHONE LOG

PERSON I TALKED TO   TELEPHONE   DATE

QUESTION/INFORMATION

FOLLOW-UP

- I PROMISED TO—

- HE/SHE PROMISED TO—

- ADDITIONAL ACTION NEEDED—
(e.g., letter documenting phone call,
others to contact, etc.)

Provided to the author by New Jersey Statewide Parent Advocacy Network (SPAN)

The Surefire Four-Step Record Decoder*

Step I: Organize

1. After obtaining the *complete set of records* from the school system, separate reports about your child (teacher reports, psychological evaluations, social history, etc.) from the correspondence.

2. Make an extra copy of the records in order to have an original and a working copy you can mark, cut, paste, and use in any way that will help you.

3. Arrange each set, reports, and extra documents, in chronological order.

*Provided to the author by Fran Rice, special education advocate

4. Secure the pages in a folder with a clip or in a loose-leaf notebook.

5. Number each report and make a chronological list that can be added on to as new records are generated.

Step II: Read

1. Read through the entire record to get overall impressions, tones of the school's view of your child.

2. In the margins of your working copy, mark with a "?" the statements or areas of the reports with which you disagree or do not understand.

Step III: Analyze

1. While rereading the reports, underline the phrases or sentences you feel best describe *both* your child's strengths and your child's problems. Put an "S" in the margin opposite a description of your child's learning strengths, a "P" opposite problems.

2. Using a worksheet, place the phrases or sentences about your child's strengths and problems within the categories of Oral Expression, Listening Comprehension, Basic Reading Skills, Reading Comprehension, Mathematical Calculation and Mathematical Reasoning, and Social Perception.

3. After each piece of data put the *source* and *date.* Often you will find trends beginning to emerge. The same observation, said in similar language, may occur in several reports over a period of time. You can indicate this by simply recording additional sources and dates to the original data.

4. List *recommendations* in the last section of the analysis sheet that are made by each evaluator: for example, services needed, classroom environment, class size, type of school setting, recommendation for further testing, specific teaching materials or methods.

Step IV: Evaluate

Using the question mark quotations you have made in the margins and your overall sense of the records from your analytical work with them, evaluate their accuracy against the following criteria:

ACCURATE—do these reports and portions of the records correspond with your own feelings, perceptions, observations, and assessments of your child?

COMPLETE—are all the documents required by the school system for the eligibility, Individualized Education Plan (IEP), and placement decision available in the file, for example, medical report, psychological examination, educational report, and others as required?

JARGON-FREE—do the reports describe your child in nontechnical terms and/or language you can understand and use? In a good report, diagnoses and technical language will be used and defined.

CURRENT—are the dates on the records recent enough to give a report of your child's present behavior and functioning?

CONSISTENT—are the reports contradictory? Is there consistency between the descriptions of your child by each evaluator?

UNDERSTANDABLE—is the language used meaningful, clear, and understandable to you? Example of an unclear statement: "She appears to have a psychological learning disability, calling for treatment involving a moderation of the special focus on interpersonal sensitivity she has received so far." WHAT DOES THAT MEAN?

OVERALL INTEGRITY—considering the records as a whole, do they make sense and lead to the given recommendations?

The Red Carpet Brigade

"I dubbed myself the 'red carpet brigade' because I would set out a red carpet wherever Drew went, to make his passage possible. That's how I define advocacy," says Iris Rothman. Since his earliest days, Drew has needed extraordinary help. In addition to severe ADHD, he also has severe learning disabilities. After second grade, it became clear to Iris that Drew would not be able to survive in a public school.

As Iris came to see, "Put him in a room with twenty-five people and you've got him used up in thirty minutes. There's nothing left to work with." A private school for kids with learning difficulties seemed to be the best alternative.

Drew, who is now finishing high school, has been in private school placements since third grade. The Rothmans have paid for all but one of those years out of their own pocket. Iris was able to get one year in a residential school funded by the school district. She had to sue them to do so. Ultimately, the Rothmans decided that they would make considerable financial sacrifices to have the autonomy of selecting the best places and programs for their son, plus avoid a yearly battle.

Though Drew didn't sail through any of the placements, some were better than others. The private school that Drew attended through eighth grade gave him the Headmaster's Award, which goes to the student who they have the most confidence in and who has grown the most. Iris believes the reason their program was so successful for her son had to do with their approach. "Drew has many needs. He couldn't possibly address them all at once. So rather than force him into situations where he would meet with little success, they gentled him and found his areas of strength." A large part of their approach was due to Iris's team effort. She never stopped problem-solving. If Drew's mood got low or his performance seemed to dip, she found out why and worked with the school to make his road less painful.

When Drew transitioned to a private residential high school hours from home for ninth grade, the results were horrible. "We just saw all the executive function issues come into play," explains Iris. With the exception of the tutor the school provided, the entire program proved to be a poor match. So Iris once again went on a school search. She found a new school that was minutes from home where he could board during the week and come home on weekends. It allowed Iris to stay more involved. Still, Drew had a terribly hard time. He was dogged by academic performance problems, slow processing speed, and constantly having to make transitions, and the year just went from bad to worse. "He lost heart," his mom says sadly. "He acted inappropriately, the whole nine yards."

Iris realized that Drew had been sending out signals. He just couldn't understand the work without one-to-one attention. His parents supplied him with the necessary tutors. He managed to hobble through another year, but at the end the Rothmans got a huge surprise. "He announced that he thought he'd take a year off from school. We said, 'Yeah, right.' Then he wrote the headmaster an eloquent letter of resignation, which indicated his decision to withdraw with the knowledge but not the permission of his parents," Iris explains.

Drew took this drastic step because, he says in no uncertain terms, "I was just fed up with the hassle of it. Summer break wasn't enough. I wanted a year off and not just to log around the house and do stuff. I wanted to hike the Appalachian Trail."

Everybody tried to convince Drew to just finish high school and take a year off before college. Drew knew he couldn't do that. "I was beat and needed a year off right then." Once Drew put it that way, his mother had a realization. She told the headmaster, "By trying to convince Drew that he can stick it out, none of us are acknowledging the pain and the effort that goes into his presence in this location known as school."

After that realization, the Rothmans decided to allow Drew to take a year's leave of absence from education. "Surprisingly, when we agreed that he would not go back to school for this one year, there was an enormous sense of relief for everybody. The relief came because we didn't have to keep him up to keep him going. We didn't have to try to emotionally support a person who in essence was like a donkey being coaxed with a carrot but being whipped by somebody at the other end. We were trying to support him, but he just couldn't make it. That just made him feel guilty, because everybody is doing everything for him but he just can't do it."

Of course, the Rothmans couldn't support Drew's plan to hike the Appalachian Trail by himself. They went to see the family counselor, who came up with an interesting alternative. Instead of just dropping out of school and heading for the hills, Drew would go to a wilderness program, where he would learn the skills necessary to someday hike the long, arduous trail.

Once again Iris found herself leading the red carpet brigade. She called an independent educational consultant. She learned what programs were available and where. Drew insisted on no academics, so she found just the program. The only problem was that Drew was underage. Due to her advocacy work, they took him anyway.

Out in the wilderness, Drew learned that his executive function problems and his learning disabilities continued to be a detriment. For instance, he could read maps but not follow them. However, the social piece was the hardest part of the program. He found it very hard to live so closely for so long with eight other people. He began to isolate himself.

The staff frequently called Iris to keep her informed of troubles that were brewing. Drew had "stopped listening." That presented a safety issue. When the group would come up with a plan of how to approach a particular trail or cross a river, Drew always had another idea. He'd argue with them over the minutest detail and insist his way was the better one. Finally the leadership had to restrict his group activities. "He was asked to leave before the fourth session, and I was very distraught," Iris remembers. She was mainly worried that instead of this being a helpful experience, the outcome might have done him harm.

It didn't. Drew says matter-of-factly, "At the end of the third part, the social discrepancies just got too much for me. If I had stayed, I wouldn't have looked back on the program as positively. Though I struggled with it a lot, I don't regret doing the program one bit. I had so much time to reflect on myself, to learn how to communicate with others, and how to plan and organize."

When Drew returned from the wilderness, his mother says, "He came back a different person." Drew sees a change, too. "I notice little things more. I care about little things more, like putting the dishes away. I think I'm happier. Of course, I gained outdoor skills. It was just a phenomenal experience."

This family has mastered the art of the alternative approach. A large part of that may be due to Drew's excellent self-advocacy skills. He's really clear about his strengths and weaknesses. And he's exceptionally grateful for his parents. "They're really accepting, and this is really nice," he says, and elaborates, "They're used to the routine with me. They got the diagnosis of ADD when I was at a very young age. My mother has learned so much. She's like an encyclopedia. There's some things she knows about me that even I don't know. And my dad's just great, too. He's also learned a lot and he's very supportive. They advocate for me with different schools and teachers and they always tell me what's going on."

What have all their efforts shown Arnie and Iris Rothman? "People will ask me," says Iris, "what his prognosis is." Her answer? "If we can get him through school, he'll be fine. He is really gonna get there. He can be a whole person, hold a job. He will always be different. He will always have issues he has to address, but I think he is better equipped since we've been working on it for so many years. Will life be easy for him? No, but I couldn't guarantee that for any of my children or anybody else's children, or even myself."

A year after the program, Drew went back to his previous private high school. He's doing great academically. Iris says, "He's fallen in love with philosophy and reads Aristotle even though it's not assigned for school." He gets tutoring for math. He's discovered set design and does the photography for the yearbook. That helps him with socialization, as he's in the mainstream but also has a task to see him through those awkward moments of random conversation that have caused him so much trouble in the past. This young man is also on the cross-country team and is learning better socialization by being part of a team effort. Iris happily says, "He's a changed student, and things there are going smashingly well."

Education Consultants/Special Placements

What Consultants Do

When our children do not thrive in school, sometimes we have to make extraordinary efforts. Clearly, the Rothmans went way beyond what many parents know or can afford to do. If you turn to the public schools for guidance, you probably will find that your school, like most public schools, won't really explore too many options beyond their normal procedures. That's where educational consultants can play a huge role in helping you to find some options for your teen. In the next chapter, I discuss the role they play with college placement. For now, let's focus on what they do and when you might need to see such a person for students during the secondary school years.

Helene Reynolds, from Princeton, New Jersey, and Barbara Posner from Katonah, New York, have their own educational consulting firms. Ms. Reynolds specializes in placements for students of all types and ages, from the great student looking for a good boarding school to students with the most severe disabilities in need of lifelong residential placements. Ms. Posner specializes in educational programs for students with learning disabilities, ADHD, and emotional issues.

"Educational consultants assess a child's life through their paperwork and their testing results. They meet with the family to help them work out how to improve their child's present school placement, and then work closely with the schools and the families to do so," Ms. Posner explains. Consultants consider the full scope of placement possibilities, which range from public school options and cooperative educational services that have special programs for various school districts to local day placements, publicly funded private schools, private schools, and residential/therapeutic programs.

"It's our responsibility to guide, advise, counsel, and provide information so the parents can make an informed and wise decision," says Ms. Reynolds. Educational consultants have very goal-directed work and mainly serve as project managers. "We can guide parents and provide a larger universe of information and choice," says Ms. Reynolds. She notes that most of her clients would rather not need her services. Parents come to her because they are confused about information or available services, or because some other professional has steered them on to a narrow course that they don't feel confident with.

Educational consultants make great problem solvers. They not only look at the information you have, but also advise you about gaps in your information that may need to be filled in order to truly find an appropriate placement. Some may also help you in your teen's IEP development, whether the teen attends a regular public school or a private placement.

When Considering Private Placement

The consultants advise parents to proceed carefully in choosing programs for their children. Many parents will often take the recommendation of other parents who've sent a child to a particular school. "That's not a very good source," says Ms. Posner. As she explains, a placement that's good for one student isn't necessarily good for another. Furthermore, private schools are collections of students and staff, and over time student and staff profiles will change. You need to be especially careful about what type of students the placement serves, and whether it still lives up to its reputation.

Another important criterion Ms. Reynolds points out is whether or not the school wants to work with students who have ADHD. She believes the school should be saying, "We're not looking for brilliant kids or successful kids. We are not looking for the kids who are minding rules and regulations. We want the kids who are out of order, who are not focused, who are not doing their homework, and who are disorganized. That is who we work with, and we do it well." Yes, there are schools that work well with teens who have ADHD. As you read in Chapter 9, there are even schools that work well with the toughest of teens. Of course, be careful that the schools actually do what they claim to specialize in, and that they are a good fit for your teen.

If you are considering a particular school, that school's staff can give you a list of parents to call for references. Your state department of special education also has a list that can be helpful, especially if you are considering a publicly funded placement through special education. Some wonderful private schools geared toward a special-needs population opt not to go through state bureaucracy. A school doesn't have to be on the state's approved list in order for a parent to get funding, although it makes it easier. Regarding special education placements, I advise parents to ask the potential school for a list of school districts in the parents' state that have paid to send students there. That will be helpful should you have a legal dispute with your school over placement.

Unless there is a crisis, Ms. Reynolds advises parents to visit at least two schools before making a decision, although she'd prefer they see even more so they can make a good comparison. "Parents need to spend a half day if they can. They need to sit in on a class or two, to go to a meal, to attend a school meeting if possible. They need to sit around and watch," she says.

Of course, talking to the students helps, too. But you need to read between the lines of what the students say. Ms. Reynolds points out that there are standard phrases. She describes visits she's made where the kids would say, "You'd be nuts to send your kid here. This place is terrible." Ms. Reynolds has found that these same students will then tell her something like, "We went to the pound today and we're in charge of taking care of three animals. I washed one and I'm going back next week." That type of comment tells you "what the child wants, what the child needs, and the child's awareness of it," says Ms. Reynolds. She's also heard "I hate this place, but I'm glad I'm here."

In selecting a placement, you want to be sure that it can serve your particular child well. Ms. Reynolds advises parents to be honest and open about their child. Otherwise they may be putting themselves, the placement, and the child at risk. "The place has to want your child with all their warts and hairs. Otherwise it's not going to work," she says. Parents may want to hide certain clinical information because they don't want the school to think poorly of their son or daughter, or because they're seeking an acceptance for a kid who desperately needs to go somewhere. Ms. Reynolds knows that within a month or two of placement, schools generally find out everything. She tells parents, "Look at this not in terms of will they want me, but will this place serve my child, and do we want them?"

Funding Private Placements

Payment for special placements usually comes through three primary sources: the parent's pocket, health insurance for any medically related expenses, or public school payment. Of course, state-sponsored social agencies and private charities may also be helpful. As mentioned earlier, if you're seeking public school placement, you probably should have an educational consultant or an attorney, preferably both. Do keep in mind that local school districts are not legally required to provide the *best* education. The law requires them to provide an *appropriate* education.

If you find that your teen needs a private school placement, try these steps.

1. Make a list of all the reasons why the public school does and does not work for this student. Keep in mind that they are responsible for education, and that includes social, emotional, and behavioral learning. If clinical problems prevent the student from receiving an education, then the school may have to provide for these needs as a related service to enable the student to be educated.
2. If possible, see an educational consultant, an attorney, or an advocate.
3. Research placements that would be appropriate given your child's needs.
4. Call your state department of education and get private school placement guidelines from them. Follow these carefully.

5. Visit placements. Select two good choices. Be sure the potential placement has thoroughly evaluated your child, in person if possible, and reviewed all records to make sure the match would work.

6. Have the placement help you determine how their program will meet your child's needs in a way that the school cannot. Create measurable goals, objectives, and benchmarks. Sound a bit like an IEP? Yep, it is. You want to come up with the IEP that your child needs and the placement best suited to carrying out that IEP. You may find that, in the long run, the local school district is the best place—provided it makes necessary program changes.

7. Work on getting eligibility first. Then make your placement case.

Crisis Placement

Sometimes parents of teens find themselves in volatile and crisis situations. Looking back, you might be able to trace these developments much the way you can see how a storm developed into a catastrophy. Still, that doesn't change the immediate need to take drastic action. The question is, how swiftly do you need to make a move? "We get a lot of crises," says Ms. Reynolds. "It's our job to assess whether something really is a crisis or whether it's better to wait a week, or a month, or a semester to gather information."

Ms. Reynolds and her staff often have parents call because their kid has gotten into trouble and will be going to a juvenile detention center unless they come up with an alternative. "In this situation, this type of placement may be a temporary safe harbor for the child so that the parents can go to court and know the kid isn't going to be hauled off to some place the parents might consider arbitrary or harmful," she explains. Of course, should that happen to you, understand that the temporary placement may become more permanent, especially if it works out well. Otherwise, you need to look further.

In the case of crisis placement, who pays? Well, that's not so easy to know. If the juvenile system pays, they usually select the placement. If you pay, you may be able to file for due process and get the school to pay. There's no way I can give guidelines for these complicated cases. You really need an attorney or a very good advocate.

Local school districts are responsible for the education of kids in psychiatric facilities and drug and alcohol treatment centers while they are in such programs. They don't pay for the program per se. In fact, some programs have a teacher on staff and ask the local school district only for the books and materials needed to advance the student along the curriculum. However, most teens don't wind up in these programs without lots of troubles. Many have disabilities. If that's the case, you may want to make a thorough assessment of your teen's total needs. If education is problematic, perhaps it's time to consider a significant change in placement.

SOME USEFUL WEB ADDRESSES

For IDEA: www.nichcy.org/idealist.htm, www.nichcy.org/regohs/ regohtoc.htm, (you will find discipline information here), www.ideapractice.org, and www.edgov/offices/osers/osep/index

For legal updates, attorneys, texts of statutes, decisions, etc.: www.edlaw.net

For advocacy organizations: www.chadd.org, www.add.org, www.ldonline.org, www.wrightslaw.com, www.c-c-d.org, and www.pacer.org

For mediation resources: www.directionservice.org/cadre

For Section 504: www.dhhs.gov/progorg/ocr/ocrhmpg.html

For ADA compliance: www.usdoj.gov

CHAPTER TWELVE

Transitions

After high school, young adults with ADHD must make a major life transition. How do we guide our teens into the right transition? What considerations must be given to the choices the teen must make? This chapter looks at the three main transition options: college, employment, and the military.

When Tyler Winston began school, most people knew ADHD by the symptom of hyperactivity. Laid-back, inattentive Tyler didn't stand much of a chance to be recognized as a student with a disability. With the exception of his mom, just about everybody saw him as unmotivated.

Tyler didn't know what to make of himself. He simply could not do well in school. After a while, he stopped caring. "It was like, well, I got another 28 on a test. I'd yell to the other kids, 'Hey, I got a 28.' In high school and elementary school, I truly didn't care. I wouldn't strive to get the lowest grade. I'd take the test and at times I'd try. Of course I'd study. And of course when I sat down I wouldn't look at the test as a joke or anything. I would be serious and think that maybe I'd do well on this one. Or maybe I don't know this question, but I'll know the next one. Then I'd get the test back with a grade of 32. So it was almost like a desensitization process—taking the test, thinking I'd at least get a 65 or 70 and then getting the test back with a 35 or whatever."

After enough bad grades despite his effort, over time Tyler came to believe that he just couldn't pass a test. Tyler's mother, Victoria, always knew her son had better ability than he demonstrated. Finally, in his high school junior year, a doctor identified his ADHD. He took medication for two days. According to his mother, "The medication had such a dramatic effect, it scared him." It was as if somebody had turned on the lights. Tyler refused to take it again.

Tyler struggled to graduate and decided to go a community college for a year. He also went to work part time in a brewery. As it turned out, Tyler was not ready for any type of college. He did, however, find out a lot about himself at work. "I got to learn hands-on from day to day. I knew what I had to do to earn my paycheck. In school, if you are not paying attention, you can sort of slip through. If you are in a hands-on, one-to-one situation and you are not paying attention, you mess up." Tyler decided he couldn't afford to mess up at work because he was getting paid.

This work experience showed that "unmotivated, lazy" Tyler did have a strong work ethic, but not for school, where he seldom saw success. He did terribly his first semester at the community college, where he planned to major in business. Still, he went back for a second term and hung in there until the last three weeks. His mom recalls he came home and said, "I will not do it anymore. I hate it here." With that he quit. Later Victoria discovered that he was failing everything. That partly helped him reach his decision to leave. He also quit because he had a moment of truth while on a mountain hike: He didn't know what he wanted to do, but he realized he had no interest in being a business major.

Nonetheless, Tyler's mother insisted he go to college. Over the summer they worked at finding a school for him. Poor high school grades prevented Tyler from even applying to his first choice. Then he found the school he currently attends and loves and wants to do well in. He had a very rocky start there. His father became terminally ill. He missed a lot of classes and ended up dropping a couple.

When winter term came, Tyler was full of plans to make a fresh start there because he really loved the school. When it came time to pay the tuition, he couldn't do it. "I decided to go to California. I got the inspiration to just drop everything and go." The cross-country trip gave Tyler an expansive view of his life.

"If I stuck with the path I was on, I would have been a business major coming out of a community college and going to a four-year school. One day my life changed," he explains. On his trip west, Tyler once again realized he was in the wrong field. He went back to school as an environmental science major. "I found everything that makes my life. I should be graduating this year with all my high school friends. I'm not." It doesn't bother Tyler that he's a few years behind schedule. Tyler told his mom just before he left for his trip out west, "Imagine if I were to go through all of college working as hard as I could just to come out and really have no clue about what I wanted to do, or worse yet, graduate and find out that I wanted to go in the opposite direction."

Tyler has just entered his senior year. He still struggles with academics. Even so, he gets decent grades now with a maximum of effort. "I don't mind school, because I truly want the degree that I'm working for," he says. Environmental science has been a tough major because he does so poorly on tests and has to work so hard in every other area to compensate for these low grades. He's so plagued by these tests, in fact, that he thought he failed his chemistry exam. Turns out he did fail it—because he forgot to hand it in. After the semester break, when he went to see his professor to find out what happened, she said, "Tyler, where's your exam?" It was in his notebook in the car.

That Tyler could forget to turn in his exam and not remember even after he struggled to pass the course seems almost unbelievable—unless you know what happens to students with ADHD. Despite his extraordinary struggle, Tyler refuses to accept that he has the disorder. Instead he sees it as an excuse he doesn't want or need. He's determined to graduate and is even thinking about going to law school. Now that he has a goal, his mother thinks he might consider medication for his working memory problem if it holds him back in law school.

The years after high school mark the beginning of a major life transition for both parents and teens. Parents must come to terms with having their teen legally able to make his or her own decisions. On top of that, teens have to figure out what's next for them in life. While some high school students can see what they're going to do after they graduate, this disorder often blurs that vision. Basically, all teens have these choices: college or vocational school, work, the military, or a combination thereof. Some teens with ADHD don't wind up in any of these tracks. They may find themselves lost, wondering "What do I do now?" Continuing an education seems like a hideous punishment to some. Others have trouble getting or keeping a job. The military, which used to sound like a great idea, a way to help someone mature, may not be the option we once thought it was, as I explain later in this chapter. Some teens with ADHD go through a "do nothing" period, maybe even more than once.

Many of us have hopes and aspirations for our teens. This late adolescent period marks the time when we realize our teens have their own ideas. For many parents, the hard part comes in accepting that what we envision may be wrong for who we've raised. Letting go is not easy. As Tyler's mother, Victoria, learned, she could not keep her son under her counseling thumb. When he decided that college was not right for him, she had to yield. To this young man's credit, he knew what was best for him. When the time was right, he made his move, but not to please his mom or anyone else. Tyler understood that if he had to struggle that much to get through college, he needed to do it for himself.

What should a teen with ADHD do after high school? There's no easy or right answer. Many teens with ADHD have a rocky time starting these major life transitions. We need to learn how to stay calm in the midst, offer guidance when we can, and let our kids learn from the consequences of their own decisions.

College

For some teens with ADHD, college is the right place. For many others, it's not. Research shows that many high school teens with ADHD have lower grade point averages than their peers without disabilities. Furthermore, a 1993 study shows that only about 20 percent of kids with ADHD enrolled in a four-year college. Of that group, only 5 percent graduate. I hesitate reporting these statistics to you, because I don't want you or your teen to think that college is too much of a reach if that's what the teen wants to do. Colleges today understand the diversity of their learners and that many academically challenged students can succeed with the right supports and services. So if your teen has put college on his or her possibility list, following are some factors and guidelines to consider.

Readiness

"We went away to look at two colleges. At one school, he nodded out in the middle of the interview. I was so embarrassed. I kicked his foot under the table to wake him," Jane Farnsworth remembers. Her son Neil's behavior should have been a huge tip-off that this young man was in no way ready for college.

What does it take to be ready for college? In general, it requires responsibility, self-awareness, good self-advocacy skills, maturity, and a willingness to work harder than ever in school for a goal that's pretty far from sight. Clearly, not all students with ADHD have these skills when they begin college. Some of these skills come with maturity. Others can be and should have been taught in high school, such as advocacy and study skills, which happen to be critical for college success.

While we can't make our teens mature, we can cultivate the environment to assist them. Some of them will thrive in an environment similar to a greenhouse, where they are nurtured with the right amount of support and independence. Others may resist any outside support and need to ripen like fruit kept in brown paper bags. You can use a greenhouse approach with a teen who willingly allows you to assist in the decision-making process, and who also wants to know how to compensate for the ADHD issues. You might have to use the brown bag approach for the teens who aren't yet ready to grow in the full light—the ones who resist help, think they have the answers, and need to learn the hard way.

Making a greenhouse environment is easy once you know the basic ingredients: structure, support, good communication, and problem solving. It's much more difficult to watch your teen shoot him- or herself in the foot. Yet, that may be equally as important for the young adult who's not yet ready to take guidance. Notice I use the words "not yet ready." If you give the teen enough space to feel the consequences of his or her decisions, he or she usually does get ready, provided the parents stay neutral. Generally, when parents keep their burning desires out of the picture, the teen has the opportunity to realize that he or she has created the life currently being lived. By being neutral, the parents provide a safe place for the teen who needs to pull a few weeds out of his or her life.

If you are the parent of a teen in need of maturity, you're not alone. Dr. Marsha Glines is dean of the College of Education at Lynn University in Florida and the executive director of TAP, the university's program for students with learning disabilities. She's been in the education business for many years and works with students who have ADHD and other learning problems. "We have to understand that many of our incoming freshman are really still developmentally functioning as adolescents. They're no worse. They're no better. They're just different," she notes. She's speaking about teens in general, not just those with ADHD.

Dr. Glines would like to see adolescents empowered with responsibility before coming to college. She suggests that they do community service. "It teaches responsibility beyond the family unit," she explains. It may also lead to student success. College students without responsibility and self-monitoring skills have a hard time coping: "Some of the students get unfocused or simply shut down."

Regarding parents of students with disabilities, Dr. Glines says, "Parents need to stop and look at the difference between accommodating and encouraging alternative approaches." That's a tough one. It's natural to want to protect a teen from mistakes and their consequences. Yet prevention may not always be the wisest course. It may be better to make and learn from mistakes in adolescence, when the stakes are lower. If parents always accommodate, the teen doesn't learn that mistakes cost.

Typical Skills of Successful College Students

- They know their learning style.
- They know their strengths and weaknesses.
- They can balance work and play.
- They know how to set priorities.
- They manage time.
- They attend classes.
- They do assignments.
- They get outside help when necessary.

What should you do if your son or daughter doesn't seem ready for college? You really need to consider the individual. As you can see, readiness includes many factors. Some of the areas of weakness can be compensated for with the appropriate college support, which I explain later in this chapter. In the meantime, talk openly and honestly with your teen about his or her reasons for wanting (or not wanting) to go on in education. Some kids may need time off between high school and college. As Dr. Zakreski says, "I don't think anything helps you grow up better than having a job where you have to be responsible and show up on time. When you have to go to work every day and remain there for eight hours or whatever your shift is to collect a paycheck, you begin to see what it takes to earn money."

Your teen may force college because he or she views not going as failure. Nothing could be farther from the truth. College isn't for everyone. And college right after high school isn't for everyone, either. The point here is to help the teen feel okay about whatever decision he or she makes. Should the teen opt for college, Dr. Glines strongly advises parents "to let the teen know that you have certain expectations for your tuition dollars or loan signatures." For example, he or she must go to classes, get extra help as needed, study, and show up for exams. Dr. Glines does not believe, however, that parents should expect good grades in return for tuition, especially if the student is trying hard and meeting the daily responsibilities.

Choosing a College

Ask not if the school wants you; ask if you want the school. A lot of teens who are not stellar students seem to settle for a particular college because they can get into it. While it's important to choose schools within academic and financial reach, a lot more needs to go into the decision-making process. First of all, you and your teen need to explore why college

---

INFORMATION LINK

If you and your teen are looking into college, you may want to contact the Heath Resource Center. They have some excellent free pamphlets to guide students with disabilities. You can call (800) 544-3284 or visit them on the Web at www.acenet.edu/programs/heath.

is the next step in life. Does the youth have a goal in mind? Is there a particular field of interest?

In the beginning of this chapter you read about Tyler Winston. He had a clear goal when he entered college—to major in business. His rocky freshman year helped him understand that the business life would not suit him. He had to take some time to "find himself." Clichéd as that sounds, he did find himself and now willingly puts out extraordinary effort to attain his goals. Was his first year or two of flunking out of college a failure? I don't think so. It brought him to a decision that would affect the quality of his life forever. Expect changes.

The Heath pamphlet "How to Choose a College" raises a number of questions teens with disabilities should answer as they begin the college admissions process. The main questions are:

- How independent am I?
- Where do I want to go to school?
- What do I want to study?
- How prepared am I academically?
- What are my goals?
- What services will I need?

Getting into the College of Choice

Most universities require applicants with disabilities to meet all the criteria of any other student seeking admission. In general, students have to meet the course requirements. Some schools that have special support programs for students with learning disabilities and ADHD may loosen their admissions standards with regard to SAT and ACT scores. For instance, Dr. Glines can make some accommodations on the SAT requirements, "particularly if the candidate has written a dynamite personal essay," she notes. However, she adds, "The more competitive the university, the less they are going to do in terms of altering those kinds of admissions criteria."

Education consultant Helene Reynolds believes students shouldn't totally rule out applying to a selective college based on the SAT or ACT cutoff requirements. Here's where an education consultant can be very helpful. As explained by Ms. Reynolds, many schools appreciate the recommendations of respected educational consultants because they know the colleges or universities very well and they know what type of student will do well in the placement. Consultants also prescreen, so admissions directors understand that when a respected consultant sends a student their way, that student deserves a more serious consideration.

If you use an educational consultant, be sure that person is honest, forthright, and well respected by the admissions directors where your teen's applying. You can find that out by asking to talk to clients who have used the consultant's services.

Do you really need an educational consultant? It depends. Understand that many high school guidance departments are snowed under by so many responsibilities and such high caseloads that they are unable to give the personalized attention that they used to. As Dr. Glines observes, "I think a consultant can be critical because guidance counselors, particularly for nontraditional students, don't have the time to really look at what a good match is versus the education consultants, who really have the time to look at the whole entire persona of the individual." A fair number of guidance departments actually streamline operations by holding parent-student seminars to give guidelines for the college selection process. They also tend to have a list of schools they've developed relationships with. That can be helpful or limiting, depending on the student. For highly personal attention, you and your teen may need to go outside the school or work extra hard to cultivate that guidance department relationship.

The Community College Route

Today's students have a lot more to choose from when selecting a college. That allows for a much better fit. Schools come in many designs. They either have open enrollment, which means that everyone who applies gets in, or selective admissions, which requires meeting the school's admissions criteria. There are private two-year programs and public community colleges that must openly enroll. In addition to the two-year and four-year programs, there are schools that do combined work/academic programs. Services for students with disabilities range from minimal to extensive.

A fair number of students with ADHD opt for the community college route. They may do so because they don't think they're ready to go away.

Some think they need to beef up their grades so they can go on to a higher degree program. This thinking can be either wise or unwise. It depends. Ted Harris opted for a community college because, he says, "I was majorly confused when I got out of high school. I wanted to be an astronomer, a pilot, an actor, do technical theater. I was so wide in thought, but I had no actual idea of what to do." After a year of floundering, he landed in a communications program. Now he's narrowed down his goal.

Dr. Zakreski finds that a number of the teens in his practice "opt for what they *perceive* to be a less challenging two-year program." Community colleges aren't necessarily easier. The same lack of study skills that dog a kid in high school will continue to affect the student in community college. It's unreasonable to think that the student will be successful in an open-enrollment two-year community college program without support. Local community colleges do offer special services to students with disabilities. However, Dr. Zakreski finds that "a lot of kids either don't know about them or are unwilling to make themselves pursue those services. That puts them at risk for further frustration and failure."

On top of these concerns, staying at home also presents another type of challenge. While it may seem a good way to ease into the transition of college or to narrow down one's possibilities, let's remember that both Ted Harris and Tyler Winston flunked a few semesters of community college. Parents might think the distractions at home are less than going away to dorm life, sororities or frat houses, and freedom, but Dr. Zakreski has found that many of his clients in community college "continue to study at home, try to prepare for classes with their stereos, TVs, and the same circle of friends that may be around. These are all distractions." They also make new friends at the community college and so have even more to draw them away from academic pursuits. Except for a few public and private community colleges with excellent support-service programs, in general, Dr. Glines does not favor the community college for nontraditional students.

In short, kids underestimate open-enrollment community college programs, and private ones, too. These programs are not necessarily watered-down courses. Students need the same skills to succeed in a two-year program as they do in a four-year school. Students need to be willing to take advantage of the special supports that most colleges have to offer. These days many schools offer a range of services for nontraditional learners.

Special Services

The legal entitlement landscape changes considerably once your teen receives a high school diploma. The rights of IDEA are no longer in effect. For instance, colleges do not have to guarantee an education, and there is no IEP for the student with disabilities. Any evaluation recommendations are up to the student to arrange, often paying out of pocket.

Even though IDEA rights end, the Americans with Disabilities Act (ADA) and Section 504 of the Rehabilitation Act remain in place throughout life. These laws do not require colleges to change their admission standards or their graduation requirements for students with disabilities. However, they do require all colleges to make reasonable accommodations to assist students with disabilities. Basically the law requires higher education to make modifications as needed to policies, practices, and procedures in order to ensure access to examinations and courses as long as it does not fundamentally alter the program.

Dr. Glines serves as her university's ADA compliance officer. She says, "The problem with the ADA is that it doesn't tell us what to do. It only gives guidelines and it gives us the language. Then it is up to individuals to interpret the law. The law tells us that we must make accommodations and offer auxiliary aids and services." The problem is the law doesn't state what's reasonable and what auxiliary services are required. Thus, these determinations are being made case by case. Consequently, I can't tell you exactly what services your college student may be entitled to, as the law's interpretation changes from place to place.

The services offered by colleges and universities basically range from compliance (the basics, no bells, no whistles) to comprehensive (the best model that money can buy). Of course, there's a range of services in between these. The compliance programs meet the basic legal requirements of the ADA and Section 504 to make reasonable accommodations. The comprehensive programs go well beyond what the law requires. As you might imagine, such programs cost extra. "One is not better than the other," says Dr. Glines, who adds, "It's entirely dependent upon individual students, and so it's student need that determines what parents look for."

What Are the Eligibility Requirements to Receive Special Services?

To begin with, your college student must be able to document having a disability. Documentation serves two purposes: It establishes that the student has a disability under ADA/504 guidelines, and it guides the college as to what services are necessary and appropriate.

Most experts believe that most, if not all, college students with ADHD should take advantage of the special services the college has to offer. You and your teen will want to make contact with the office of the director of student disability services or its equivalent at any college he or she considers. This office has the responsibility for designing and implementing the range of services the student needs. To do so, they require fairly recent evaluations—usually within the last three years.

Colleges are under no legal obligation to evaluate students with disabilities to determine whether they need services and if so, what kind. You can obtain an evaluation in two ways: through the high school or through an independent licensed practitioner, such as a psychologist. IDEA requires public elementary and secondary schools to do a reevaluation of students with disabilities every three years to determine the need for continued services. While that reevaluation doesn't have to be as comprehensive as the initial eligibility evaluation, it does fulfill the documentation requirements for colleges under the ADA.

Dr. Glines finds that many students now go to outside agencies or professionals for more specific testing, including a precollege battery. Here again is another use for educational consultants. They can interpret these test results for the college and make recommendations totally geared to the individual student. The recommendations they make, however, are not binding. They help the office of student disability services, but the school is under no obligation to follow these recommendations. For a fee, many colleges will also interpret and make recommendations through the office of student disability services.

Psychoeducational batteries can be costly. High schools can give these

> **KEY POINTS ABOUT DOCUMENTATION**
>
> - Evaluation data must be fairly current—usually no more than three years old.
> - Public school evaluations under IDEA or Section 504 can be used.
> - A student need not receive services before college to be eligible for accommodations in college.
> - Private evaluations by licensed professionals serve as documentation.

tests. If your teen has to have them done privately, based on Dr. Glines' recommendation, the two tests you'll definitely want are the Wechslar Adult Intelligence Scale, Revised (WAIS-R) for IQ and the Woodcock-Johnson for achievement. Of all the achievement tests, Dr. Glines prefers the Woodcock-Johnson because it is very specific and allows personnel to truly get a sharp picture of the student's areas of strength and weakness.

Take note: A student with a disability does not have to be classified in high school in order to receive services in college. A licensed professional can do an evaluation and provide the necessary documentation. Documentation provides the record of disability and the accommodations necessary to provide the student with access to courses and examinations depending on the individual's impairment. For instance, not all students with ADHD will require extended time on tests, nor will all students who are paraplegic.

The Application Process

What Should Be Taken into Consideration When Applying to Colleges?

First of all, students with ADHD need to take heart. Dr. Zakreski points out, "Status as a student with ADHD doesn't make you ineligible for college. Many kids go on to college and are quite successful, so there's every reason for a kid with ADHD to go to college. They just have to understand that the skills required are demanding and they have to be prepared to meet those challenges." Students with ADHD can succeed with the right supports.

The student and family who take time up front to narrow their search

Once the student determines that college is an attainable goal, then comes the grueling decision of which college. In its guide "Getting Ready for College," the Heath Resource Center advises students with disabilities to take a three-pronged approach to school selection. See www.acenet.edu/programs/heath or call (800) 544-3284.

and target schools will have a better chance of finding the right match. Ms. Reynolds believes that parents need to take on more of a guidance role in the selection process. As she explains, "By the very nature of the age and the level of education, that youngster needs to be involved front and center in making these choices. Let the youngster do as much work as possible."

When we parents want our kids to go to college, we very often take the bull by the horns, especially given that many students with ADHD let details fall through the cracks. If the student can't handle the guidance or won't do any of the footwork, even with help, then parents need to consider whether they want to make a financial investment at this point in time. Ms. Reynolds finds that in such cases, chances are the student will not succeed. What you can do is get outside help, such as from an educational consultant or a treatment professional, to help your son or daughter think through the choices and take action to meet his or her goals. That's the same principle you've heard repeated numerous times throughout this book: *Build the scaffolding to enable the youth, but don't disable the youth by doing his or her work.* Besides, taking care of somebody else's business usually comes back to haunt you.

Assuming the student has done his or her legwork, the college visitation provides other useful and sometimes vital information. Dr. Glines believes that prospective students must consider the culture of the campus. She raises these points for consideration:

- Is it a large public institution, with a football team and sororities and frats, or a small private school where the faculty know every student by first name?

- Is it a compliance program (minimal supports), or a comprehensive program (all the bells and whistles)?
- Is the comprehensive program run by a special department, like a school within a school, or is it part of the mainstream university where the support program is more integrated into the campus and not segregated?
- Do students receive peer support, group support, or individual support?
- Is this a student who can sit in a large lecture hall, or does this student need personal attention, that is, faculty who know his or her name and who would be able to say, "Hey, you weren't in class for two weeks. What's up with that?"
- Does the college or university have a great support program but not the degree program the student needs?

As we all know, it's hard to pick a college from a catalogue or Web site. They all look so wonderfully perfect. A visit usually tells a more accurate story. Dr. Glines notes that many parents want to sit in on classes during visits. "We do that, but that's not the answer," she says. "The parent who really knows what he or she is doing will have lunch in the cafeteria or go into student services where they really find out what the culture of the university is. They won't get that sitting in a classroom."

When Applying, Should the Student Disclose That He or She Has a Disability?

Schools may ask prospective students if they have a disability, but students are not required to disclose this information. Still, disclosure may help the student with the admissions process. By law, it cannot be used to discriminate against the student. While having a disability does not require schools to alter their admissions criteria, it may help an admissions director understand certain discrepancies in transcripts. Also, some schools may have a track record for working with students with ADHD and appreciate the candidate all the more.

Dr. Glines strongly encourages applicants to self-disclose. In fact, she's impressed by applications that come with recommendations that let her know the student has received support and with that support has been successful for a variety of reasons. She also likes to read personal essays that explain the struggle, what the student has learned from it, and why the student is going to be an asset to the university because of that struggle. She prefers this type of application to the one where, as she has found, "the student makes believe there is no issue and maybe comes in but does not get the support and is not successful—which does happen."

When applying, you need to check carefully about the school's process. Most colleges and universities will require students with disclosed disabilities to apply through the regular admissions procedure first. Others want the students to make dual applications through the regular channels and the disability services office. Regardless of whether or not the school requires single or dual applications, make a call to the disability services office and establish a relationship early on so that they know who your student is and that an application is being made. In schools that have comprehensive programs, very often the director of admissions of that program can make recommendations or assist the student with any appeal should admission be denied.

What Can Be Expected in College?

Most students can expect to have a continuation of the types of problems they had in high school. As the famous line from the movie *Casablanca* goes, "I'll round up the usual suspects." Attention, memory, and executive function problems will continue. Your son or daughter needs to be aware of the types of problems he or she can expect, and what to do to compensate in these areas that have the potential to derail progress. Dr. Glines strongly feels that "the student has to learn to be an advocate in high school. Support is not going to find him. He should really know what the vehicle is to find that support."

Don't be surprised if your college student wants to leave ADHD back home with you. After years of struggle and special education, your son or daughter may say, "Enough already! I'm fine now. I don't need any extra help. I can do it on my own. I'm grown-up." Who can blame the student? No one wants to walk around with a scarlet *ADHD* on his or her chest. Yet whatever you can do to help your son or daughter understand that the mature person accepts his or her limitations along with the strengths will help immensely.

College is not the time to bid farewell to advocacy efforts. Doing well isn't necessariliy about motivation. As Dr. Glines says, "It's really about just sort of self-monitoring, self-regulating, and understanding the whole gestalt of it. Why is it important? Well, you are going to feel better if you really do get to class on time and your notebook is in order. It has to be internalized."

About Particular Problems

Educational problems have been covered in Chapter 10. You and your teen might want to review the lists of problems in that chapter and this one. Circle those that apply. That's how you know what needs special attention. In general, expect these types of problems—especially during the first four semesters:

Data In/Data Out Issues
- reading large amounts of text
- note taking
- written language
- higher-order thinking skills such as inference, analysis, and synthesis
- problems with attention
- problems with working memory, storage and retrieval of information

Executive Function Issues
- time management—late to class, absenteeism, underestimating time required to complete assignments, missing appointments
- organizational management—making and keeping appointments, writing down assignments, using a day planner, keeping track of long-term assignments, losing things, poor workspace, forgetting to hand in assignments, poor scheduling—for instance, scheduling back-to-back classes with no decompression time, or too many courses
- emotional control—being easily overwhelmed, being unable to delay gratification or sustain effort for long-term gain, giving up, getting angry, quitting before problems are solved

- poor study skills and learning strategies—no memorization techniques, weak test-taking skills, no test preparation, poor microsizing, not reading for purpose, not using active learning strategies
- the "cat's away" syndrome—No meds, no bed, no being fed right, too much partying, too little self-care or preservation

As you know, the law requires schools to offer reasonable accommodations on an "as-needed" basis. Colleges and universities have the right to charge fees for services that go beyond the minimum compliance accommodations. What you may not know is that the courts have rules that while the school must make reasonable accommodations available, *it's up to the student to take advantage of the disability-related accommodations.* That means the school does not have to hunt the student down and ask, "Do you need a note taker?" or, "Did you take advantage of course waivers?" As you can imagine, students with ADHD will need reminders. They usually need a case manager or coach to guide them.

Furthermore, the law does not treat reasonable accommodations as a grocery list. A student can't have everything in the store. Instead, the law requires that the accommodations be effective for the particular student. Thus, a student should not expect extended test time, for example, just because he or she has a documented disability. The student has to need the accommodations and it has to be shown to help the student.

Some colleges and universities have comprehensive support programs. For instance, Lynn University's TAP program, directed by Dr. Glines, provides a very intensive level of service. Among the services

 INFORMATION LINK

Looking for that special gift for your college student?
How about a book of strategies written by two Ivy League college students with ADHD and learning disabilities? Jonathan Mooney and David Cole, *Learning Outside the Lines*, Simon and Schuster, New York, 2000.

INFORMATION LINK

Many older teens, adults, and parents benefit from using an ADHD coach. Coaches help people with ADHD add structure to their lives and to be self-advocates. For more information contact The American Coaching Association, www.Americoach.com, or The International Coaching Federation, www.coachfederation.org.

offered are a thorough evaluation of the student's learning needs and a lot of personal attention, including a fourteen-week, three-credit course that teaches the student study and advocacy skills. In addition, students are assigned trained tutors. Both the parents and the student receive more frequent feedback.

Colleges and universities have the right to charge extra fees for services that go beyond the minimum compliance accommodations. Following are examples of the types and range of services that may be offered. I've divided the possible accommodations and auxiliary services and supports into three levels of service: minimum, moderate, and comprehensive. Please note: The categories I have created are artificial, which means individual schools may differ as to what they consider necessary for compliance and what goes above and beyond. Thus, you really need to check the school's policy. I've made this list to give you an idea of what's out there for help. Funding for some of these fee-based programs may be available through special programs, such as vocational rehabilitation.

Examples of Accommodations for Compliance: The Minimum
- reduced course load
- extended time for tests and assignments
- extended time to complete degree requirements
- note-taking help (many schools now have a pool of designated note takers)
- substitutions of nonessential courses
- quiet test room
- possible alternative test format

INFORMATION LINK

For more information, see Heath Resource Center, "Creating Options: A Resource on Financial Aid for Students with Disabilities," and "1999 Financial Aid for Students with Disabilities," http://search.acenet.edu (click on Information from Heath in the New Releases section).

- books on tape (not everyone agrees that this format works well for ADHD; it has a better chance if the student reads along with the text, uses a highlighter, etc.)

Examples of Moderate-Level Accommodations and Services
- all of the minimum accommodations
- student support groups
- priority registration
- special academic advising for courses and disability-friendly faculty
- guidance for dropping or adding courses before penalty
- a copy of course syllabi ahead of time to see if student can handle the work
- computer assistance
- counseling to provide individual assistance with planning, organization, and other coping strategies

Examples of Comprehensive Programs
- all of the minimum and moderate-level accommodations
- case managers
- study skills and learning strategies courses
- study groups
- tutoring in individual and content areas
- academic aides
- special summer programs
- designated course sections
- special advisers

About Medication

Most colleges and universities do not have a policy for dispensing medications to their students. Dr. Glines believes that "by the time they get to college, they should be able to self-medicate." However, she also notes that many students do not take their meds because they want to party, which usually includes drinking. That problem may be handled through timing of doses. Of course, we don't do careful dosing to accommodate drinking or pot smoking—but there is a better reason to consider changing the dosage schedule. As Dr. Zakreski notes, "We usually recommend the students obtain four-hour tablets if they are using Ritalin, as opposed to the longer-acting tablet, because that gives them more control over the timing. They're using the medication for class or study periods." In college, students have a fair amount of "down time," when medication may not be needed. It depends on the individual's treatment needs.

Regarding monitoring, if a student has self-disclosed that he or she takes medication, Dr. Glines will intervene a bit. She has no problem saying something like, "Hey, you feeling all right? You're not looking real great. Taking your medication?" Dr. Glines makes such comments, "assuming I have a relationship close enough with the student, which is often the case. Then I can say that." Without that personal relationship, students are on their own.

Nothing Is Forever

"He was unsure of what he wanted to do," says Charley Holman, recalling those years before his son Dylan found his passion. "Because he hadn't taken the SAT, he needed to go to a community college, which was not a problem. He pulled a 4.0 his first semester. Then we got a phone call about halfway through his first year. He decided to quit school."

"The only way I could cope was just to back away," says Dylan's mother, Shirley, an education therapist. "I had given it my best effort. I just figured whatever's going to be will be. There's really nothing more I can do until he's ready. Then when he decided to go to a community college, it was heartbreaking. All his friends were going off to the university, and yet he knew he wasn't ready."

Dylan had planned to go into psychology, like his dad. Once he began that track, it didn't wear well. After giving it the good old college try, he dropped all his courses except one he was barely passing but had fallen in love with—anatomy. At that point Dylan had been accepted to a four-year school but declined because he wanted to spend another year at the community college and take as many biology classes as he could. This young man had decided to go to medical school, where he would marry his two loves, sports and medicine.

When he went on to the four-year school, he became president of the sports medicine club. As an undergraduate, he also taught two of the classes he was enrolled in. "He's really good and gentle and compassionate," says his dad. "And because of all the struggles he's been through, he really relates well to people who have struggled." It may have taken Dylan until age 25 to get his B.S., but he got it and is presently in medical school.

"I think there's a place for every student," says Dr. Glines. "The difficulty is finding the right match." She finds that sometimes it can take three or four tries to find the right place for a student. Parents should not be upset if their son or daughter switches schools. That seems to go with the territory. In fact, when she interviews families, Dr. Glines tells them, "You and your student make the best decision you can on as much information as you have available." She recalls one student who left his program because he missed the mountains. "He ended up coming back to us, but he had to leave us to realize it wasn't about the mountains." By the same token, Dr. Glines has had students leave to pursue a degree program at a larger university. "Students develop and become successful, excited, and passionate about a major," she explains. "They need to move to a different institution, and that's a good thing."

Other students simply wash out of school. As Dr. Glines has told parents, "If your son or daughter can't get up and come to class no matter what I say or how many times we call, let's look at other options. Maybe the student needs to go home and work for a while. Maybe he's just not ready, so give him or her a year to work and grow up." Many students with ADHD need time to decompress after the first twelve years of school. College is not the best model for every student.

Work

After high school, some adolescents elect to go to work rather than continue schooling. They may make this decision because they truly want to work or because they believe they'll do better in the workforce than in college. Some are fried from so many years of trying to get by in the school environment, which demands competence in their areas of weakness. Others may romanticize the notion of work and the paycheck. Or they may have work as a fallback position after leaving college without a degree.

Employment Task Force Adviser Dr. Horne says, "We have to change the attitude that evolution is four years of high school, four years of college, and then go to work. It isn't anymore. We come in and out of lifelong learning at many different points in our life." Ultimately, we all want our kids to have successful outcomes: working, living independently, and having a good quality of life. The question remains, How does that happen?

We are a country that loves success stories. It's easy to look at the successful entrepreneur who worked his or her way up from the mailroom to the boardroom and think such things are possible. They are, but not for too many people. For people with disabilities, the challenges don't stop with the end of formal education. In fact, the post-high-school employment statistics leave a lot to be desired. Young people with disabilities get hired at the same rate as their peers, but often in part-time or minimum-wage jobs. They receive little job counseling and usually acquire positions through family friends and relatives.

Consider the skills needed to succeed in the workplace:

- Job-related academic skills
- Specific vocational skills to perform entry-level personal services jobs, e.g., plumber, electrician
- Interpersonal skills—good work habits and attitude, good communication skills

Many students with ADHD find that after high school they don't have what they need to be successful in the workplace. I hate to burst a bubble, but I think we erroneously consider the workplace as a fallback position for kids who can't make it in college. I have serious concerns about the underestimation that our teens with ADHD bring to the work aspect of life. ADHD isn't just a disorder of poor school performance. Depending on the severity and the comorbid problems, it can be tough stuff to handle. We, the adults in their lives, may play a part in their lack of understanding about work and its demands. Do we really prepare these young men and women for life? Do we provide the scaffolding they need to transition effectively into the workplace? I'm not sure.

It's not that these youth can't pick up good work habits and skills. They can. But they often fail to realize they need further training, whether it's on the job or through a trade school or some of the other school-to-work opportunities mentioned in Chapter 11. I'm bothered by what happens to their hearts and souls when they go out expecting to succeed and find out that ADHD lives on. We need to do preparation and failure prevention for work as much as we do for school.

Following are the top ten reasons, in rank order, of why the job applications of young adults with disabilities get rejected. This list is from a 1976 study by J. M. Brown. (Source: "The Role of Special Education in LD Adolescents' Transition from School to Work," by Okolo and Sitlington. *Learning Disability Quarterly,* Vol. II, Summer 1988.)

1. poor reason for wanting the job
2. past job hopping
3. inability to communicate during an interview
4. health record
5. immaturity
6. personal appearance
7. manners and mannerisms
8. personality
9. lack of specific job skills
10. poorly filled-out application

Knowledge is power. Young adults looking for employment need to be coached in how to get a job. That begins with preparing a good application and having a positive personal interview. We all do well to remember the old advertising slogan "Because you don't get a second chance to make a first impression."

What does it take to succeed in the workforce? In addition to the pre-requisite academic and vocational skills, social/interpersonal skills play a major part. For instance, knowing how to read people's moods and silent signals, having empathy, knowing how to give and receive criticism, and being able to communicate effectively with supervisors are skills that go a long way toward workplace success.

Finding a Job Match

We want to help our teens avoid trial-and-error employment. Upon entry into the workforce, they need to take inventory. Each individual needs to know areas of strength and interest, along with areas that undermine successful employment. These areas may or may not be disability-related. It's much better if young adults with ADHD target potential employment where they are likely to have success and satisfaction.

Career counseling helps here. Once a young adult identifies fields of interest and aptitude, then he or she can go about gaining any necessary skills and polish needed to land and keep a job. Career counseling centers can be found in community colleges, in some local high schools, through your state's division of vocational rehabilitation, and through private clinicians. Check the employment classifieds in your local paper.

While finding and keeping jobs is the responsibility of the young adult, guidance remains the parent's role. Clearly, some teens won't want parental help. That's why it's good to go outside the home to a counselor. Inside the home, you can supply your teen with information. How you do that will depend on your relationship. If the teen really doesn't like you "butting in," you can always leave print information lying around.

 INFORMATION LINK

For teens and young adults, Wilma Feldman, *Finding a Career That Works For You*, Speciality Press: Plantation, Florida, 2000.

Wilma Fellman created twenty questions to help prospective employees identify their areas of individual strengths that may lead them to certain types of careers.*

1. What are my passions—those interests that really light me up?
2. What have my accomplishments been thus far?
3. What personality factors contribute to my ease of handling life?
4. What are the specifics that feel as natural and automatic as working with my dominant hand?
5. What are my priority values that must be considered to feel good about myself?
6. What are my aptitude levels that maximize success?
7. What is my energy pattern throughout the day, week, month?
8. What are my dreams and how do they relate to the real world of work?
9. What are the pieces of jobs that always attracted me and how can those pieces be threaded together?
10. How realistic are my related options in terms of today's job-market needs?
11. How much do I really know about the related options?
12. How can the options be tested out before going full steam ahead and thus raising the possibility of failure?
13. What special challenges do I have?
14. How do the challenges impact me?
15. How might my challenges impact on work options?
16. How could appropriate strategies and interventions overcome the challenges?
17. How great is the degree of match between the option and the real me?
18. Can we test out the degree of match before pursuing the field?
19. How could I enter and sustain the chosen work environment?
20. What supports can be put in place to ensure long-term success?

*Used with permission

You've probably gathered that these questions require your teen to give more than one-word or even one-sentence answers. However, time spent on them may save time and trouble later on. There are also interest inventories and personality tests that help narrow the choices. These instruments need to be meshed with personal preference, lifestyle, and values. Whether we're talking work instead of college or after college, it's important that our young adults approach the employment picture with serious effort, rather than fall into something and hope it works out.

As reported in the article by Cynthia Okolo and Patricia Sitlington, the Brown study cited the leading reasons for employee termination: absence, disinterest, frequent and costly mistakes, following directions poorly, and resistance to learning. It's easy to see how unmanaged ADHD can lead to significant job problems.

About ADHD and ADA in the Workplace

ADHD may interfere with job performance. Thus, workers with the disability may seek protections under the Americans with Disabilities Act. Part of this act protects workers with disabilities who can perform essential job functions when reasonable accommodations are made. ADA and the workplace is a rather complicated subject and too extensive to be covered in this book. Following is some information of interest and an information link for those who need more.

Workers with ADHD would do well to make a list of ways the disorder affects their job performance, along with what, if any, reasonable accommodations might help them to satisfactorily perform duties. Reasonable accommodations might include:

- allowing breaks in between chunks of work
- permitting the worker to leave the building for a brisk walk or other physical exercise to relieve stress
- prioritizing tasks
- highlighting important details in task
- creating a quiet, individual workspace
- providing a computer for written tasks
- providing written job instructions

INFORMATION LINK

> The ADA is a rather complicated subject and too extensive to be covered in this book. For more information contact: CHADD, www.chadd.org or (800) 233-4050 for a fact sheet, or the National Council on Disability, www.ncd.gov or (202) 272-2004.

Before disclosing that they have a disability or asking for accommodations, young adults with ADHD entering the workforce have a lot to consider. First of all, does the worker want the employer to know? If so, how should disclosure be made and when? What accommodations are needed, and does the employer have to provide them? If accommodations are sought, might the job be jeopardized?

Employers do not have to make accommodations that are unreasonable, nor can the accommodations create undue hardship for them. Consideration must be given to the size and financial resources of the employer, the nature of the workplace, and the impact on the operations. Furthermore, workers with disabilities don't have to accept accommodations if they don't want them. They do, however, have to meet their job responsibilities.

The Military

Jim Maresca did not get diagnosed with ADHD until his junior year of high school. By then, he had a lot to make up. His mother, Connie, had been misinformed by her son's school district for many years. As she explains, "He wasn't in special education because his intelligence tested way too high." His IQ is 125. Jim also has a photographic memory. Still, he struggled with school and had to take extra courses at night to make up for those he failed before he discovered he had ADHD and was placed on medication. That treatment made a world of difference. Jim soared through his senior year, finishing it with a 3.8 average. "He got an award from a county-based men's club for having the most improved grade point average in the county," Connie says proudly. "It was such an amazing thing for someone who had been beaten up by the system for so long," she adds.

Jim decided he wanted to operate heavy equipment like his dad. The family discussed the best way for him to get the necessary training. That's when the army entered into the picture. He chose to enlist to get some skills. He'd been in the army a little over two years when I spoke with his mom. The reports have been great. Jim really does well, and Connie can't say enough about what a great environment the military has turned out to be for her son. He functions fine without medication. "I think it's a perfect place," she tells me. "Everything is taken care of for you. He doesn't have to fix his meals. He has to exercise every day, which helps him with the stress. I just think the structure is extremely helpful for him." Apparently so—Jim was one of three people promoted out of the basic training group of 120 people. Since then, he's been promoted every time he's been up for it. "Though the army did not pan out to be all that he expected," Connie says, "it has been a real growing experience for him."

The military may not be an option for some teens with ADHD because the disorder can be considered a disqualifying condition. Each branch of the military has its own guidelines to determine whether or not the disorder (or any other disorder) will disqualify a candidate or a member. Should your teen be considering military service as an option, it will be helpful to find out about disqualifying information ahead of time.

Following are some key points from "ADHD and the Military," by William Hathaway:

- ADHD per se is not a disqualifying condition. To be so, it must produce a pattern of recent impairments that contraindicates military duty.

 INFORMATION LINK

In the October 1997 issue of *The ADHD Report,* William Hathaway wrote an excellent piece titled "ADHD and the Military." It's the most detailed information I've seen on this topic. If your son or daughter is considering the military, you might want to order a reprint of this article from Guilford Publications at www.news@guilford.com or (800) 365-7006.

- Current treatment with medication is disqualifying.
- Past treatment with medication does not necessarily disqualify an applicant.
- Recent treatment with medication may disqualify an applicant. It's up to the branch of the service and its medical examiner to determine what "recent" means.
- Misrepresentation of one's medical/psychiatric history can be grounds for separation from duty.
- Even if ADHD does not render a service member ineligible for service, it may restrict him or her from specific types of duties and clearances.
- A Disability Evaluation System (DES) exists to determine suitability of active members when personnel become aware that an active duty member has a disability. They may retain, give limited assignments, medically retire, or separate such an active duty member.

What's a Parent to Do?

As parents, we cannot decide what life our young adults will have. We can only hope that our guidance is well received. We can also hone our communication skills. When our sons or daughters come home frustrated and fed up, we may get upset or worry about the future. It's better to hold back on our fears and lend a supportive ear. When the young adult is more receptive to guidance, offer that as well.

There's another thorny transition issue that many parents face when their teens drop out, flunk out, or opt not to go to college or into the military. That's the independence issue. I know a fair number of parents who've had difficulty getting their teens to work, or to contribute to their personal expenses, or to pay rent of some sort. While it's easier to avoid confrontation, the tough part of the parents' job is to create opportunities for our teens to become independent, fully functioning members of society. These years between late adolescence and early adulthood are precisely for this purpose.

I don't want to overstep my bounds by defining your family's values. I do think it's important to say a word or two about enabling our sons and daughters to avoid the responsibilities of adult life by not holding them accountable or by protecting them from life's natural consequences. While we need to give a little leeway, especially under extenuating circumstances, it's important to create a structure that will eventually lead the youth down the road of independence. It's hard to look down that curvy road and imagine how today defines tomorrow. We do know that responsibility develops when people are given it and expected to meet it. Teens and young adults with ADHD need to be held accountable for their actions and the decisions that shape their lives. Like any young adult, they need to be helped to become independent by having to follow rules and meet reasonable expectations. The good news is that a great many teens with ADHD can and do handle life well. Their lessons may be hard, but through your loving guidance and support, they learn they can make it through and even beyond whatever challenges ADHD brings.

CHAPTER THIRTEEN

Learned Hopefulness

The story of ADHD, like many of life's stories, is the story of struggle and overcoming odds. How do teens and their families weather the storms? What factors contribute to a positive outcome? This chapter explores the nature of resilience and what people with ADHD and their families have done to adapt and respond to the challenges presented by this disorder.

When my children were little, a popular toy commercial had this silly little jingle: "Weebles wobble, but they don't fall down." If you know these toys, then you know you can't destroy them. They're little egg-shaped characters made out of superhard plastic—and they float. I know for a fact that they live forever, because my son dropped one down the bathtub drain. I must have poured a thousand gallons of Drano on that Weeble. Still the drain ran slow. The plumber snaked the drain to no avail. He told me my only other option was to rip apart the walls and replace the entire drainpipe. I learned to live with the effects of the Weeble. Admittedly, some days it annoyed me more than others. Once it even caused a total drain clog just as a prospective buyer came to look at the house. Ironically, at the end of my son's adolescence and the last chapter of this book, that Weeble has popped into my consciousness once again as my symbol for resilience.

The word *resilience* means the ability to recover quickly, to bounce back, to return to the initial state after being squished, bent, or stretched out of shape. Researcher Ann Masten, chair of the Department of Psychology at the University of Minnesota, has studied resilience extensively. She defines resilience as the ability to successfully adapt despite challenging or threatening circumstances. Life brings trials and tribulations. Being resilient does not make us less vulnerable or leave us unscathed. Like my Weeble buddy, it allows us to do better than expected under extraordinary circumstances.

Some people are more resilient than others. Despite extraordinary adversity, they do reasonably well. Understanding the why behind this phenomenon has captured the interest of researchers, writers, poets, and general observers for centuries. Today's resilience researchers have identified vulnerability and protective factors that help explain why one child, adolescent, or adult manages to do better than survive adversity, while another succumbs to the risks, either temporarily or permanently.

Risk Creators and Risk Reducers

When life fills our plates with adversity, we become vulnerable, or at risk. Dr. Masten defines a vulnerability factor as anything that creates the potential for risk. We know that outcomes vary for people who grapple with ADHD. Some youth grow up and have a minimum of life problems. Others may wind up in constant struggle or have very negative outcomes. Certainly the type and severity of ADHD factor into the outcome picture, but they don't write the whole story.

We need to understand that ADHD, though it may be especially challenging, is still but one risk factor for our kids. When we use the management tools mentioned throughout this book, the risks from ADHD lessen. Furthermore, our youth with ADHD have protective factors. As Dr. Masten writes, "Resilient children teach us that humans have a tremendous capacity for adaptation unless their basic tools for resilience are damaged."

Fortunately, life graces us with the possibility of many protective factors. These are not ADHD-specific. They don't need to be, because the protections that guard against vulnerabilities help whoever has them to be resilient in the face of adversity. Dr. Masten cites the following as protective factors for youth:

- parents who care
- connections to other competent, caring adults
- the ability to problem-solve
- the belief in one's own capability
- talents valued by self or society (as these lead to mentoring relationships with competent, caring adults)
- socioeconomic advantage
- faith and religious affiliations
- good schools
- community resources

Toward a Positive Outcome

Of all of the protective factors, or risk reducers, Dr. Masten writes, "The two most widely reported predictors of resilience appear to be a relationship with a caring, prosocial adult and good intellectual functioning." Both of these conditions seem to guard against the development of antisocial behavior. Time and again, adults with ADHD told researchers that they attributed their success or positive life adjustment to *having someone who believed in them.* In many instances, that someone turned out to be one or both parents.

Though we parents and our teens may have to put forth extraordinary effort, we don't necessarily have to take extraordinary measures. Sometimes we just have to keep it simple. That's what Tina Lyons's mother did. Tina is an adult now, with a child of her own. She learned she had ADHD when her son was diagnosed. She finds a little humor about finally coming to understand herself as a child.

"My mom always said there was something special about me. My brother and sister thought I was her favorite. Mom said it wasn't that I was her favorite. I was the easiest and the most fun. I just had an outlook on things that was different. And I always kept her going. She saw my personality as strength. I was a straight-A student and expected to be a lawyer or a doctor." That expectation had special meaning in Tina's family. She's an African-American woman who grew up in the inner city. No one from her family had gone to college. Few had graduated from high school.

Despite her good grades, Tina did have school difficulties. "I was always in trouble and being suspended in grammar school. My mother had a personal relationship with the principal. He would call her and say, 'She's at it again, Mrs. Lyons. I'm bringing her home.' He'd drive me and my mother would meet me at the door. I'd get out of the car and she'd say, 'Have a better day tomorrow, okay?'" Tina did have many good days.

Tina happens to be so bright that she did not have to study in junior and senior high school. As a result, she had no skills. When she got to college, she says, "I felt like I was having a nervous breakdown. I finally went to someone and they put me in a study skills course." Tina got her degree, became pregnant, raised a son alone, and worked for seven years. She went to graduate school. Today Tina has a master's degree in social work and is currently working on her Ph.D.

Shirley Holman also has a beautifully nurturing relationship with her son, who's now in medical school. Despite his poor academic performance throughout most of his precollege schooling, Dylan found his areas of strength. His parents supported him in these wholeheartedly. "He's a great entertainer," his mom says with pride. "He can really understand what's necessary in a character. He's also a hardworking athlete. His football coaches nominated him for most valuable player. People found him to be the most inspirational player, too. The other place where he was very successful was with people. He is nice to everybody, and everybody just adores him because of his big heart."

When I ask Shirley what's been the hardest part of raising her son, tears came. "He's so courageous." Though she tried to parent ADHD out of Dylan, she came to accept it and appreciate his struggles. Her tears are tears of release. "It's been hard to watch somebody who had to be on the battleground so many hours a day and to watch him carve a path for himself in other areas. He believes in himself today," she says, happy now that she didn't push the education issue back in the days when he struggled.

What do these two mothers have in common? They abandoned expectations of what they believed their kids should be and worked with the kids they had. They sent their teens a message of acceptance, love, and support. They made home the safe shore. That allowed these teens to feel secure enough to develop their areas of competence. It also gave them opportunities to find their unique strengths and talents.

People with ADHD who find their passion work passionately to succeed at it. Behind that success is this belief: "I can do it." How do we protect our teens from getting on a downhill track? Help them find what they are good at. Notice the word *good*. Resilience and positive outcome don't require greatness. Good seems to be good enough for life adjustment.

Many of the people I interviewed for this book spoke to this very point. They understood, as Dr. Masten notes, that "mastery taps into the self-efficacy/learned hopefulness system that motivates human adaptation."

Work Around Limitations

Limitations can be seen as opportunities to develop elsewhere. Author and clinician Dr. Robin says, "If someone really had a choice, I could not recommend having ADHD. It's a condition that creates adversity in life. Yet I think the core characteristics of ADHD are double-edged swords. They are positive in certain contexts. I think the challenge for people with ADHD is to learn what context their ADHD characteristics are positive in. They have to maximize those areas and figure out how to eliminate or compensate for the negatives."

Philip Banks is a successful physician. But getting through medical school and passing his boards didn't promise him a full range of opportunity. He had to figure out how he could practice medicine given his difficulties with organization and management. He went to work for a health care system. As he explains, "It wouldn't be possible for me to run a medical practice of my own. I know my limitations. I knew finishing my fellowship that it was beyond imagination for me to go out and get an office and hire staff. My wife manages all the finances at home. I can't do that. I can't run a business. I wouldn't even know how or where to start. It works out much better for me to work for someone else."

Limitations can also be seen as ways to get what the Holmans calls "in shape." As Charley explains, "It might take Dylan five hours to study what takes somebody else two hours. At the beginning he was asking, 'Why me? Why do I have to go through this? This isn't fair.' Then he got accustomed to it. He's taken something that's a liability and really turned it into an asset. He's just very intense. He knows what he needs to do to accomplish a task, and he does it without complaining and without worrying about it much because he knows what it takes to get to that level."

Finding Areas of Competence

As mentioned earlier, an important ADHD treatment tool has to do with helping our teens to find their niche, that place where they do well. Sometimes they find they do extraordinarily well. For instance, Connie Maresca tells us that her son "excelled in weight-lifting because it was just a competition with himself. They have a wall of fame in the weight-lifting room for people who set a record on weight/strength ratio for size. His name has been on that wall, and nobody has been able to beat him."

That just fills me with joy. Yet I think it's important to make another point. To be competent, our teens don't have to make it to a "wall of fame." Competence means having adequate skill or ability. We need to be careful not to give our teens mixed messages when we encourage them to find and develop their places of competence. They don't have to be great.

Consider the experience of 18-year-old Adam O'Leary. "I like playing on the drum set, and I play in the youth corps and stuff. I like reading music and working on that. It's really hard, but it's really cool when you get everything together. Marching and playing at the same time, plus memorizing your notes and where you are supposed to be and what foot you're supposed to be on at the exact time takes a lot of practice and a lot of training as a whole group. Once we finish, it's really great. It sounds cool and looks cool." Adam shows us that competence develops out of practice and work. It's when our skills come up to par with the demands of the task. We can be competent in many aspects of life, for example, our jobs, our relationships, or in the ways we handle our moods.

Competence also develops over time and through experience. As 22-year-old Ted Harris reminds us, "Kids with ADHD need a big goal, but they have to have small goals to make the big goals, because if they have one big goal, it's gonna throw them off. My big goal was to make Eagle Scout, but I had little goals in between. I had to make merit badges, and then I made rank. Then I had to go camping and be a leader.

There are so many things you have to make, and kids need to see the things in between or they never make it."

Acceptance

Perhaps the biggest challenge for ADHD is accepting it. That's a process that unfolds as struggles are overcome. As 17-year-old Drew Rothman observes, "It definitely does not hold you back in life in any way. The only way it would at all hold me back is the stereotypes people draw. If you accept it and come to terms with it, then you are fine. You have to work with it instead of just pretending it's not there and letting it mess you up. You definitely see different sides to things, a harder side. You're prepared for the struggle of life a lot quicker, which is a good thing."

Some people move beyond acceptance to actually embracing some aspects of ADHD. For instance, father David Milstein says, "Joel was once on a TV program. They asked him how he would feel if there were a magic pill to get rid of his ADHD. He said he wouldn't take it because there are many things that are positive about ADHD and that he didn't want to lose them. He loves the way he thinks, for instance. He certainly doesn't bore you to death. I love the way his mind works, too. It's not that linear fashion. It's superb."

Hope

In *Emotional Intelligence*, author Daniel Goleman cites the work of R. C. Snyder, who has identified certain traits shared by people with high levels of hope. As Goleman writes, those traits include the following: "being able to motivate themselves, feeling resourceful enough to find ways to accomplish their objectives, reassuring themselves when in a tight spot that things will get better, being flexible enough to find different ways to get their goals or to switch goals if one becomes impossible, and having the sense to break down a formidable task into smaller, manageable pieces."

Both Ted Harris and Drew Rothman have gotten very adept at keeping their spirits up. "Sometimes I get dispirited," says Drew. "That's when

I take a minute and sit back and survey the situation. I look at what's going on around me. I figure out what I have to do, and then figure out what I have to do first—what's the thing I should do when I'm clear-headed. Then I get to work."

Ted, on the other hand, doesn't get dispirited. "My psychologist told me that people with ADHD tend to prosper later in life because things take a longer time to generate. I keep thinking about what he said." This psychologist also told Ted, "You know, right now you feel you're stupid because you see the world doing stuff that you're not doing. Just wait ten or fifteen years down the road, when you have a family and you have a job and you're happy with it." Ted has hung on to those pearls along with the belief his psychologist planted in his mind. Ted says he told him, "The day will come when I'll feel fine."

What does a person do in the meantime? As Dr. Glines, the director of Lynn University's student disability program, phrases it, "We have to give them hope in spite of their failure. We have to believe that every young person can make a difference. It doesn't matter if they are not traditional and they haven't got a great academic history. It doesn't mean that they can't be agents of change. They need to understand that they can make a difference. We have to provide the notion and the belief that it's okay to fail. Where's the positive thread? 'Well, you got out there. You took a risk. How cool is that? That's a great thing.'"

We who are ordinary humans taking care of those with extraordinary needs have our own special blend of resilient qualities. The strongest among these, I believe, is hope. How do we keep hope alive and well in the midst of sometimes dark and chaotic days? The book *Simple Abundance* teaches us to look for the brightness in ordinary events. The author suggests everyone keep a daily gratitude journal. In it, she tells us to write down at least five things that we are grateful for every day. I found this exercise extremely helpful to train my mind and attitude to look at the positive things in life no matter how grand or small. That's in keeping with an old saying, "Take care of the pennies and the dollars will take care of themselves."

Take care of the mind, body, and spirit, too. Humor, exercise, meditation, and decent food do wonders to get you in physical, spiritual, and emotional shape. ADHD can become all-consuming, especially when our kids are in crisis. Even in noncrisis times, it can make life chaotic. As flight attendants tell passengers, if you're traveling with small children and the oxygen masks drop down, put the mask over your face first, then attend to the child. Parents who take care of themselves have a better shot at taking care of their kids more effectively. ADHD requires a lot of patience and energy. We can deplete those resources rapidly. The best way to guard against that is to find some way each day to replenish your personal resources. Try to give yourself at least a half hour a day—more if possible—to do something constructive that makes you feel good.

There's nothing magical about the coping tools we bring to our tough situations. In fact, as Dr. Masten notes, "The biggest surprise in the research is the *ordinariness* of resilience." What are those protective systems that allow us to handle extraordinary circumstances? Dr. Masten believes what has been preserved and protected in our evolution are these human capabilities:

- to think
- to hope
- to make meaning of life
- to take action or to stop one's own behavior
- to respond to opportunity
- to seek relationships that are healthy for development
- to adapt to changing circumstances

Want to know how to help yourself, your teen, and your family—or anyone else, for that matter—make it through hard times? Look over the above list. It's the blueprint for Weebles who wobble but don't fall down.

INFORMATION LINK

The following books offer a closer look at this topic:
Sam Goldstein and Robert Brooks, *Raising Resilient Children: Fostering Strength, Hope, and Optimism in Your Child,* McGraw-Hill, New York, 2001.
Robert Brooks, *The Self-Esteem Teacher,* American Guidance Service, Circle Pines, MN, 1991.

Words of Encouragement and Advice

When dealing with chronic conditions such as ADHD, we have to become our own healers to a large degree. Throughout the interviews I did for this book, I never ceased to be amazed by or grateful for the words of encouragement or advice given by every person I spoke with.

Drew Rothman has this advice for teens with ADHD: "Learn to self-advocate. Figure out what it is that you actually have trouble with and then try to fix it. If you can't fix it, at least you know what's wrong, and that gives you some sort of peace of mind. I know myself very well, actually better than other kids, because I've needed to learn how to figure out what's going on and advocate for myself. Stick with things as much as you can and even if you don't want to. Know when to quit, but don't quit too early. If you think you are ready to quit, stay at it a little longer."

Victoria Winston wants everyone to know this about teens with ADHD: "They are great kids. My boy was just the greatest kid going through school. He was a 10 in everything except school. I totally believe once you get them through whatever schooling they have to do, they're gonna go fly. If I can give any message or any sort of encouragement to people reading this book, it would be this: Don't ever give up on your child. You are the only advocate your child has. If you stop believing in him, then he's finished. I never ever gave up on that child, and I never ever let him think I was wavering."

Sometimes we can inadvertently send our teens messages that we don't really intend to send. Though Ted Harris' parents always told him that ADHD was but one aspect to who he was, his experience as the son of parents who ran a support group for many years led him to offer this advice: "One thing parents should never say is 'That's just the way he is.' There's gonna be a lot coming along in life, and they need to be patient and optimistic."

Over the years Ted has had an opportunity to overhear many conversations from parents who called in search of help and to field a lot of the calls as well. It made him defensive and angry when parents told him, "Oh, my child did this or that." Ted never responded to the negative comments he heard for fear he'd say the wrong thing. But, he says, he'd say to himself, "If the kid has a lot of energy, that can be a really good thing."

"I don't want a mother to say, 'Well, my kid has ADHD,' and all of a sudden get a frown on her face," Ted says emphatically, and adds, "The kid has ADHD, and it just means that they have a different style of learning and stuff. That's all it means. I know there are famous people who have ADHD and they've made it. They've come a long way, and that's because they weren't told, 'This is all you can do.' You can never tell a kid with ADHD that he can't learn or that's the way it's always going to be. You need to give them a challenge and the challenge has to be motivating enough—at least for me."

I am grateful for Ted's comments. He's so right to remind us that we need to separate the person from the disorder. It's very important to give people their dignity. One way to do that is to respect their individual, unique natures. The Navajo rug weavers have a lot to teach us in this respect. They never make a rug that's totally symmetrical or otherwise perfect in design. To do so, they believe, misrepresents nature, which is seen as a world of constant movement seeking to balance itself.

The weavers have had to work hard to honor this belief. When mass market demand for Navajo weavings grew, traders tried to require perfect symmetry from the weavers. Rugs that did not have the same pattern from top to bottom and from right to left were considered "flawed." Of course, this concept clashed with the Navajo belief system. To sell their goods, the weavers became very adept at making their rugs *look* perfectly balanced. The very skilled weaver always managed to get that slight imperfection into her work. But, unlike the coyote trickster, she did not weave in destructive imbalance.

In the natural order of things, there is no perfection, at least not in the way most humans conceive of perfection. In fact, to weave a pattern that's perfectly in order is to stop the natural movement of the sun and the earth. The Navajo weavers seek to show the balance in nature, not nonexistent perfection. It is our differences that make us who we are. Though ADHD may create adversity and challenge, with the right weavers, pieces slightly out of harmony make interesting, unique tapestries. No two days or nights are exactly the same, ever.

Index

attorneys and, 269
Behavioral Intervention Plan
(BIP), 283–84
development, 269–70
Functional Behavioral Assessment
(FBA), 283
inclusion of teen in creation of,
268, 269
information link, 274
"least restrictive environment"
requirement, 271, 278
major requirements for IEP
content, 270–72
manifestation determination
review, 287–89
parent involvement, 268, 276
PLEP (present level of educational
performance) and, 267, 270
school responsibilities for
implementing, 274
team and transition plan, 273
teen resistance to, 269
transition plan, 272–74
who is on the IEP team, 268
Interventions for out-of-control
teens
dealing with the courts, advice for
parents, 201–3
drug and alcohol involvement,
203–7
five minimum home rules, 194
halfway houses, 205
information links, 194, 209
inpatient centers, 205
insurance coverage, 205–6
involving the juvenile justice
system, 195–200
outpatient counseling centers, 204
placement decisions, 192–93
referrals, 209
residential centers, 192, 193, 204,
207–15

school referrals to police, 200–201
therapeutic communities, 204–5

Judgment, adolescent vs. adult, 15
Juvenile justice system, 195–203
detention facilities, 193
filing petition, 198
how the system operates, 197–99
lack of appropriate facilities,
196–97
school referral to police, 200–201
shortcomings of, 199
suggestions for parents whose
teens have to appear before a
judge, 201–203
when to seek help from courts,
195–97

Law-enforcement intervention,
195–203
after police are called, 195–97
age and considerations, 199–200
arrest of teen, 201–2, 207
bullies and, 188–89
drug and alcohol involvement,
203–7
out-of-control teen, 191–92
school referral to police, 200–201
Late bloomers, 19
Learned helplessness, 110, 172
Learning disabilities (LD), 60–61
ADHD with, 61, 296
information link, 61
oppositionality and, 168
Listening
active, 146–47
parental, 17, 18, 111

Manipulative behavior, 174–75
Marijuana, 63, 64, 89–90, 206
Medical intervention
abuse of stimulants, 88–89

JOYCE BLOCK

MARY FOWLER has more than twenty years of experience as the parent of a son who has ADHD. She is considered a leading lay authority on the disorder. As the former vice president of government affairs of CHADD, the national ADHD support group, Ms. Fowler was instrumental in leading the national advocacy movement, which led to the inclusion of ADHD in the Individuals with Disabilities Education Act (IDEA). She has testified before Congress, worked with numerous advocacy groups, and served as an ADHD consultant to many professional organizations, scientific committees, and universities. She has been on numerous television and radio talk shows, including *Today* and NPR. She lectures internationally on topics related to ADHD and is the author of the very successful *Maybe You Know My Kid: A Parent's Guide to Helping Your Child with Attention Deficit Hyperactivity Disorder*. Ms. Fowler is also an ADHD coach. Visit her Web site at www.maryfowler.com.